Mahler Remembered

Born in London in 1948, Norman Lebrecht studied sociology and psychology at university. As a television news producer he covered wars, elections and revolutions before becoming a fulltime writer at thirty. His nine books on music, including *The Maestro Myth* and *The Companion to 20th Century Music* have been translated into many languages, from Japanese to modern Hebrew, and his weekly column in the *Daily Telegraph* has been described as 'required reading for anyone interested in music.'

Norman Lebrecht has made many television and radio documentaries for the BBC and other broadcasters. He is founder editor of the *20th-Century Composers* series for Phaidon Press, and is an acknowledged authority on the life and work of Gustav Mahler.

Norman Lebrecht is married to the archivist and food writer Elbie Lebrecht and lives in central London with their three daughters.

in the same series

BARTÓK REMEMBERED
Malcolm Gillies

BRUCKNER REMEMBERED
Stephen Johnson

DEBUSSY REMEMBERED
Roger Nichols

GERSHWIN REMEMBERED
Edward Jablonski

MENDELSSOHN REMEMBERED
Roger Nichols

PURCELL REMEMBERED
Michael Burden

RAVEL REMEMBERED
Roger Nichols

SATIE REMEMBERED
Robert Orledge

SHOSTAKOVICH: A LIFE REMEMBERED
Elizabeth Wilson

MAHLER
REMEMBERED

NORMAN LEBRECHT

faber and faber
LONDON · BOSTON

In memory of

ANNA MAHLER
(b. Vienna 1904, d. London 1988)
and
ELEANOR ROSÉ
(b. Vienna 1894, d. London 1992)

First published in 1987
by Faber and Faber Limited
3 Queen Square London WC1N 3AU
This reissue published in 1998

Typeset by RefineCatch Limited, Bungay, Suffolk
Printed in England by Clays Ltd, St Ives plc

A CIP record for this book
is available from the British Library

ISBN 0–571–14692–9

2 4 6 8 10 9 7 5 3 1

Contents

Introduction:
Seeking Gustav Mahler

No composer has had greater influence on the music of the twentieth century than Gustav Mahler; none wrote more of himself into his music. These truths are as inseparable as they are becoming self-evident.

Mahler was the first composer to seek personal spiritual solutions in music. Where Beethoven addressed himself to universal suffering and Wagner to altering the values of art and society, Mahler from his earliest symphony delved into private experiences and traumas — domestic brutality, bereavement, alienation — searching within himself for remedies to the human condition.

This quest is the key to the remarkable resurrection of Mahler's music half a century after his death. The first surge of acclamation in the 1960s owed much to the currents of self-awareness and introspection that fostered the Me Generation. But his creations penetrated the underlying culture more permanently than any of the decade's crop of individualist cults.

A survey of orchestral concerts in London, where Mahler was played only sporadically before 1960, finds him entering the list of the ten most performed symphonists in 1962 and rising steadily every year thereafter. In 1986 he overtook the perennially popular Tchaikovsky to claim fifth place with more than twenty-six complete symphonic performances.[1]

The first cycle of Mahler symphonies on record was completed by Leonard Bernstein in autumn 1967. In the next twenty years, no fewer than eight conductors have recorded the entire works; several others are in mid-cycle, while Bernard Haitink and Bernstein himself are recording them a second time.[2] The demand for Mahler discs seems insatiable.

The enthusiasm is most marked, and to many programmers most puzzling, among the under-twenties. Greeted by a sea of luminous

---

1. Figures compiled by David Chesterman, counting symphonic performances at the Royal Albert Hall, South Bank, Barbican and St John's Smith Square each year since 1951. The exact figure is 26⅔ symphonies, including performances of the uncompleted Tenth Symphony and the abandoned *Blumine* movement of the First.
2. Complete cycles have been recorded by Leonard Bernstein (New York Philharmonic; CBS), Rafael Kubelik (Bavarian RSO; DG PolyGram), Sir Georg Solti (Chicago SO; Decca London), Bernard Haitink (Concertgebouw; Philips Phonogram), Vaclav Neumann (Czech Philharmonic; Supraphon), Lorin Maazel (Vienna Philharmonic; CBS), Wyn Morris (Symphonica of London; Symphonica Ltd.), Klaus Tennstedt (London Philharmonic; EMI Angel) and Eliahu Inbal (Frankfurt RSO; Denon Nippon Columbia). Maurice Abraranel (Utah SO; Vanguard) recorded all the symphonies except *Das Lied von der Erde*.

punk hair-styles at Mahler's Sixth Symphony at a London promenade concert, Klaus Tennstedt reflected: 'Young people are searching for values that have been destroyed. Long after his death, Mahler fights on against a terrible world. He gives people back their sense of feeling, and fear, and outrage.'[3] 'Perhaps', suggests Claudio Abbado, 'young people can find all the great matters of life and death in Mahler'.[4]

Like Sigmund Freud, Mahler examined himself less as a singular specimen than as a prototype of tormented humankind. 'Every injustice done to me', he declared, 'is an injustice towards the whole universe and must hurt the almighty spirit.'[5] 'The whole world concerns me,'[6] he thundered at a narrow-minded musician who, pondering his outburst, concluded that Mahler 'pursued a constant search for the divine, both in the individual and in man as a whole.'[7]

Apostles regarded his sense of mission as Messianic, opponents as megalomanic. He and his music provoked extreme reactions because they encompassed unrestrained extremes of emotion and ambition. The richness and contradictions of his vast personality are inextricable from his music, and consequently from all music after him. For, through his own works and the trail of his followers Schoenberg, Webern and Berg, as well as through such diverse connections as Busoni, Varèse and Alfredo Casella, Mahler has influenced every dominant strand in twentieth-century composing apart from the Debussyist, the nationalist and the party-line Stalinist (see Fig. 1). Mahler, writes Pierre Boulez, is 'indispensable to anyone reflecting today on the future of music.'[8]

Almost every composer after Mahler has adopted, knowingly or not, at least half of his utilitarian attitude to music: as a means of self-examination, or as a route to moral regeneration. None of his major contemporaries envisaged such aims for their art. Strauss was frankly bewildered when Mahler talked to him of seeking redemption in music. 'I don't know what am I supposed to be redeemed from,' he complained.[9] Debussy dined with Mahler, then walked out of his Second Symphony.

'The symphony must be like the world,' Mahler told Sibelius, 'it must embrace *everything*!'[10] His own symphonies invoke both the violent contrasts of the outer world and those of his volatile inner

---

3. Interview with the author, *Sunday Times* colour magazine, 15 September 1985.
4. Quoted in *Barbican* magazine, December 1986.
5. Specht, p. 55. (See Select Bibliography, p. xvii, for abbreviated source references.)
6. See p. 252.
7. See p. 174.
8. Pierre Boulez, *Orientations*, London (Faber and Faber), 1986, p. 303.
9. See p. 50.
10. See p. 218.

nature, a temperament that hovered on the brink of the clinical manic-depression that has afflicted many of the greatest artists.[11]

The complexities of his character have intrigued psychiatrists,[12] biographers and novelists[13] alike. The present book is intended as a basic guide to Mahler's personality, a half-explored continent with awesome topographic contours.

Images of Mahler

The prevailing profile of Mahler is founded on three primary documents: correspondence published by his widow in 1924,[14] her own memoirs sixteen years later,[15] and the notes of his adoring companion, Natalie Bauer-Lechner.[16] Vital as they are, these volumes have inspired almost as much fantasy as fact. Many concert-goers firmly believe, for example, that the Mahler they are hearing is the hapless hero of Ken Russell's movie, itself an imaginative distillation of Alma's memoirs filtered through English landscapes and the director's personal predilections.[17]

Any clearer understanding of Mahler can only be obtained by setting aside these overworked sources and seeking out further testimonies to corroborate, balance or refute existing conceptions. The more such materials I assembled, the more I became convinced that Mahler was best perceived directly through the eyes of his contemporaries.

Alma Mahler's famous memoir appeared in Amsterdam in 1940, at a time when 'Germany is deprived of his music and the memory of

---

11. For recent assessments of manic-depression in artists see Kay R. Jamison and Robert Winter, *Moods and Music*, programme book of concert staged on 19 May 1985 by the Neuropsychiatric Institute and Department of Music, UCLA, Los Angeles. Dr Jamison's study 'Manic-depressive illness and accomplishment' will appear as Chapter 18 in F. K. Goodwin and Kay R. Jamison, *Manic-Depressive Illness*, to be published by Oxford University Press.
12. Among them: Theodore Reik, *The Haunting Melody*, New York (Farrar, Straus and Young), 1953, and David Holbrook, *Mahler and the Courage To Be,* London (Vision Press), 1975. For a trenchant attack on the neuropsychiatric approach to Mahler see Dika Newlin, 'The "Mahler's Brother Syndrome": necropsychiatry and the artist', *The Musical Quarterly*, vol. 66 (1980), pp.296–304.
13. Thomas Mann borrowed aspects of Mahler for both *Death in Venice* and *Doctor Faustus*. Episodes from his biography are conferred on a character in *Of Lena Geyer* (New York, 1936), by Marcia Davenport, daughter of Alma Gluck who sang with Mahler. At least two novels based on Mahler's domestic tragedies are currently in progress.
14. GML.
15. AMM.
16. NBL.
17. *Mahler* (1974) was filmed in the Lake District and in a house in the Portobello Road, West London (information obtained from Ken Russell, March 1985).

his life and compositions is carefully effaced.'[18] Having written it 'many years ago' [19] from her diaries, she brought it smartly up to date in order to settle some burning scores: 'I therefore have no scruple in saying openly what I know from experience of persons who live their lives and play their parts in the Third Reich.' In particular: 'All that I say of Richard Strauss is taken from the daily entries in my diary.'[20]

Her tales of Strauss, like much else in the memoir, are a subtle blend of truth and malicious gossip. Her original dislike of the composer and his wife was reinforced by anger at his acquiescence to Nazism and his refusal to release his correspondence with Mahler.

Strauss is one of many instances where Alma's long-standing grievances outweighed any regard for historical accuracy. Much else in her book is prejudiced by personal animosity, a casual attitude to chronology and downright perjury designed to expiate guilt feelings and excuse her marital infidelities.

She portrays Mahler from the outset as prematurely old, in poor health and a confirmed virgin. He was, in point of fact, forty-one years old when they met, in unparalleled command of the world's most problematic opera-house, approaching his prime as a composer, prodigiously athletic and a veteran of sexual experiences with several singers.

In her autobiography twenty years later,[21] Alma admits that she became sick of Mahler and his music at different times; she often sent her small daughter to represent her at concerts.[22] The scholarly consensus that Alma 'is nearly always reliable where she speaks of aesthetic judgements or emotional reactions; it becomes risky to trust her in questions of fact or chronology'[23] is no longer tenable. She deliberately misleads too often for her book, compulsively readable though it remains, to be used as the principal basis for considering Mahler's character. 'I had known much about Mahler,' she reflected in a candid, late confession, 'but ignored his essence.'[24]

Nor can Natalie Bauer-Lechner's account, loyal though she was to Mahler, be taken as read. Mahler called certain of his friends 'my

---

18. AMM. p. xxix.
19. Examination of the draft manuscript at the Bibliothèque Gustav Mahler, Paris, reveals from such statements as 'it is now ten years since his death' that the greater part of the book was written in 1921.
20. AMM, p. xxix.
21. AML.
22. Statement by Anna Mahler to the author, December 1985.
23. Kurt Blaukopf, *Gustav Mahler*, London (Futura paperback edition), p. 259.
24. Alma Mahler-Werfel, *And the Bridge is Love*, London (Hutchinson), 1959, p. 271. This admission appears only in the English version of Alma's autobiography, and not in the German AML.

dear Eckermann', implying that he knew they were taking down his words, like Goethe's acolyte, for future publication. Well before his thirtieth birthday, he displayed an awareness of his historical importance that in a lesser man would be deplored as mere vanity. In the presence of scribes, he plainly tailored some utterances to mould his image for posterity.

Natalie's *Erinnerungen* circulated in Vienna for years in typed versions before her nephew 'edited' a truncated selection in 1923. An expanded edition lately issued by her family in West Germany is not nearly as revealing as the original typescripts owned by Baron Henry-Louis de La Grange, Mahler's paramount biographer, who has generously allowed me to study and reproduce previously unquoted passages.[25]

The few other books about Mahler by close associates are in varying degrees unsatisfactory. Bruno Walter wrote a dry, uneasy profile in 1936; his own autobiography is notably more interesting, as are his private letters.[26] But Walter's most vivid account, written in a musical journal months after Mahler's death, has never since been reprinted.[27] The musicologist Guido Adler, Mahler's lifelong friend and supporter, wrote a biography that analyses the music at some distance from the man; and two critics close to Mahler, Paul Stefan and Richard Specht, wrote early studies, one influenced by Adler, the other by Alma.

The most vivid descriptions of Mahler are mainly to be found in articles in pre-1921 Austrian and German periodicals. I have selected those memoirs where the memory is freshest, apart from a few instances – notably the autobiographies of J. B. Foerster and Ludwig Karpath – where prolonged reflection has produced a fuller portrait.

I have also gained access to a variety of eye-witness materials that have never previously been printed in any form. These include autobiographical manuscripts by Arnold Schoenberg, Carl Moll and Berta Zuckerkandl, and tape-recorded interviews with Anna Mahler and various individuals who knew and worked with him.

Mahler and his friends

People who have shared the privilege of friendship with a genius are notoriously prone to exaggerate the virtues and ameliorate the faults. Mahler's circle, however, was so infected by his questioning mind

25. See pp. 6–14.
26. See Select Bibliography on p. xvii.
27. See pp. 81–5, 127–30.

and his dedication to absolute, unattainable truths that they wrote with an honesty that spared neither his sins nor inconsistencies. Others who described Mahler in paeans of unqualified praise are those who knew him least, and may usually be disregarded.[28]

In almost every aspect of his personality, the reliable evidence is contradictory to an astonishing degree. He was compassionate and callous, co-operative and tyrannical; a childlike innocence alternated with a machiavellian cunning, pantheism with a belief in the one God. Even physical descriptions of Mahler are conflicting. Many remember him as small, weak and ugly; Alfred Roller's objective portrait of his naked frame shows him to have been powerfully built and supremely fit.[29] From his photographs, most women find him sexually attractive; his own lovers seemed almost indifferent to his carnality – or so it appears from their reports of him.

He is repeatedly likened to Kapellmeister Kreisler, E.T.A. Hoffmann's sardonic and extravagant caricature of a Romantic conductor.[30] Yet some observers immediately retract this comparison when recalling Mahler's asceticism and search for God. These antipodes of elation and sorrow, idealism and irony, are hallmarks of his works. 'Whatever quality is perceptible and definable in his music, the diametrically opposite quality is equally so. Of what other composer can this be said?' challenges Leonard Bernstein.[31]

Richard Specht and Paul Stefan, accomplished writers who knew Mahler for more than a decade, admitted defeat when it came to defining the essence of the man. Specht begins his book: 'I do not think anyone really knew Mahler.[32] Stefan declares that Mahler 'defies description: he is at once just as portrayed and yet quite different.'[33]

Already as an immature, provincial musician, he attracted a stream of followers. He did not encourage sycophants: his disciples were rebels and reformers who scorned the trappings of high office yet could not resist his allure. Mahler, for his part, needed their

---

28. Exception must be made here for Arnold Schoenberg whose posthumous beatification of Mahler (see pp. 315–6) was founded on guilt feelings for having shown him insufficient respect.

29. See pp. 154–5.

30. Struggling to support himself as a musician when he took up writing in his thirties, Hoffmann copied much of Johannes Kreisler from himself. He appears in the *Kreisleriana* cycle of 1815 and again as the central character in the unfinished novel *Kater Murr*. Kreisler is one of the towering figures of Romantic literature, his wild, almost schizoid duality constituting his most prominent feature.

31. *High Fidelity* magazine, September 1967.

32. 'Ich glaube nicht dass einen Menschen gegeben hat, der Mahler wirklich gekannt hat.' (Specht, p. 23.)

33. NBL, p. viii.

reassurance that he belonged to a progressive trend. He required the combative stimulus of their disputiveness; his was an interactive nature that thrived upon animated exchanges and new ideas.

The ability to give and receive friendship was among his most endearing traits. Numerous reports tell of the moment when Mahler suddenly, as if in priestly blessing, 'shone his countenance' upon a lesser mortal and declared him his friend. Stefan found him 'unusually shy',[34] but to close friends he exposed his innermost concerns. The Czech composer J. B. Foerster relates how Mahler, during a crisis of creative self-doubt, talked freely of his intimate life but uttered not a word about his compositions.[35] Certainly some of the portraits of Mahler by his friends are among the most revealing that exist of any major musician.

That he sometimes shed people unsentimentally does not detract from the warmth he gave during the relationship. Siegfried Lipiner, an old friend ejected from Mahler's circle by Alma's antagonism, accused him of 'contempt for his fellow men . . . we are all just *objects* to you.'[36] Ferdinand Pfohl, one of several associates discarded when Mahler left Hamburg for Vienna, wrote: 'He was a bad friend, because in anger he would forget all friendship.'[37] Specht notes that 'most people only meant to him as much as they could give him.'[38] Yet egotism and ingratitude apart, the experience of his friendship was intense and abiding, even to those he eventually wronged. Hans Pfitzner, a fellow composer, concluded: 'In ihm ist Liebe' – in him is love.[39]

In an important essay entitled 'Mahler's friends',[40] Paul Stefan compiles a list beginning with Anton Bruckner – 'not his teacher, but a paternal guide' – and Mahler's college contemporaries, Adler, Lipiner, the archaeologist Friedrich Löhr and the lawyer Emil Freund. Next come Natalie Bauer-Lechner, Walter and Foerster, pillars of his Hamburg period. Marriage to Alma introduced him to the leading Viennese artists Klimt, Roller and Carl Moll, as well as to the young musicians Zemlinsky and Schoenberg.

Other musical comrades included the composers Richard Strauss, Josef Marx, Alfredo Casella and Julius Bittner, the conductors Willem Mengelberg and Oskar Fried, several critics, his last

34. op. cit., p. viii.
35. See p. 76.
36. Letter in the possession of Henry-Louis de La Grange. See HLG1, p. 697.
37. Ferdinand Pfohl, *Gustav Mahler*, Hamburg (Verlag der Musikalienhandlung Karl Dieter Wagner), 1973, p. 20.
38. See p. 185.
39. Contribution to fiftieth-birthday tributes to Mahler.
40. 'Mahlers Freunde', in *Musikblätter des Anbruch*, vol. 2 (April 1920), (Gustav Mahler Heft) pp. 287–9.

publisher Emil Hertzka and some singers, Kurz, Mildenburg and Gutheil-Schoder. The twin poles of his life, says Stefan, were his favourite sister, Justine, and his wife, Alma. Like many others, Stefan proudly recalls the moment Mahler said to him: 'You are now my friend . . .'

In the same journal, Richard Specht contributes an opposing article: 'Mahler's enemies'.[41] The contrast is stark and unyielding. Those who loved Mahler were, on the whole, agents of advancement, humanity and light. Many of those who opposed him are revealed as the primeval forces that soon plunged Europe into double holocaust and devastation.

The powers of darkness detested Mahler because he would not tolerate comfortable compromise and commonplace art. They loathed his undeniable genius and feared his naked ambition. They despised, above all else, his racial origin and they made his heritage the cross upon which Vienna ultimately nailed him.

Mahler and his origins

Mahler's Jewishness has been a topic of controversy from his own time to the present, but much of the argument is founded on false premises and subjective analysis. Although he rarely talked of his background, he made no secret of its importance. 'The songs which a child assimilates in his youth will determine his musical manhood,' he declared.[42] Guido Adler, raised in the same small town in Bohemia, underlined the importance of the folk-tunes and military marches they both heard as boys. 'The impressions of Mahler's youth extend like a scarlet thread through the creations of his entire life.'[43]

Adler was keen to gloss over any trace of Jewishness in Mahler's composition, whether out of personal unease or because it would not help in the prevailing social climate to win recognition for his music. In recent years, however, enough new information has come to light to gain a truer impression of Mahler's origins. And while it is impossible to accept Max Brod's thesis that Jewish music suffused his symphonies at the subconscious level,[44] there is enough evidence

41. 'Mahlers Feinde', op. cit., pp. 285–7.
42. Newspaper interview, 1910; see p. 289.
43. Guido Adler, *Gustav Mahler*, Vienna (Universal Edition), 1916; trans. in Edward R. Reilly, *Gustav Mahler and Guido Adler, Records of a Friendship*, Cambridge (Cambridge University Press), 1983, p. 18.
44. Brod (1884–1968) argued in 1915 that Mahler was 'unconsciously impelled' to compose 'by the same wellsprings within himself that produced the beautiful Chassidic songs' (article in *Der Jude*, vol. 51 (1915), reprinted in Brod, *Israel's*

to show that Mahler was familiar with his own heritage and that among the songs 'assimilated in his youth' were traditional Hebrew hymns and chants.

He was born of Jewish parents, Bernhard and Maria Mahler, in Kalischt, Bohemia, on 7 July 1860. It may be safely assumed that seven days after his birth he was ritually circumcised, a rite then universal among Jews. During the ceremony, he was given a Hebrew personal name, which has not yet been ascertained. Since a new-born maternal cousin was also named Gustav,[45] it is likely that, following ancient custom, both babies were given the Hebrew and secular forenames of a lately deceased ancestor.

The only trace of musical or religious devotion among his forebears was a great-great-grandfather, Abraham Mahler (1720–1800), said to have been a cantor and supervisor of dietary laws.[46] Two generations later, Mahler's grandfather and father were distillers and barkeepers, yet their communal attachment remained strong. When he moved to Iglau in December 1860, Bernhard Mahler soon became friendly with the cantor at the newly formed synagogue. The cantor, leader of divine worship and a man well versed in Scripture, was godfather in 1868 to his eighth child, Justine. [47]

Bernhard thirsted after secular knowledge and lusted, like many another bourgeois paterfamilias, after servant girls. He is sometimes described as an assimilated Jew, but this is contridicted by his close

Music, Tel Aviv (Sefer Press), 1951). Many of the songs of Chassidism, however, have their roots in the indigenous central European folk-music that Mahler heard as a child. For a thoughtful recent assessment of the Jewishness of Mahler's music, see Henry A. Lea, *Gustav Mahler, Man on the Margin*, Bonn (Bouvier Verlag), 1985, pp. 52–65.
45. Gustav Frank, born 14 September 1859 at Wlaschim, Bohemia, was a first cousin on his mother's side who studied art in Vienna at the same time as Mahler and remained in friendly contact with him. He became a high-ranking official in St Petersburg, where Mahler met him in 1907, and was in the Munich audience for the première of the Eighth Symphony, Mahler's last European appearance, in September 1910.
   Maria Mahler named her first-born son Isidor (1858–9) presumably after her paternal grandfather Isaac Hermann (died 1836), whose biblical Hebrew name he would have received (Isidor is a secular equivalent for the Hebrew Itzhak). Her third son Ernst (1861–75) may have been given the Hebrew name of her late father, Abraham Hermann, but where Gustav got his name remains undetected. Sigmund Freud, born of similar stock in Moravia, was named after his paternal grandfather Shlomo (Solomon). The fact of Mahler's circumcision can be taken for granted. Only the most alienated of Jews gave up this practice. One source of the surname Mahler is that it reflected the occupation of its bearer: *Mohel*, Hebrew for circumciser.
46. See Jaroslav Sanda, 'The family history of Gustav Mahler', *Jewish Quarterly*, vol. 33/3 (1986), pp. 53–4.
47. HLG1, p. 841.

connection with a religious officiant, by Gustav's attendance at synagogue services[48] and by Bernhard's own election in 1878 by a large majority of fellow congregants to the Committee of the Iglau Jewish Community, serving on its education board.[49] He could not possibly have stood for office in a traditional community if, as one researcher states,[50] he was a free-thinker who 'shut the door upon every religious usage of traditional Hebraism'.

The onus for Gustav's religious indoctrination rested with his mother, who was unquestionably devout. The hypersensitive Gustav was raised therefore amid a domestic dichotomy of religious observance and sensual amorality, simple faith and sordid hypocrisy. Small wonder that he acquired a scepticism for established religion while retaining his mother's unwavering belief in an all-powerful deity. His faith as a child must have pleaed the ill-treated Maria. It is reflected in his first school report in 1870, which shows Religious Studies (Mosaic) as the only subject graded 'excellent'.[51]

The largest lacuna in Mahler's religious background concerns his bar mitzvah, the occasion when, at his thirteenth birthday, a Jewish boy reads a portion of the Law and enters the community as a fully fledged member. Even among half-assimilated Jews, some form of bar mitzvah ceremony is observed: Theodore Herzl in Budapest and Arthur Schnitzler in Vienna, both throughly Germanized, celebrated a bar mitzvah at this time. It is an occasion for familial pride and not a little anxiety. It is Judaism's most important rite of passage.

As the son of a pious mother and a prominent member of the community, Mahler must have had a bar mitzvah ceremony. In April 1873, a matter of weeks beforehand, a local newspaper reports a service at the Iglau synagogue for Archduchess Gisela's wedding and continues with news of 'the young virtuoso Mahler' playing the piano at a celebratory concert.[52] His links with the synagogue and the community are undeniable. They have been obscured by the Nazi destruction of communal records, by Alma's anxicty to Christianize his image and by the reticence of his early friends who were, almost without exception, Jews who had converted to Christianity.[53]

---

48. See p. 11. De La Grange writes of 'one of his first visits to the synagogue', implying repeated attendance (HLG1, p. 15).
49. HLG1, p. 84.
50. Hans Holländer, quoted in DM1, p. 5. Lea also avers, quite erroneously, that 'Mahler was an assimilated Jew, who had no ethnic roots.' (Lea, op.cit., p. 1.)
51. HLG1, p. 22.
52. KBD, p. 150.
53. Almost all of Mahler's close men friends were born Jews. Among his student circle, Siegfried Lipiner and Victor Adler were baptized in the 1880s, Guido Adler, Löhr (born Löwi or Lewi) and Freund may have taken the same course. Neumann in Prague, Steinitzer in Leipzig, Behn, Arnold Berliner and Bruno Walter in Hamburg

Mahler himself never sought to hide or renounce his Jewish origins. 'Rather,' writes Alma, 'he emphasized it.'[54] He spoke of the Jews as 'a formidable people'[55] and blended pride with pain in his axioms:

An artist who is a Jew has to achieve twice as much as one who is not, just as a swimmer with short arms has to make double efforts.[56]

I am three times homeless: as a native of Bohemia in Austria, as an Austrian among Germans and as Jew throughout the world. Everywhere an intruder, never welcomed.[57]

Exactly when Mahler parted philosophically from the Jewish faith is undetermined, but the indications are that it came about in two stages. When Mahler went to study in Vienna in 1875 he presumably ceased any formal observances. It was common for Jews leaving a provincial home to adopt a cosmopolitan way of life.[58]

By 1879 the student Mahler was swept up in a tide of German nationalism and Wagnerolatry that supplanted the ancestral faith. On 1 November 1880 he commemorated 'the first All Souls' Day I have ever known',[59] mourning a Catholic girl-friend who took her own life. Some[60] believe this marks his transition to Christianity, but in the same year, unemployed and near despair, he declined to become Kapellmeister in Iglau 'because of my family',[61] implying that he would not publicly desecrate the sabbath in the town where his parents lived.

Their death in 1889 released Mahler from his last obligations to Judaism. Assuming responsibility for the upkeep and education of his brothers and sisters, he placed two in the care of a Catholic

---

were all Jews, as were Karpath, Stefan, Schoenberg, Fried, Pringsheim, Gabrilowitsch, Klemperer, Zuckerkandl, Decsey and Hertzka in Vienna. Several of them converted, from either conviction or convenience.
54. AMM, p. 101.
55. NBLe, p. 76.
56. Max Graf, *Legends of a Musical City*, New York, (The Philosophical Library), 1945, p. 212.
57. AMM, p. 109.
58. This was the case, for example, with Freud's father, who moved to Vienna in 1860.
59. GMB, p. 14.
60. Knud Martner is one, in his notes to GML, p. 388.

priest. Yet he still refused to follow the easy route to Christianity taken by most of his friends.

Four years later, when composing the resurrective verses of his Second Symphony, he set the first four stanzas of Klopstock's ode, then abruptly shied away at the line where the poem first mentions Jesus. The taboo of apostasy still held sway and, though Christian images abound in the Third Symphony, he did not formally change faith until it became absolutely essential if he was to achieve his lifelong ambition.

Mahler was baptized a Roman Catholic in Hamburg on 23 February 1897 as a means of qualifying for the job he was about to be offered at the Vienna Court Opera. He recognized that high office in the Hapsburg court was reserved for men who subscribed to the state religion; he confided to a friend that he had acted 'from an instinct of self-preservation' and that it had 'cost me a great deal'.[62]

A conversion undertaken for such pragmatic purposes is unlikely to be heartfelt. Alma called Mahler *ein Christgläubiger Jude*,[63] a Jew who believed in Christ, and made much of his fascination with Christian mysticism. But Mahler never went to church, never confessed, never celebrated religious rites or festivals. The deity he prayed to *in extremis* in the frantic graffiti scribbled on the score of his Tenth Symphony[64] is not a trinity but the ancient, monotheistic God.

No one, recalled Alma, 'dared tell him funny stories about Jews; they made him seriously angry.'[65] He was himself derided on racial grounds from the day he first raised a baton at the summer theatre in Bad Hall.

A spoor of anti-Semitic smears pursued him from post to post in the Austro-German provinces, climaxing in an unfettered campaign of racial abuse when he reached Vienna. Two days after his appointment, the nationalist newspapers *Deutsche Zeitung* and *Deutsches Volksblatt* objected to the 'Jewification' of the Opera.[66] The *Reichspost* generously postponed comment on 'this unadulterated Jew' until 'Herr Mahler starts his Jew-boy antics at the podium.'[67] It has been claimed that Mahler's radicalism and insensitive conduct provoked anti-Semitic reactions: there is ample proof

---

62. Ludwig Karpath, *Begegnung mit dem Genius*, p. 62.
63. AMM, p. 101.
64. Published in facsimile, Vienna, 1924.
65. AMM, p. 101. He did utter derogatory remarks to Alma about the Eastern Jews he saw in Poland, but these reflect a common anti-*Ostjuden* prejudice among Germanized western Jews, faithful or converted.
66. HLG1, p. 418.
67. KBD, p. 210.

that racist opposition lay in wait for him in Vienna well before he could begin to trample on any hallowed tradition.

That the stock clichés of anti-Semitic propaganda were singularly inapposite to Mahler and his music did not prevent the racists from churning them out regardless. It fell to Arthur Schnitzler to expose the inherent anomaly: 'If you didn't know which, Mahler or Richard Strauss, was the Jew, you would certainly think that the erotic, exuberant sensuality, the unbridled oriental imagination, the taste for extraneous effect and . . . the skill [Strauss] applies to the economic exploitation of his talent were properly Semitic characteristics. In contrast, one takes Mahler, a man of mystic ruminations . . . the chaste *Wunderhorn* singer . . . the folk-based composer . . . idealistic . . . the perfect type of German artist.'[68]

Mahler endured the attacks silently. 'We can do nothing about our being Jewish, our chief mistake,' he told Oskar Fried mournfully in 1906.[69] 'We must merely try to moderate those aspects of our nature that really *do* disturb.' After nine years of Viennese innuendo he had, it seems, come to believe some of the libels levelled against the Jews and himself.

It is curious that so forthright a personality did nothing to combat the persistent slanders. In Mahler's era in Vienna, a political response to ingrained anti-Semitism was beginning to emerge in Theodor Herzl's concept of political Zionism. Herzl, a formidable public figure – front-page *feuilleton* editor of the *Neue Freie Presse*, novelist and playwright – was driven to seek his solution when reporting the Dreyfus ugliness in Paris, an affair followed attentively by Mahler, who later befriended Colonel Picquart, Dreyfus's liberator.[70]

Mahler and Herzl were exact contemporaries, born within two months of one another and fellow students at the University of Vienna. In 1878 they were virtual neighbours, Herzl living comfortably with his parents at Praterstrasse 25,[71] Mahler in meagre student lodgings nearby. Both joined Germanic fraternities. Then and in adulthood they shared many mutual acquaintances, including the writers Schnitzler, Bahr and Zweig. [72] In the year Herzl published *The Jewish State*, Mahler presented his Resurrection Symphony,

---

68. HLG3, p. 366.
69. GMUL, p. 55.
70. For the Picquart connections, see Berta Zuckerkandl's published memoirs, quoted in KBD, p.245.
71. Amos Elon, *Herzl*, New York (Schocken Books), 1973, p. 32.
72. Bahr was swept up in the anti-Semitic fervour of the early 1880s and had Herzl drummed out of his student fraternity. He later relented and became a supporter and daily visitor of the Zionist visionary. Schnitzler sympathized with Herzl's ambitions. Zweig took his first journalistic steps as a Herzl protégé on the *Neue Freie Presse*.

one proclaiming national, the other individual, salvation.

Herzl, a man of the theatre, cannot have failed to notice Mahler's role at the Opera. Mahler, alert to new political ideas, must have taken note of the national solution to the Jewish dilemma. Neither, however, is recorded as ever having mentioned the other.

Turn-of-century Vienna is usually envisaged as a cultural village in which all the great minds were connected somehow across a vast network of creativity. The dull reality was that, although they rubbed shoulders in coffee-houses and patrons' palatial homes, the degree of spiritual cross-fertilization was minimal. Hofmannsthal and Herzl, Schoenberg and Freud, Wittgenstein and Klimt, had little ostensibly in common. Where they came together in an ethos and a cohesive culture was in their contact with Gustav Mahler.

Mahler and the Viennese Renaissance

Mahler in the decade of his dominance was, after the Emperor, the most famous man in Vienna. Cab-drivers stopped at that sight of him, murmuring 'Der Mahler!'[73] A man of Schnitzler's eminence would find himself involuntarily following Mahler down a street, fascinated by his gait.[74] 'The intensity of his nature seemed to fill the entire city,' noted the author Felix Salten.[75]

With political progress stifled by the lazy repressions of an anachronistic oligarchy, social ferment was channelled intc intellectual and artistic pursuits. It was an epoch 'which seemed to live particularly for the sake of cultural purposes'.[76] In it, Mahler reigned supreme, a living affront to hidebound traditionalists and a beacon to the young. A café full of Mahler-baiters would empty in an instant as patrons rushed to the window to catch a glimpse of the Director striding past.[77] The whole opera-house knew when Mahler, unannounced, entered the pit. 'For my parents' generation,' writes a current Viennese authority, 'the Mahler era was *the* great experience, *the* great event.'[78]

As the omnipotent cultural figure in a society where culture was king, Mahler sprang to Gustav Klimt's mind as the hero figure for his *Beethoven-frieze*. When Klimt planned the painting, he knew

---

73. Walter GM, p. 35.
74. See p. 309.
75. Salten (1869–1947), theatre critic of *Die Zeit*, is best known for his children's tale, *Bambi*. He describes Mahler in *Geister der Zeit*, Vienna (Zsolnay). 1924, pp. 62–5.
76. Walter TV, p. 56, quoting Jacob Burckhardt.
77. See p. 264.
78. Marcel Prawy in Sigrid Wiesmann (ed.), *Gustav Mahler in Vienna*, London (Thames and Hudson), 1976, p. 77.

Mahler only by reputation; Mahler's association with visual artists dates from his marriage to Alma. From the same circle, the architects Otto Wagner and Adolf Loos looked to Mahler's musical example when stripping Vienna's new buildings of encrusted traditions of ornamentation.

To leading writers he was no less of a hero. Schnitzler, Stefan Zweig, Salten, Bahr and Hofmannsthal, all adulated him. Young musicians when they set up their own concert society automatically chose Mahler as president. He stood at the epicentre of artistic activity (See Fig. 2).[79]

The small-town incestuousness of intellectual life in the capital of the Austro-Hungarian Empire ran deep into its sub-terrain. The creators may not have cross-pollinated, but Mahler fostered an atmosphere of striving and aspiration in which many shared. Take, for example, the separate realms of the composer Mahler and the philosopher Ludwig Wittgenstein (1889–1951), one chafing at the limits of tonality, the other defining the boundaries of language.

Wittgenstein had, so far as is known, no direct contact with Mahler. He was twenty-two years old when Mahler died, the youngest son of Karl Wittgenstein, an industrial millionaire and arts patron who financed Klimt's Secession building and the Society of Creative Musicians founded by Schoenberg and Zemlinsky. Brahms and Mahler were visitors at his palace; three of his children were gifted musicians.[80]

Ludwig Wittgenstein was raised in Mahler's Vienna. Music, say his biographers, was foremost among his broader interests. He subscribed, like Mahler, to Schopenhauer's view that music has greater expressive power than language or philosophy. One day in Cambridge, the ageing philosopher sat a young jazzman down at his piano and demanded a concise analysis of the structure and development of jazz.[81] This persistent anxiety to penetrate the essence of an art is typical of the ethos that Mahler fostered.

Mahler's era in Vienna is usually said to have ended on 9 December 1907, the day he left for America. His influence, however, persisted to the end of his life, reinforced each summer when

---

79. A recent biographer of Karl Kraus seeks to portray the satirist at the centre of concentric circles of Viennese creativity. With due allowance for special pleading, it is hard to see the commentator in any sense as creative instigator. See Edward Timms, *Karl Kraus*, London (Thames and Hudson), 1986.
80. For the Wittgenstein family and its musical connections see Allan Janik and Stephen Toulmin, *Wittgenstein's Vienna*, New York (Simon and Schuster), 1973, Chapter 6. Wittgenstein's elder brother Paul (1887–1961) lost his right arm in the First World War but founded a successful concert career on concertos for the left hand alone commissioned from Ravel, Prokofiev, Britten, Richard Strauss and Schmidt.
81. Janik and Toulmin, op. cit., pp. 175–6.

he returned to compose, conduct and reinvigorate those who shared his ideals. So long as Mahler was alive, even if he no longer lived there, Vienna sustained its musical energy. The day he died marked the end of Vienna as a source of music. Within six months, the city was stripped bare of musical creativity. Arnold Schoenberg moved in October 1911 to Berlin where for the first time he obtained genuine recognition. His brother-in-law Zemlinsky, perhaps Mahler's most worshipful disciple, transferred to Prague and offered a job there to Webern. In emotional turmoil, Webern followed Schoenberg to Berlin, then went on to Stettin. Alban Berg remained in Vienna, bitterly demoralized and barely able to compose.

The literary and artistic revival subsided more slowly, but had been substantially snuffed out by the time world war stilled the most stubborn of the Viennese muses. If *fin-de-siècle* Vienna is now regarded as 'the crucible of contemporary culture',[82] source of present-day pleasures and dilemmas, its discoveries were made possible and publishable by a particular climate. They were sparked off not by one another but, to an overwhelming extent, by the unique atmosphere created by Gustav Mahler in his revolutionary decade as Director at the Opera.

---

82. Phrase coined by George Steiner in South Bank television lecture, 1985.

Preface to the Reissue of
Mahler Remembered

The decade since this book first appeared has witnessed yet another shift in Gustav Mahler's public reception. Having risen from half a century of politically led neglect to inspire a restless generation with his ceaseless self-questioning, Mahler in the closing years of the millennium became established as standard concert fare – which is to say, he was embraced by the social and political establishments that control musical provision in western societies. 'My time will come,' he famously proclaimed. Measured in terms of popular recognition and exposure, that prophecy has been richly fulfilled – though not, perhaps, in quite the way he intended.

Mahler is no longer a voice in the wilderness preaching redemption ('I don't know what I am supposed to be redeemed from,' said Richard Strauss), no longer the searcher of hearts and mender of minds, no longer a subversive creator. Rather, in postmodern culture, he has become an all-purpose box-office attraction – a honey-toned entertainer of the moneyed classes. When an orchestra needs to make a splash or a conductor his career, they announce a cycle of Mahler symphonies, knowing that support for so *safe* a composer can be guaranteed. Raising their batons before a conspicuously corporate audience, some conductors are tempted to tone down the anger, the irony, the shrieking polemicism that might upset copper-bottomed concert-goers. Mahler is served up all too often nowadays as a palliative rather than a provocateur – overplayed, power-steered and under-penetrated.

The embers have dimmed in the Mahler debate, now that Mahler has been firmly installed among the Great Composers. He is an icon of sanitized heritage, inviolably non-controversial, universally accepted like a credit card. It has reached the point where maestros who privately dislike his music are obliged to perform it, and where critics who doubt his pertinence are discreetly advised to suppress their reservations. There may come a time when dedicated Mahlerians cry out for a rest from Mahler, before his music loses its capacity to shock.

The last decade of the twentieth century has produced a surfeit of Mahler biographies, symphonic studies, recordings and discographies – many of them piously recycling myths and falsehoods, as befits an object of mass veneration. Then there are the T-shirts, the medallions, the memorabilia; a visiting card with Mahler's signature scrawled upon it can fetch $1,000 at auction.

The Vienna Staatsoper has finally hung a huge portrait of Mahler and named a lobby in his memory. Initiatives are afoot to assemble a birthplace museum at Kaliste, in the Czech Republic. There is a Mahler Bibliothèque in Paris; a winter festival in Boulder, Colorado; a fan club in Japan; and a statue in the village square of Dobbiaco, high in the Italian Dolomites. Mahler, in short, needs no further advocacy anywhere in the world.

Yet as time passes, distorting his image in its Versailles mirror, it becomes all the more essential to return to original sources, to those who had living experience of Mahler and were able to convey a true sense of the man and the musician. *Mahler Remembered* brought to light authentic testimonies from many individuals and brought its fortunate author into contact with the last people still alive who had known Mahler in the flesh. Two women, in particular, possessed immaculate memories and left indelible impressions.

I got to know Anna Mahler, the composer's daughter, in the last two years of her life. We struck up a friendship that involved twice-weekly correspondence and violent disagreements over every topic under the sun, from socialism to sensuality. Anna loved a good argument and was endlessly curious about other people's views of the world, just as her father had been.

Not that we talked much about Mahler. Anna was a remarkable artist in her own right, a sculptor in stone and clay who seemed to cut right through the skin of her subjects to reveal inner character. Nowhere has Klemperer appeared more granitic, Schoenberg more appealing, Arthur Bliss more officious and Alban Berg more shifty than in Anna Mahler's unsparing busts. Much of her work was destroyed in Vienna between 1938 and 1945; she never looked back, rebuilding her life in London, Los Angeles and Spoleto, Italy.

Anna was an extraordinary woman who married five times and never lost her faith in love, with an intellect that did not stop asking questions even in our final conversation, on her deathbed in London. She was preparing an exhibition for the Salzburg Festival when her strength gave out; she was laid to rest in Highgate Cemetery, a few plots away from Karl Marx.

I had been planning to bring Anna together with another Mahler survivor in London. Eleanor Rosé was the niece of two brothers who married Mahler's two sisters. Her father, Alexander Rosé, organized the premiere of *Das Klagende Lied*. Eleanor grew up within Mahler's family circle and, aged eight, attended Mahler's wedding and was sent home for being naughty. 'What did you do?' I asked. 'I imitated his walk,' she grinned, and on the boards of her dilapidated living-room, this ninety-year-old lady demonstrated the arhythmic limp that afflicted Mahler in moments of stress.

Eleanor was removed from Vienna in 1904, when her parents divorced, but, as a budding violinist, attended all rehearsals and the first performance of Mahler's Eighth Symphony in Munich. I came to know her when, by divine coincidence, I took a flat in the same London house in the very month that *Mahler Remembered* was published. 'Do you know who's moving here?' she asked the workman sanding my floors. 'He's written a book about *Mahler*!'

Cut off from the Mahler milieu in childhood, Eleanor possessed a trove of unique memories and jealously guarded their accuracy. 'You can't quote that,' she would say, after relating a tantalizing episode: 'I'm not sure if I witnessed the incident or it was related to me.' Her devotion to truth and her rage against its misrepresentation were rock-solid Mahlerian values. Sadly, she never got to meet Anna Mahler. I have rededicated this edition fondly to their memories.

Norman Lebrecht
St John's Wood, London
July 1997

Select Bibliography

The basic Mahler literature

The following works are indicated by abbreviated titles:

AMM   Alma Mahler, *Gustav Mahler, Memories and Letters,* 2nd (enlarged) edition, trans. Basil Creighton, London (John Murray), 1968.

AML   Alma Mahler-Werfel, *Mein Leben*, Frankfurt am Main (Fischer), 1960.

DM1   Donald Mitchell, *Gustav Mahler: The Early Years,* London (Rockliff), 1958.

DM1r   (revised edition of DM1), London (Faber and Faber), 1980.

DM2   Donald Mitchell, *Gustav Mahler: The Wunderhorn Years,* London (Faber and Faber), 1975.

DM3   Donald Mitchell, *Gustav Mahler: Songs and Symphonies of Love and Death,* London (Faber and Faber), 1985.

GMB   *Gustav Mahler Briefe, 1879–1911*, ed. Alma Maria Mahler, Berlin and Vienna (Paul Zsolnay Verlag), 1924.

GML   *Selected Letters of Gustav Mahler*, ed. Knud Martner, London (Faber and Faber), 1979 (enlargement and translation of GMB).

GMBR   *Gustav Mahler Briefe*, ed. Herta Blaukopf, Berlin and Vienna (Paul Zsolnay Verlag), 1982 (further enlargement).

GMRS   Herta Blaukopf (ed.) *Gustav Mahler – Richard Strauss Correspondence 1888–1911,* trans. Edmund Jephcott, London (Faber and Faber), 1984.

GMUL   Herta Blaukopf (ed.), *Mahler's Unknown Letters*, trans. Richard Stokes, London (Victor Gollancz), 1986.

HLG1   Henry-Louis de La Grange, *Mahler*, vol. 1, London (Victor Gollancz), 1974.

HLG2   Henry-Louis de La Grange, *Mahler, L'âge d'or de Vienne*, vol. 2, Paris (Fayard), 1983.

HLG3   Henry-Louis de La Grange, *Mahler, Le génie foudroyé*, vol. 3, Paris (Fayard), 1984.

KBD   Kurt Blaukopf (ed.), *Mahler: A Documentary Study*, New York (Oxford University Press), 1976.

Mahlerthon	Eight-hour radio programme by William Malloch, containing recollections by musicians who knew Mahler, broadcast 7 July 1960 (Pacifica KPFK), 4–5 May 1974 (KFAC Los Angeles) and twice by CBC Canada. Part of the programme was used to fill side 4 of Leonard Bernstein's CBS recording of Mahler's Sixth Symphony.
NBL	Natalie Bauer-Lechner, *Erinnerungen an Gustav Mahler*, Leipzig and Vienna (E. P. Tal), 1923.
NBLe	*Recollections of Gustav Mahler*, London (Faber Music), 1980 (NBL, trans. Dika Newlin).
NBLg	Herbert Killian, *Gustav Mahler in der Erinnerungen von Natalie Bauer-Lechner*, Hamburg (Verlag der Musikalienhandlung Karl Dieter Wagner), 1984 (expanded version of NBL).
Roller	Alfred Roller (ed.), *Die Bildnisse von Gustav Mahler,* Leipzig and Vienna (E. P. Tal), 1922.
Specht	Richard Specht, *Gustav Mahler*, Stuttgart and Berlin (DVA), 1913; 2nd edition, 1918; 18th impression, 1925.
Stefan, *Studie*	Paul Stefan, *Gustav Mahler: eine Studie über Persönlichkeit und Werk*, Munich (Piper & Co.), 1910, 2nd edition, 1913.
Walter GM	Bruno Walter, *Gustav Mahler*, trans. James Galston, London (Kegan Paul, Trench, Trubner & Co.), 1937.
Walter TV	Bruno Walter, *Theme and Variations*, trans. James Galston, New York (Alfred A. Knopf), 1946.

Further Reading

The important three-volume Mahler biography by Henry-Louis de La Grange will be published complete in English translation before the end of the decade. Donald Mitchell's analysis of the music has filled three volumes, with a fourth yet to come. These two enterprises provide the most comprehensive and up-to-date assessment of Mahler and his works.

Regrettably, shorter studies are either outdated or inaccurate, with the exception of Michael Kennedy's serviceable *Mahler* (London, J. M. Dent, 1974) and Deryck Cooke's astute *Gustav Mahler: An Introduction to his Music* (London, Faber Music, 1980). Kurt Blaukopf's documentary study (KBD) is pictorially fascinating. Knud Martner's selection of letters (GML) is absorbing.

The portraits of Mahler by Alma Mahler (AMM) and Natalie Bauer-Lechner (NBL) are essential reading for Mahler-seekers. Those by Bruno Walter and Guido Adler are sporadically interesting.

Acknowledgements

The selflessness of Mahler scholarship is a delight that awaits any researcher. I am indebted to a number of specialists for assistance and advice, above all to Henry-Louis de La Grange and Donald Mitchell, to whom this book is humbly dedicated.

Irene Fröhlich-Wiener and Gordon Fielden helped me translate German texts. Patrick Carnegy has been the very paragon of an editor. In addition, I have received mental, material and moral aid from the following:

United Kingdom: H. Baron, Eileen Bell, Roxy Bellamy and Terri Robson, Stephen Boyd, David Chesterman, Judy Grahame, Jane Krivine, Ginny Macbeth, Fiona Maddocks, Mark Ottaway, Dieter Pevsner, Eric Shanes, Clive Sinclair, Daniel Snowman, Richard Stoker, Christel Wallbaum, Dr Michael Weitzman.

France: René and Gusti Klein, Mmes Marie-Jo Blavette, Thérèse Beutz (Bibliothèque Gustav Mahler), Annie Neuburger.

Austria: Mmes Herta Blaukopf, Emmy Hauswirth, Gerda Hanf, Alma Zsolnay (Internationale Gustav Mahler Gesellschaft), Professor Erwin Ringel (Vienna), Gasthaus Föttinger (Steinbach am Attersee), Dr Adolf Lex (Kulturamt, Klagenfurt).

Switzerland: Mme Lotte Klemperer.

Italy: Mmes Anna Mahler (Spoleto), Nuria Schoenberg-Nono (Venice); Herbert Santer (Dobbiaco).

Federal Republic of Germany: Inge and Klaus Tennstedt (Kiel), Antony Beaumont (Cologne).

Netherlands: Mme Desi Halban.

United States: Gilbert E. Kaplan, Jerry Bruck, Louise Bloomfield, Louise Zemlinsky (New York); Professor Elliott Galkin (Johns Hopkins University, Baltimore), Professor Edward Reilly (Vassar College), Dr Kay Jamison (UCLA Neuropsychiatric Institute), Lawrence Schoenberg, Jerry McBride (Arnold Schoenberg Institute, University of Southern California, Los Angeles), William Malloch (California), the late Jack Diether.

Canada: Professor K. Pringsheim.

The author is indebted to the following individuals and institutions for permission to reproduce text and illustrations (full bibliographic references to all published sources are given with each extract):

Bibliothèque Gustav Mahler, Paris and Baron Henry-Louis de La Grange for the manuscripts of Natalie Bauer-Lechner's 'Mahleriana', Carl Moll's *Mein Leben*, Berta Szeps-Zuckerkandl's *Mahlers*

ACKNOWLEDGEMENTS

Abschied and Maurice Baumfeld's *Erinnerungen*, for access to various periodicals and for the illustrations on pp. 106, 113, 115, 274, 289; Emile Zuckerkandl, Palo Alto, for *Mahlers Abschied*; Internationale Gustav Mahler Gesellschaft, Vienna, for memoirs by Theodor Fischer and Hans Bruckmüller and for illustrations reproduced on pp. 16, 34, 248; Donald Mitchell, Anna Mahler and John Murray Ltd for extracts from AMM; Dr Mitchell and Faber and Faber for Julius Epstein's memoir in DM1; Lotte Klemperer and Toccata Press for passages from *Klemperer on Music*; Martin Anderson and Toccata Press for Franz Schmidt's autobiographical sketch; the Arnold Schoenberg Institute, California, Lawrence Schoenberg and Nuria Schoenberg-Nono for the Schoenberg manuscripts; William Malloch for extracts from his legendary Mahlerthon; Eric Shanes for the illustrations on pp. 18, 21, 156, 233; David Higham Associates for Ethel Smyth's reminiscences; Kurt Blaukopf and Penguin Books for the Apponyi commendation; the Canadian Music Journal for Alfred Rosé's article; Artia publishers, Prague, for J. B. Foerster's memoirs; Verlag der Musikalienhandlung Karl Dieter Wagner, Hamburg, for Ferdinand Pfohl's account; Rowohlt Verlag, Hamburg, for Leo Slezak's *Werke*; Revue Musicale Suisse and Josef Ritter-Tcherv for William Ritter's memoir; Hans Moldenhauer and Victor Gollancz Ltd for Webern's diaries; Thames and Hudson Ltd for Willi Reich, *The Life and Work of Alban Berg*; the Estate of Egon Wellesz for *Reminiscences of Mahler*; the Estate of Ernst Decsey for *Stunden mit Mahler*; Harper and Row and Hamish Hamilton for Samuel Chotzinoff, *Day's at the Morn*; Sigmund Freud Copyrights for letters on pp. 280–84; Alfred A. Knopf Inc. for Katia Mann's *Unwritten Memories* and *The Letters of Thomas Mann*; E. P. Dutton & Co. Inc. for *Great Composers through the Eyes of their Contemporaries*; Antony Beaumont, Faber and Faber and Dietrich Fischer-Dieskau for the Busoni letter on p. 303; the estate of Stefan Zweig for *Gustav Mahlers Wiederkehr*; Österreichische Nationalbibliothek for illustrations on pp. 101, 135, 137, 150, 183, 227, 250.

Every reasonable effort has been made to ascertain and contact copyright holders. Any who have not received proper acknowledgement are requested to notify the publisher for amendment to be made in subsequent editions.

All illustrations and texts not otherwise credited are from the author's private collection.

I

Songs of a travelling apprentice (1860–88)

Chronology of Mahler's Life and Work

1860	7 July	Gustav Mahler is born at Kalischt, Bohemia.
	Dec.	Moves with family to Iglau.
1868	Dec.	Birth of his favourite sister, Justine (Justi).
1870	13 Oct.	First public recital, Iglau.
1871–2	Sept.–Mar.	Sent to Prague Gymnasium to improve his scholastic record.
1875	13 Apr.	Death of his favourite brother, Ernst, 13.
	summer	Attempts an opera, *Ernst von Schwaben*.
	20 Sept.	Enters the musical conservatory in Vienna.
1876	June	Wins piano prize at the conservatory, playing Schubert's A minor Sonata.
	July	Wins composition prize for a piano quintet.

Chronology of Contemporary Events

1860   In the twelfth year of Franz Joseph's reign as Emperor of Austria,
        Italy wages its fight for independence.
        Abraham Lincoln is elected President of the USA.
        Theodor Herzl is born in Pesth, May 2.
        Arthur Schopenhauer, 72, dies in Frankfurt. Mahler at an early age
        absorbs his philosophical influence.
        10 July: a competition is announced in Vienna for the building of a
        new Court Opera house.

1861   The Kingdom of Italy is proclaimed.

1864   11 June: Richard Strauss is born in Munich.

1865   Lincoln is assassinated.
        Wagner, *Tristan and Isolde*.

1866   Prussia defeats Austria in the Seven Weeks War.
        Friedrich Rückert, orientalist and poet, dies near Coburg.

1867   The Austrian Empire becomes the Dual Monarchy of Austria–
        Hungary.
        Ibsen's *Peer Gynt*.

1869   Opening of the Suez Canal.
        Tolstoy completes *War and Peace*.
        The Court Opera building opens on the new Ring in Vienna.

1870   Franco–Prussian War.

1871   The German Empire is proclaimed at Versailles; the Prussian army
        besieges Paris.
        Aida is staged in Cairo.

1872   Rückert's *Kindertotenlieder*, mourning the death of his son Ernst,
        are published posthumously.

1875   Collapse of the Austrian stock market.
        Bizet's *Carmen* opens in Paris; the composer, 36, dies three months
        later.
        Alexander Graham Bell invents the telephone.

1876   The first *Ring* is staged by Wagner at Bayreuth.
        Mark Twain, *Tom Sawyer*.

1877		Makes two-piano version for Bruckner of his Third Symphony.
		Befriends and shares lodgings with Hugo Wolf.
1878		Leaves conservatory, graduates from Iglau High School and enrols to study philosophy and art history at the University of Vienna. Starts composing *Das klagende Lied*.
1879	31 Aug.	Alma Schindler, Mahler's future wife, is born in Vienna.
1880	summer	First job: conducting at summer resort of Bad Hall.
		Suicide of one friend, insanity of another; Mahler becomes ideologically vegetarian and Wagnerian.
1881–2		Conductor at Laibach (Ljubljana); begins an opera, *Rübezahl*.
1883	Jan.	Conductor at Olmütz, where he lasts three months.
	July	Visits Bayreuth.
	21 Aug.	Starts work as assistant conductor at Kassel Court Theatre.
1884		Begins First Symphony.
		In love with singer, Johanna Richter.
	Dec.	*Lieder eines fahrenden Gesellen*.
1885	1 Aug.	Leaves Kassel, moving to Prague as third conductor at the German Theatre.
1886	1 Aug.	Appointed second conductor to Artur Nikisch at Leipzig.
1887		Completes Weber's opera *Die drei Pintos* while in love with the wife of the composer's grandson.
	13 Oct.	Meets Richard Strauss.
1888	20 Jan.	Conducts the première of *Die drei Pintos*.
	29 Mar.	Completes First Symphony.
	17 May	Resigns at Leipzig after conflict with the director.
	10 Aug.	Finishes *Totenfeier* movement of Second Symphony.
	1 Oct.	Named Musical Director at the Royal Budapest Opera.

1877   Thomas Alva Edison patents the gramophone.

1878   Tolstoy, *Anna Karenina*.

1880   Dostoevsky publishes *The Brothers Karamazov*, Mahler's favourite
        novel.
        New York streets are lit electrically.

1881   Tsar Alexander II is assassinated in St Petersburg.
        US President James Garfield is shot dead.

1882   Austro–Hungary, Germany and Italy form a secret Triple Alliance.
        Georg von Schönerer organizes Austrian political anti-Semitism.
        Parsifal at Bayreuth.

1883   Feb. 13, Venice: death of Wagner.
        Prague: Czech National Theatre is built. Kafka is born.

1886   Daimler manufactures the first automobile.

1887   Eiffel Tower is built for the Paris Exhibition.

1888   Wilhelm II becomes Emperor of Germany.
        Vienna inaugurates its new Burgtheater.

Natalie BAUER-LECHNER
(1858–1921)

Mahler did not readily talk of his childhood, confiding only in two women who loved him. His wife made notes of some of his reminiscences and rewrote them in the third person, sometimes contentiously. His previous confidante, though, preserved his own account more or less verbatim.

Natalie Lechner was born in Vienna on 9 May 1858, daughter of a bookseller and publisher. She met Mahler as a student at the Conservatoire and was his closest woman friend from the early 1890s until he met Alma in 1901. She had been married (1875–85) to a schoolteacher, Alexander Bauer, and earned her living independently as a professional violist, playing in the Soldat-Röger quartet. She longed to marry Mahler and attempted on at least one occasion to seduce him, but he did not find her physically attractive and exercised his passions elsewhere. Natalie shut her eyes somehow to his sexual relationship in Hamburg with the singer Anna von Mildenburg, with whom she was quite friendly.

But his engagement to Alma, twenty-one years her junior, forced Natalie to give up hope of marrying him. She bowed out of his life painfully but with great dignity and died destitute in Vienna on 8 June 1921,[1] just over ten years after Mahler's death. She had been among the first to recognize his greatness, although her ranking of genius was not altogether sound. In her will, dated 10 June 1918, she writes: 'What I thank Heaven for most is that my life has been allowed to encounter those two great spirits, Lipiner and Mahler.'[2] In that order.

Extracts of her Mahler recollections first appeared in issues of the magazines *Der Merker* (April 1913) and *Musikblätter des Anbruch* (April 1920). After her death, a savagely cut-down version was published by her nephew as a book.[3] Her manuscript, of which she made several copies, had circulated for years among friends in musical Vienna and 'various unknown persons had torn up numerous pages'.[4] An expanded version of her book[5] has been published lately in Germany by another relative, but is by no means

---

1. The cause of death was *'Altersschwäche, Melancholie'* (NBLg, p. 12).
2. NBLg, p. 13.
3. *Erinnerungen an Gustav Mahler von Natalie Bauer-Lechner*, ed. J. Killian, Leipzig, Vienna and Zurich (E. P. Tal & Co.) 1921.
4. HLG1, p. 700.
5. Herbert Killian: *Gustav Mahler in der Erinnerungen von Natalie Bauer-Lechner*, Hamburg (Verlag der Musikalienhandlung Karl Dieter Wagner), 1984.

ERINNERUNGEN AN

GUSTAV MAHLER

VON

NATALIE BAUER-LECHNER

Natalie Bauer-Lechner
geb. am 9. Mai 1858, gest. am 8. Juni 1921

1923

E. P. TAL & CO. VERLAG
LEIPZIG   WIEN   ZÜRICH

Frontispiece of Natalie's published memoir.

as comprehensive or as vital as the fullest surviving text, owned by Henry-Louis de La Grange. The extract below is reproduced for the first time.

In the times we chatted, G. told me something about his childhood. The first thing he composed on paper at the age of six was a polka, to which he added a funeral march as an introduction. He produced this in response to a promise from his mother that he would receive two crowns – although a condition was firmly attached that there must not be any blots on the paper. (G., it should be said, was great at making blots!) So he prayed to God before he went to work that he would not cause him to make any splashes, and secure in the thought that God would see to it that he didn't, he merrily dipped his pen in the ink without taking any care. He had a non-spill inkwell to preserve him from the worst disasters. But, oh dear, when he was on the very first notes he made a huge

puddle so that the lovely clean paper and all his prepara-
tions were ruined from the start. The messy little child
had to begin all over again. 'My faith in God suffered
quite a setback,' concluded G. with a laugh.

'My second attempt was when my father gave me the
task of setting a poem to music. Again a few crowns were
promised as a reward – my various sallies into art were
always for the sake of sordid gain. I settled upon a
curious poem by Lessing that goes something like this:

'The Turks have lovely daughters
Kept safe by harem guards.
A Turk can marry many girls.
I'd love to be a Turk.

To think of nothing but love,
To live for love alone.
But Turkish people drink no wine.
No, no, I'll not be a Turk!'

'You made a fine choice for a little boy,' I chuckled. 'I
must say, it suits you – considering that nowadays you
don't drink wine and are such a hermit as far as the ladies
are concerned – you really hit the nail on the head!'

'Heaven knows how I came to pick a thing like that and
what got into my head. I suppose I chose it because it
was short, though it did seem dreadfully poetic: "To live
for love alone!" [*der Liebe nur zu leben!*]

'Later on I did become keener on composing of my
own accord: a sonata for violin and piano, a nocturne for
the cello: all sorts of things for piano, and finally an opera
with a libretto that a schoolfriend wrote with me. It was
on the basis of this fragment (because I never got round
to finishing it) that I had the great misfortune to be
accepted by Hellmesberger (that idiot) for the composition class at the Vienna Conservatory, missing out on the
harmony and counterpoint classes.

'Before that, when I went to Grünfeld's in Prague as a
boy of ten, I amazed my fellow inmates by simultaneously transcribing everything they played to me on the

piano, even the most difficult pieces, without a single mistake, just from listening to them. Something that is so hard to do that it astonishes me, even today.'

G. enjoyed telling me about how his musical gifts first came to light when, as a child, his mother and father were taking him to his grandparents who lived just a day trip away. 'It seems I should have been happier lying in my cot than being taken for a ride along the highway in the big coach. So I cried so furiously that my father and mother were forced to spend most of the time nursing me in their arms: and when that did not help, to climb out and walk beside the coach, rocking and singing songs to me until in this entertaining fashion we arrived at our destination.

'Apparently I was still a babe in arms when I copied little songs and sang them back. Then, when I must have been about three, I was given an accordion and by working out the notes of the things I had heard I was soon able to play them perfectly.

'One day when I was not yet four a funny thing happened. A military band – something I delighted in all my childhood – came marching past our house one morning. I no sooner heard it then I shot out of the living-room. Wearing scarcely more than a chemise – they hadn't dressed me yet – I trailed after the soldiers with my little accordion until quite some time later a couple of the ladies from nearby discovered me at the market-place. By that time I was feeling a bit frightened and they said they would only promise to take me home if I played them something the soldiers had been playing, on my accordion. I did so straight away, up on a fruit stall where they set me, to the utter delight of the market women, cooks and other bystanders. At that, amid shouts and laughter they bore me back to my parents, who were already in a great panic over my disappearance.

'There was another occasion somewhat later when I came across a military band on my way home from school. I was so fascinated that I stood there heaven knows how long without being able to tear myself away – despite an urgent call of nature that soon filled my pants.

People began backing away in disgust until I found myself in the middle of a big empty circle.

'My first acquaintance with the piano was made on another visit to my grandparents in Ledeč. There was a battered old instrument in the attic which I came across by chance when we were clambering around and exploring the upper regions of the house. This jangling hulk excited my curiosity. I was still so small that I could only reach the keys with my hands held high above my head, but in this uncomfortable position and with my tiny fingers I plonked out all sorts of things I had heard, so recognizably that my parents and grandparents, who could hear down below – and then discovered that it came from me – were absolutely astonished. When Grandpa asked me whether I would enjoy having a big toy like that, I said yes with gusto, and the very next day, to my indescribable delight, the monstrosity arrived in Iglau, trundled over on an ox-cart.

'They soon engaged a teacher for me and I know for a fact that, to please my mother who always sat nearby when I was practising, I worked hard at the task. I made such rapid progress that by the age of six I played in a public concert, for which in order for me to operate the pedals, because my short legs would not reach, they had to devise their own special attachment.[6] At this and other early concerts that followed, they tell me there was no way I could be made to bow. Instead I would rush up to the piano, straight as an arrow, and begin to play, and when I had done my bit, despite the applause, I would rush straight off again and out of the hall.

'Very early on I began to give piano lessons. To make my pupil – about a year younger than myself, a lad of six or seven – play properly, I would rest my arm on his shoulder while he was playing, with my open hand against his cheek. The moment he hit a false note, he received a box over the ears! I also punished him for such

---

6. This performance is undocumented; Mahler's earliest reported concert was given when he was ten.

sins by, for instance, making him write out a hundred times: "I must play C sharp instead of C". Of course, with my Draconian methods it was not long before this teaching job came to an end.

'During the instruction I was giving to another boy, I got into such a fuss one day over his awful playing that I burst into tears of anger and ran home weeping to my mother. When she asked in fright what had happened, I stamped my foot and, with the tears pouring out, bawled: "That ass of a boy plays so badly that I won't teach him the piano for another minute, no, no, no!" Nevertheless he remained my pupil for years, until I went to Prague, and the lessons (at five crowns an hour) bore such good fruit that they praised me for his progress in the top grades.'

One more story comes to mind that G. told me about his childhood. He was about eight years old when one day after the evening meal Emma, the seven-year-old daughter of the schoolmaster who lived in the Mahlers' house [on the top floor], sent the maid down with the order to ask G. if he would tell her how to compose.

Willingly and in complete earnest he explained to the maid that Emma should simply sit at the piano and play whatever came into her head. She should identify the main theme and write it down, transpose it a bit, elaborate and vary it until a complete piece had developed. The maid reported all this faithfully, and one or two evenings later she came running back. 'I must come upstairs quickly: Emma had composed something but could not write it down.' So G. dashed up to help as fast as he could, asked her to play him what she had worked out and jotted it down on paper (probably something had stuck in her head from one of her piano exercises or somewhere). That was the first and last time Emma composed anything. 'But,' said G., 'it's by that method which I gave her at the age of eight that most so-called composers proceed all their lives.'

Around the age of three, Mahler was taken to the synagogue by his parents. Suddenly he interrupted the singing of the community with shouts and screams: 'Be quiet, be quiet, that's horrible!' And when, from his mother's arms, he succeeded in stopping everything, when the whole congregation was in consternation and had all stopped singing, he demanded – singing a verse for them – that they should all sing 'Eits a binkel Kasi [Hrasi?]',[7] one of his favourite songs from earliest childhood.

Regarding the childhood photographs of Gustav: this is what G. told me about the small picture showing him as a five- or six-year-old boy holding a piece of music: 'The picture-taking session was almost abandoned because I had got the idea that in order to appear on the sheet of cardboard, when I stood in front of the scarifying apparatus I, G., would suddenly be whisked, plonk, into the box through some sort of magic spell uttered by the man behind it. And then I should be stuck fast on the paper. This gave rise to a huge outburst of tears because I didn't want it to happen at any price. In fact it was the first time my father had to take strong measures with me. It was only the next day, when the photographer arranged for himself to be photographed before my eyes and I saw that, despite the image they showed me on the plate, he was still there in one piece even after the fearful procedure – only then could I be persuaded to pose in front of this photographer-cum-black magician.'

As an influence on his character, G. recalled an episode from his school-days. He was standing at the gate of the Gymnasium where the pupils had to wait for their reports to be handed out. He was tortured by an indescribable impatience to know what his testimonial said about him: and as it seemed to be taking longer and

---

7. Song untraced. Mahler was telling this story to an Austrian Gentile, unfamiliar with either Czech or Hebrew. It is conceivable that the song he loved was 'Etz Hayyim Hi' (The Torah is a tree of life), a synagogue hymn sung softly when the Scroll of the Law is returned to the Ark, a focal moment in sabbath and festival services that creates a strong impression on the young. An alternative suggestion is that it is a Moravian street song, 'At'se pinkl házi' ('the bundle should swing back and forth'), popular in Prague in the 1860s. See *News About Mahler Research*, 17, Internationale Gustav Mahler Gesellschaft, Vienna, April 1987.

longer before the revelation came, he thought he would
go crazy. However, my dear G. pulled himself together
and said to his rebellious soul: now just calm down and
drive out the devil of impatience that is within you! One
day you'll be grown-up and there will be lots of times
when you think that something you can hardly bear to
wait for will never happen. Just remember this moment
and tell yourself: in exactly the same way that this finally
came to an end, other highly unpleasant times will be
survived.

G. told me that when his mother had a headache, as a
small boy of three or four he would hide behind her bed
and pray that she would soon recover. Then he would go
and ask whether she felt a bit better now. And when she
said she was, in order to please him, he would eagerly go
straight back to praying.

From earliest childhood, G. associated concrete ideas
with all compositions. He would think up for himself and
recount long stories to do with them, and from time to
time he would recite them with musical accompaniment
to his parents and to visiting friends of theirs. He would
curtain off the windows to create an air of magic and
festivity and was often so moved by his own stories that
he could not stop himself weeping profusely. For example, to Beethoven's clarinet trio (variations on 'Ich bin
der Schneider Kakadu'),[8] he invented the story of the
tailor's [*Schneider*] entire life, right up to the grave: trial,
tribulation and poverty and finally his burial – with a
parody of a funeral march – which to him conveyed the
meaning: 'Now this poor beggar is the same as any king.'

'Mahleriana', manuscripts owned by H. L. de La Grange, Paris.

---

8. Op. 121a.

Theodor FISCHER
(1859–1934)

Mahler's childhood neighbour and playmate was the son of Heinrich
Fischer (1828–1917), Iglau choirmaster and briefly music director at
the local theatre. The elder Fischer was one of Mahler's music
teachers, instructing him in harmony and conducting him in choral
performances at the St James Church[1] and in municipal concerts.
Mahler remembered him affectionately and on his golden jubilee as
choirmaster in 1908 cabled congratulations from New York.
Fischer's son, Theodor, eight months older than Mahler, was his
class-mate at school and Vienna University. Theodor Fischer returned to Iglau as a lawyer, rising to be a chief magistrate. He gave his
recollections at a Mahler memorial meeting in the town theatre on 21
March 1931.[2]

Mahler himself often stressed that, above all else, childhood impressions determine the nature of artistically
gifted men. It will therefore contribute to an understanding of Mahler's personality and creative urges if we
become better acquainted with the spiritual atmosphere
and human relationships in which he grew up, the
earliest childhood impressions that survive in the artistic
subconscious and influence its creativity.

In December of the year Gustav Mahler was born, his
parents Bernhard and Marie Mahler moved to Iglau.

At 265 (later No. 4) Pirnitzergasse (now renamed
Znaimergasse), his father in the 1860s and early 1870s
ran a business manufacturing and serving liquor.[3] The
first floor of the house was the large family's home, an
apartment consisting of a big kitchen, a hall and two

1. It was not considered unnatural in Iglau, where religious tolerance prevailed, for a
Jewish boy to sing in church or to hear music there. See p. 21, note 3. According to
Fischer, Mahler attended church performances of Mozart's Requiem, Haydn's *Seven
Last Words*, Beethoven's *Christ on the Mount of Olives* and the Rossini *Stabat Mater*.
2. By a strange coincidence, the earliest reminiscence of Beethoven is by a man named
Fischer, a Bonn neighbour ten years his junior (see O. G. Sonneck, *Beethoven:
Impressions by his Contemporaries*, New York (G. Schirmer Inc.) 1926, p. 3):
Theodor Fischer's text presented here is as printed in *Deutsche Heimat*. It differs in
significant details from the typescript transcribed in KBD, pp. 148–9.
3. There is some dispute as to whether Bernhard Mahler actually ran a bar, but the
word used here, *Ausschank*, is unequivocal.

The Mahler home and tavern (centre) on Pirnitzergasse.

rooms. The larger room served, in conventional style, as a 'Salon' decorated with stereotyped furnishings; there was his father's glass-framed certificate granting him the freedom of Iglau, a glass case with porcelain, glasses and all kinds of rare objects, a glass-fronted bookcase stacked with classical and contemporary works which Gustav Mahler read at an early age, and a piano on which he practised and studied as soon as he began to take lessons.

Mahler went with me to the Royal and Imperial Junior School on Brünnergasse and from 1869 to 1875 to the German Gymnasium [secondary school] in a building erected by Jesuits behind St Ignatius Church. One school term he studied in Prague.[4]

Next door to the Mahlers, in a house owned by my grandmother,[5] there lived with his young family my father, who had returned after studies at the Prague Conservatorium and was artistic director of the German choral society, subsequently city music director[6] and choirmaster of both Iglau churches. The Pirnitzergasse, courtyard of our house, was young Gustav's favourite playspot. It had disused workshops with many silent and dark corners where we children could have adventures and scare one another. In the courtyard we would play 'robbers and soldiers' and similar games, all except Gustav and his favourite younger brother Ernst,[7] whom he positively mothered and would properly correct when he was disobedient.

There was a children's maid in my family, Nanni, who knew lots of fairy-tales. On rainy afternoons when we

---

4. Mahler's schoolwork was so poor in 1871 that his abitious father sent him to the Neustädter Gymnasium, Prague, boarding at the home of Moritz Grünfeld, a leather merchant with eleven children two of whom, Alfred (1852–1924) and Heinrich (1855–1931), became distinguished musicians. Mahler told his wife (AMM, p. 7) that he was kept hungry and cold, his clothes and shoes were taken from him and his bid to save a maid from apparent rape by one of the Grünfeld sons was rebuffed by both coital partners. Bernhard, on discovering his misery, restored Gustav to Iglau.
5. The widow Fischer (née Proksch). In 1872 Bernhard bought the house next door (264) from her and moved his business and family there.
6. For three seasons, 1868–9, 1873–4, 1875–6.
7. A year younger than Gustav, Ernst was a weakly child. His prolonged illness and death in 1875 of pericarditis were understandably traumatic.

Iglau, general view.

could not go out, Gustav and I listened avidly to her tales. Among the stories was, I recall, *Des klagenden Lied* [Song of Sorrow], which may have given rise to one of Mahler's subsequent compositions.

As we grew older, the municipal swimming pool became the playground where we quickly learned to swim and row boats. Gustav Mahler was a permanent guest in our house. Our school and playtime camaraderie developed into a youthful friendship that persisted into our university years; later, admittedly, our professions drew us apart.

His musical talent developed very soon; from earliest childhood he played by ear and with amazing skill on the concertina[8] all kinds of tunes and songs that he had heard from guests in his father's tavern. He had his first piano lesson at six years old from one of the players in the town

8. A gift for his third birthday (HLG1, p. 14).

orchestra [*Stadtkapelle*], then from Kapellmeister [Franz] Viktorin of the Iglau theatre, and eventually from piano teacher [Johannes] Brosch . . .

As a pianist, Gustav Mahler made such progress that he soon emerged as a *Wunderkind* and in 1870 appeared at the piano in a public concert at the city theatre. *The Vermittler*, an Iglau weekly, reported:

On 13 October 1870 there was a non-subscription concert at which a boy of nine,[9] son of a Jewish businessman called Mahler, made his first public appearance at the piano before a large audience. The future piano virtuoso achieved a great success that was much to his credit, but a better instrument might have been found to match his fine playing. If the rising artist's former teacher, Kapellmeister Viktorin, hears of yesterday's success, he can feel well pleased with his pupil.

. . . An infantry regiment was permanently stationed at the Iglau garrison and we children would obviously always be there when the army marched out with fife and drum, staged exercises and played light music or at military funerals; we would blow childish imitations of signals which, as Guido Adler [10] notes in his study, made such an impression that they crop up in Mahler's songs and instrumental works.

On family outings to Iglau's richly forested surroundings Mahler learned to love nature, a love to which he was loyal for the rest of his life. Often, we children would take part as spectators in folk festivities when townspeople and farmers – in summer in forest clearings, in autumn and winter in the local pubs – would have music, dancing and singing. The dances were played by the authentic Iglau country band (*Bauernkapelle*; it consisted of three stringed instruments and a double-bass with bow and handle). Among the peasant dances, the *Hatschô* stands out in its authenticity.

---

9. It was common nineteenth-century practice to diminish the published age of prodigies to excite greater astonishment at their accomplishment. Mahler was ten years old in 1870.
10. See p. 22.

The musical impressions that Mahler gained from hearing folk-music and songs can be found in his works. In particular, the themes of the third movement of his First Symphony bear a definite relationship to the dance style of the *Hatschô*.

. . . At school, Mahler was distracted, absent-minded – one of his secondary school teachers called him 'quicksilver personified' – too immersed in his own thoughts and transported from reality to see what the teacher was writing on the board. Even though he often imposed his will on his brothers, sisters and playmates, his nature was founded upon a superior sense of justice which could neither commit nor condone unfairness, and demonstrated tolerance, humanity and sympathy with poverty and distress; in the later years of childhood he could not pass a beggar without giving alms. These characteristics, so evident in youth, persisted throughout his life.

Theodor Fischer, 'Aus Gustav Mahlers Jugendzeit',
Deutsche Heimat, vol. 7 (1931), pp. 264–8.

Guido ADLER
(1855–1941)

Adler and Mahler were raised in the same small town, Iglau, but met for the first time as students in Vienna.[1] From the beginning of Mahler's career Adler, father of modern musicology in Austria, campaigned discreetly for his advancement. Mahler's marriage strained their friendship and his departure from Vienna in 1907 was a personal blow, but Adler's devotion never wavered. He wrote a short biography of Mahler[2] and many essays that contributed greatly to the appreciation of his music.

We enter a small provincial town on the border of

1. Sometime between 1875 and 1878. See Edward R. Reilly, *Gustav Mahler and Guido Adler*, Cambridge (Cambridge University Press), 1982, p. 81.
2. *Gustav Mahler*, Vienna (Universal Edition), 1916.

Iglau, main square.

Moravia and Bohemia: a nationally isolated German-speaking enclave with an ancient culture, a mining privilege and a cloth-workers' guild dating from the Middle Ages; the different faiths live peaceably side by side;[3] the Czech minority has rising aspirations in respect of the propertied Germans, who control the government and lead it conscientiously.

A large, broad square with historic buildings stands at the centre of town. There in a corner is the Catholic church and beside it the barracks, its alternating garrisons enlivening the settled society; the young officers bring colour to the town's main street and excitement to young girls' hearts. In the university holidays, returning students – members of the Iglavia Association – add further colour with their bright, gay hats.

3. In his autobiography, Adler wrote: 'Catholic priests and the rabbi, Dr J. J. Unger, promoted religious education in family life, and tolerance was the highest principle taught at school.' *Wollen und Wirken*, Vienna (Universal Edition), 1935, p. 3.

In this town, Gustav Mahler and I spent our childhood, he five years younger than I. The impressions of this small-town life remain for life: the tiny theatre with its massive pillars, so like the ones Mahler dominated when he took his first steps in provincial theatres.

For Mahler, the German and Czech folk-songs of his homeland were a solid anchor in his work as a composer. The military bugle-calls, reveille and last post, exercise and drill motifs, were transformed in him to sound images that conveyed the figure of the old German foot-soldier. March rhythms accompanied his imagination throughout his life.[4]

A deep impression was left by the graceful surroundings, the wooded slopes and particular magical places. The great Park Heilos and the broad tree-ringed parade-ground were favourite playgrounds for youngsters. Fresh air blew in from the plateau that is Iglau's floor . . . The boy grew up in a close-knit family circle, remaining devoted throughout his life to his sisters and friends. His life's struggle toughened his nerves; he experienced personally the truth of the old folk saying: poverty is the mother of all art.

'Gustav Mahlers Persönlichkeit', lecture at the Mahler-Fest, Amsterdam, May 1920, printed in C. Rudolf Mengelberg (ed.), *Das Mahler-Fest*, Vienna (Universal Edition), 1920, p. 17.

4. The composer Ernst Křenek, son of an army officer, had an uncle who was born in Iglau around the same time as Mahler. He visited the town on various occasions and was acquainted with the family of Gustav Spitz, an Iglau lawyer related to Mahler.

What kind of town was Iglau?

A hick town, as we say in America, nothing remarkable about it. Inhabited partly by Germans partly by Czechs.

Do you remember it as a military town?

Not at all. There are stories that Mahler picked up his horn calls while hearing them played at the garrison in Iglau. There was no garrison, no military at all. The first military came there in 1866 – and they were Prussians, after the defeat of Austria.

He could only have heard horn signals from six years old?

Possibly. But that Prussian horn signals inspired him in his symphonies, I would rather doubt. He just invented them. He didn't have to hear them.

Julius EPSTEIN
(1832–1926)

Professor of piano at the Conservatory of the Gesellschaft der Musikfreunde in Vienna, 1867–1901; editor of the complete Schubert sonatas. Epstein's affection for Mahler led him to engage the impecunious student as piano tutor to his own son, Richard.

It was 1875. I was giving lectures at the Conservatoire, when a visitor was announced. A man came to me, and asked for my advice. He was accompanied by a boy of fourteen or fifteen. 'My name is Mahler, and I have a spirit factory [distillery] in Iglau', began the elderly man. He gestured towards the boy. 'This is my son Gustav – he is absolutely set on being a musician. I would prefer him to study at the technical college and the university; so that eventually he can take over my factory, but the boy does not want to . . .'

The man's voice became troubled . . . unwillingly I examined his son . . . there was something unusual, and special about his appearance. I replied: 'I decide on his future? That is a very difficult request. But I shall try. Play something for me!' This addressed to the young man. 'What?' he asked, quite undeterred. On the contrary, he gave the impression that he was perfectly capable of forging his own destiny, and removing any obstacles.

'It doesn't matter. Just begin,' I urged.

I cannot even remember what he played, and at most it lasted five minutes. My judgement was firm. I put it in these words: 'Mr Mahler, your son is a born musician!'

Mr Mahler looked at me surprised, and even somewhat dismayed, and said: 'Forgive me, Professor, but just now you said it was difficult to decide on a person's future. You have barely listened for five minutes, and you have already made up your mind . . . '

'I am not being unreasonable,' I explained. '*In this case I could not be wrong. This young man has spirit, but he will never take over his father's spirit factory . . .*'

Julius Epstein (with gun), talent-potting.

But he talked to Natalie Bauer-Lechner about watching parades as a child. And Adler speaks of a garrison.

Later they established a garrison. In his childhood there was no military establishment.

(Interview with Ernst Křenek, London, June 1987.)

I remember clearly the grateful look that these words aroused in the young man's eyes.

Mahler entered the Conservatoire. I taught him the piano, and Krenn[1] gave him lessons in theory. At this point I must mention the fact that *Mahler was never a pupil of Bruckner*, an error that is always included in biographical notes.

Neues Wiener Journal, 19 May 1911, trans. in DM2, pp. 397–8.

Theodor FISCHER[2]

In the course of his first university year in Vienna, Mahler, his future legal adviser Dr Emil Freund, his cousin the copper-engraver Gustav Frank and I formed a literary club. Our meetings would debate literary and current concerns and usually ended in us wandering half the night bewitched in the moonlight by the glorious buildings of Old Vienna and totally abandoned to romantic enthusiasms.

Mahler lived in the fourth district, Margarethenstrasse 7, fourth floor, door 40. So far as I can recall he gave piano lessons and acted frequently as piano accompanist in solo concerts at the Bösendorfer Hall. I myself went to various of these concerts; at one of them Mahler trod on the train of the advancing singer's dress, earning an enraged glance. At another concert with a Polish violinist, he forgot himself in the accompaniment thinking of God alone knows what until the virtuoso had to stamp out the beat with his foot to awaken Mahler from his self-engrossment.

Theodor Fischer, 'Aus Gustav Mahlers Jugendzeit', *Deutsche Heimat*, vol. 7 (1931), p. 267.

---

1. Franz Krenn (1816–97), known as 'Old Krenn' for his dusty manner, was Mahler's composition teacher. Robert Fuchs (1847–1927), a prolific composer of insubstantial works, taught him harmony.
2. See p. 15.

Friedrich ECKSTEIN
(1861–1939)

Musician and man about town, pupil of Bruckner's and a popular figure in *fin-de-siècle* society.

In the heart of the best part of Vienna, set among old palaces and imposing government offices, stood our obscure vegetarian restaurant – on the corner of the dreamy, quiet Wallnerstrasse and the dark Fahnengasse, barely two metres wide. A small glass door led down from the street into the half-dark cellar, where the wretched gaslights burned from dawn till dusk . . .

The autumn of 1880 brought us an unexpected and important event. The October issue of the *Bayreuther Blätter*, which had for some years broadcast Richard Wagner's views, carried a great article by the Master entitled 'Religion and Art'. In it, arising from the same emotions as the newly finished *Parsifal*, Wagner argued passionately for vegetarianism, which he called the last hope of salvation for the degenerate human race . . . The result was that our vegetarian circle gained many new members, mainly young musicians who, inspired by 'Religion and Art', joined our campaign for a bloodless diet.

One day, a slim, young fair-haired man, pale-faced with fluff on his chin and upper lip, and piercing eyes, entered the restaurant. He uttered few words, except in a rare, wary growl. His name, I learned later, was Hugo Wolf and he had composed some beautiful songs . . .

More young men arrived, friends of Heinrich and Otto Braun[1] and of Lipiner.[2] One of them was shortish,

1. Brothers-in-law of Dr Victor Adler (1852–1918), founder of Austrian socialism; Heinrich Braun was an eminent sociologist. Others listed by Eckstein as daily *habitués* of their student circle are Heinrich Friedjung (1851–1920), eminent historian, Thomas Masaryk (1850–1937), future president of Czechoslovakia, and Hermann Bahr (1863–1934), a successful playwright who subsequently married Mahler's Hamburg mistress, Anna von Mildenburg.
2. 'That shy, melancholy, sensitive poet', as Eckstein describes Siegfried Lipiner (1856–1911), was around twenty-four years old when he met Mahler and became one

betraying a certain irritability in his uneven gait. His small face, framed by a full brown beard, was intellectually alive and tense; he spoke wittily in a strong Austrian brogue. He always carried a bundle of books or scores under his arm and conversation with him was sporadic.

His name was Gustav Mahler.[3] He had studied law, and completed his studies at the Vienna Conservatory. He came to our notice because he was the first to make a piano transcription of a Bruckner symphony. In later years I often discussed Mahler with Bruckner, who had only praise for the younger man's great talent.[4]

Gustav Mahler and Hugo Wolf had known each other from their conservatory days and were like old schoolfriends. Many years later Hugo Wolf told me that, when they were very young, he had met Mahler in the Herrengasse with a roll of music under his arm. Asked what it was, Mahler replied some songs he had just composed; could Wolf take a look? In the middle of the street, Wolf read the manuscript through and, beaming, declared: 'Very good! Excellent! I like them tremendously.' Mahler, delighted by his opinion, dropped his eyes, hesitated shyly and said: 'Well, I think we've got Mendelssohn licked!'

Some other time, I forget when, we held a vegetarian dinner with speeches and music in the dining-room of an old hotel. All the guests were vegetarian. Cyrill Hynais, a Bruckner pupil, played his Ocean Symphony on the

---

of the strongest influences on his intellectual development. His writings had already made an impression on Wagner and Nietzsche, but he published nothing after 1880 and lived out his life as Librarian of Parliament in Vienna. It is probably from Lipiner that Mahler received the idea of personal salvation through artistic endeavour.

3. On 1 November 1880 Mahler wrote to Emil Freund: 'For a month now I have been a total vegetarian. The moral effect of this way of life, with its voluntary castigation of the body, causing one's material needs to diminish, is enormous . . . I expect of it nothing less than the *regeneration* of humanity . . . Eat suitable food (compost-grown, stone-ground, wholemeal bread) and you will soon see the fruit of your endeavours.'

4. Bruckner's publisher, Theodor Rättig, told Paul Stefan that 'Bruckner always spoke of Mahler with the greatest respect . . . whenever Mahler visited, he always insisted on accompanying the young man down the four flights of stairs, hat in hand.' (Stefan Studie, p. 13.)

Mahler, 18, as a student in Vienna.

piano; Josef Reiff-Heissiger, a young opera singer, sang Loewe ballads and I gave Mozart's 'In diesen heiligen Hallen'. At the piano was Mr Gustav Mahler, twenty-one years old.[5]

Alte unnennbare Tage!, Vienna (Herbert Reichner Verlag), 1936, pp. 105–13.

Jacques MANHEIT[1]

In January 1883, aged twenty-two, Mahler took over as opera conductor at the municipal theatre in Olmütz, the second city in his native Moravia, with a population of 20,176,[2] two-thirds of them German. He had an orchestra of thirty musicians, a chorus of twenty, and a cast of nonentities;[3] he left after three months. Manheit, a baritone who later joined Mahler in Budapest, wrote his memories of the Olmütz period in a letter to the journalist Ludwig Karpath.

In Olmütz on 10 January 1883 our Kapellmeister, one Herr Kaiser, was conducting [Meyerbeer's] *L'Africaine* when in the fourth act something so terrible happened (I cannot say more) that he was not allowed to conduct to the end. Our director, Emmanuel Raul, was in despair: we no longer had a conductor. He sent telegrams everywhere but it seemed impossible in mid-season to find a suitable conductor. Three days later, however, he surprised us with news that he had found a young conductor, said to be a genius but also a very curious individual.

His name was Gustav Mahler. Next morning at nine,

---

5. At a political meeting of the same circle, Adler and Friedjung led the singing of 'Deutschland, Deutschland über alles', which Mahler accompanied 'passionately' on the piano to the militaristic tune of 'O du Deutschland, ich muß marschieren'. The political complexion of these Wagnerophile, hyper-nationalist groups is examined in the manuscript autobiography of one member, Richard von Kralik (Wiener Stadtbibliothek, Ms. I. N. 106.071, f.2). See William J. McGrath, 'Student Radicalism in Vienna', *Journal of Contemporary History* (1967), pp. 183–201.

1. Dates unknown.
2. KBD, p. 166.

he took his first chorus rehearsal. The singers emerged in despair, declaring they were hoarse and could not work with the new conductor. An hour later we soloists went into rehearsal. Mahler did not introduce himself to anyone. We regarded him with overt antipathy, but he did not respond to interruptions, merely demanded that we obey his instructions. And, curiously, no one dared contradict the young man.

Two days later we saw him on the podium for the first time, conducting [Meyerbeer's] *Les Huguenots*. At the end of the first act, the bass who was singing Marcel burst breathlessly into the dressing-room shouting: 'I can't sing with this man. He holds the baton first in the right hand, then in the left, moving his free hand over his face so I can't see his cues.' When Mahler heard this serious complaint he replied quite pleasantly that conducting made him very hot, the perspiration dislodged his pince-nez and he kept having to readjust it. He called the wardrobe master for a broad ribbon, tied it to his pince-nez and hooked it round his ears. But now he looked so comic that we could hardly stop ourselves laughing on stage and barely survived the performance.

Afterwards we went to our favourite bar at the Goliath Restaurant, where members of the company, theatre-goers, officers and journalists gathered. I was the only one who had introduced myself to Mahler, and he appreciated it. Even in the bar, he introduced himself to no one; I had to make the introductions. Ignoring the mockery of the wine and beer drinkers at our table, he ordered a bottle of water, two portions of spinach cooked in water and a few apples. Mahler was then a vegetarian and an enthusiastic follower of Professor Jäger's wool theories.[4] He spoke so passionately about these matters that other diners warned me to take him outside or there would be trouble. I persuaded Mahler to come to the café next door, where we played billiards. 'What exercises are

3. HLG1, pp. 87–93. Manheit lists a chorus of ten men and twelve women.
4. Jäger's book advocating the wearing of wool next to the skin was published in 1878, launching a rapid, far-reaching fad.

you performing, my dear conductor?' I asked, as he waved his cue about in great circles. 'Carry on with your game,' he replied, 'I am conducting the first act of *Les Huguenots*. Your colleagues are so tough with me that I have been practising giving them cues.'

Gradually the little provincial town got used to the peculiarities of the young conductor. He was not liked, but they learned to fear him. His manner of demanding and commanding was so decisive that no one dared oppose him, especially since performances had greatly improved under his direction. He hardly knew a single opera, learning each work as he went along. He did not mind that no one sought his company; all he demanded was that each did his duty. I considered myself lucky to see him often. I soon realized whose spiritual child he was.

The following episode is highly characteristic. One day I found Mahler in the café, utterly self-absorbed. When I asked why he was so sad, he replied that he had received bad news from home, his father was ill. Next morning on my way to the theatre I saw a man running demented, weeping loudly, through the streets. With some difficulty, I recognized Mahler. Remembering the previous day's events, I asked anxiously, 'In heaven's name, has something happened to your father?' 'Worse, worse, much worse,' howled Mahler. 'The worst has happened. The Master has died!' It was 13 February 1883, Richard Wagner had been taken from us. It was impossible to talk to Mahler for days afterwards. He came to rehearsals and performances, but remained inaccessible to everyone for a long time.

Towards the end of the season Mahler had his benefit. He wanted to perform Méhul's *Joseph*. . . . I shall never forget the rehearsals. Mahler jumped from the podium over the double-bass players on to the stage, directed, produced and conducted. The performance was attended by Herr Ueberhorst, senior stage director of the Dresden Court Opera, who had come to hear me sing. As we sat together in the restaurant afterwards, Ueberhorst said to me: 'A man who can bring off a performance like that is

something astonishing.' I pointed at Mahler, sitting at
another table, and observed that he would love to go to
Dresden. Ueberhorst looked him up and down, then
burst out laughing. 'No, no, that figure, that appearance.
In Dresden that would be quite impossible!'

Ludwig Karpath, 'Aus Gustav Mahlers Umfängen',
Wiener Journal, 5 February 1930.[5]

Hans BRUCKMÜLLER[1]

After auditioning successfully for the assistant conductor's job at
Kassel, Mahler returned to Iglau in the summer of 1883 and on 11
August agreed to play in a Red Cross charity concert for victims of
the Ischia earthquake. Bruckmüller, a young acquaintance with
whom he had played piano four-handed 'with vigour, perseverance
and enthusiasm for hours on end', volunteered to assist. But Mahler
could no longer tolerate amateurishness, and this was to be his last
public appearance in his home town.

> Among other pieces, he was to accompany on the piano a
> Singspiel,[2] *The Coffee Party*. Things started to go badly
> wrong at rehearsal. He had no interest at all in the utterly
> trivial music with humorous asides he could not grasp.
> He accompanied distractedly, uttered ironic remarks
> about the music and the ladies singing it, failed to keep
> time and provoked considerable discord.
>
> At the public general rehearsal, Mahler sat at a piano
> raised on a podium in the middle of the orchestra pit. I
> sat beside him, turning pages. Mahler played bad-

---

5. Karpath published a slightly longer version of Manheit's letter on 18 May 1908. It
contains a brief reminiscence of Mahler in Budapest: 'We had lunch together. And
then I really had to laugh. The man whose devotion to Richard Wagner had once
made him a vegetarian now ate knuckle-bone and horse-radish sauce with the greatest
enjoyment. He displayed his enthusiasm for Wagner in another way.' (KBD,
pp. 166–7).

1. Dates unknown.
2. Opera with spoken dialogue.

temperedly. They had got barely half-way through the Singspiel when Mahler, with his customary vehemence, kicked his chair over, slammed down the piano lid, glared at the dilettantish ladies singing on stage and said to me, loud enough so that his voice carried to the front rows of the stalls: 'Go on, Bruckmüller, you accompany this damned nonsense. It's too difficult for me.' With that, he stamped out of the pit, leaving me to pick up the accompaniment as best I could and play through to the end.

At the concert itself,[3] Mahler played Beethoven's 'Kreutzer' Sonata with the virtuoso violinist Fräulein Ott von Ottenfeld[4] and I, once again, turned pages for him. In his impatience, he could never wait for the moment the page was to be turned, but kicked me repeatedly well ahead of time, presumably to remind me of my duty. I let it pass once or twice, then began to get my own kick in first.

He played divinely. I turned over faultlessly, and the audience was unaware there had been a kicking-match under the piano. As we stood to receive the loud applause, Mahler shouted at me: 'You *Schweinehund!*'[5] Fräulein von Ott, thinking this was intended for her, asked, all the while acknowledging the public acclaim, 'Who is?' And Mahler burst out laughing at me.[6]

'Aus Gustav Mahlers Jugendzeit', article in December 1932 issue of *Igel-Land*, a supplement to the *Mährische Grenzboten*, newspaper of the German-speaking populace of Iglau. Copy in the archives of the Internationale Gustav Mahler Gesellschaft, Vienna.

---

3. Attended by royalty in the person of Archduke Eugen (HLG1, p. 107).
4. Camilla Ott, Edle von Ottenfeld, had known Mahler as a student. She gave up her performing career on marriage, becoming a successful violin teacher in Vienna under her married name, Camilla von Stefanovic-Viloska. She wrote in 1897 to congratulate Mahler on his appointment to the Vienna Opera and received a cordial reply (GML, p. 222).
5. You bastard!
6. Bruckmüller relates that when he saw Mahler once again, after he had conducted his First Symphony in Brünn (Brno) in 1906, Mahler asked laughingly if he still remembered their kicking-match.

Löhr.

Friedrich (Fritz) LÖHR
(1859–1924)

A member of Mahler's student circle in Vienna, Löhr was an archaeologist and philologist, one of the founders of the Austrian Archaeological Institute and for many years its secretary. He played an unsung role in the birth of Mahler's Eighth Symphony[1] and in 1924 helped edit the first collection of his letters.

Though acquainted as students, they were not drawn closely to each other until June 1883, when Löhr's twenty-six-year-old brother died in Kassel, where Mahler, the new assistant conductor, had befriended him. A shared sense of loss bound them together. For the next two years their friendship 'was at a peak of intensity that could not be sustained, as our careers took us in different directions.'[2] They corresponded copiously and spent walking holidays together. Mahler, Löhr discovered, had an *orgiastic* worship of nature.

Mahler arrived at our house in Perchtoldsdorf on 1 July [1884] and remained until after his birthday . . . Two things predominated: our walks, and many hours of music. Despite the summer heat, we shut the windows of my first-floor room overlooking the market-place, yet people always stood outside listening in amazement. How few today can imagine what it meant then to hear Mahler at the piano.

Granted, he said he had been a better pianist five or six years earlier. But never before or since have I experienced such dematerialization of the human and technical process of playing. Mahler rose indescribably above what his hands did. He could not have explained it himself; every technical problem was annulled, everything was disembodied, cerebral, passionately and spiritually intent on all that passed, without conscious contact, from the keys into himself.

. . . In Beethoven's Op. 111, the opening storm broke in a fearsome maestoso, shatteringly intense, with a ferocity wilder than I have ever heard; while the finale faded out luminously into the loveliest beauty, softly and

1. See p. 254.
2. Note by Löhr in GML, p. 392 (GMB, p. 473).

softer still, from earthliness into eternity.

How can words convey the effect of his playing? Looking back, I am awestruck by the sublime and exclusive privilege of hearing him in the Beethoven sonatas, Bach's *Well-tempered Clavier* and much else by the most-loved masters – and, one unforgettable afternoon in the long house beside the Karlskirche where Mahler then had his lodgings in Vienna, Beethoven's *Missa solemnis* in one fell swoop. Soon afterwards Mahler lost interest in playing the piano: he had achieved the same mastery over the orchestra . . .

GMB, pp. 473–4.

Angelo NEUMANN
(1838-1910)

A retired tenor, Neumann formed a touring company to introduce Wagner's *Ring* to several European capitals, then became director at Leipzig and Bremen. In 1885 he took over the failing Deutsches Landestheater in Prague. A canny judge of conductors, he had already launched the careers of Artur Nikisch and Anton Seidl[1] and now became the first to advance Mahler's prospects.[2] Though their brief association was marred by artistic collisions, they parted amicably.

When at the beginning of 1885 the newspapers reported that I had been appointed to lead the Royal German Theatre at Prague, one of the first letters I received offering his services was from a young man whose name was quite unknown to me. He was chorus-master at Kassel, where he was unable to make much progress, restricted to the likes of *Der Waffenschmied* and *Zar und Zimmermann*. He wanted to be engaged as conductor in Prague.

---

1. Anton Seidl (1850–98), born in Budapest, assisted in preparing parts for the first *Ring* and on Wagner's recommendation was engaged at Leipzig by Neumann. In 1885 he left Prague to conduct at the Metropolitan Opera and subsequently the New York Philharmonic Orchestra. He died in New York of food poisoning. For Nikisch see p. 39.

Angelo Neumann in 1883.

I cannot really say why the style and content of this letter, among the many applications for the Kapellmeister vacancy,[3] made me send an immediate, cautiously encouraging reply. I wrote that matters in Prague were not yet finalized, as he could see from the newspapers, but if he wanted a situation he should come forward and report to me in person. After a single conversation with the young musician, I engaged him.

Even before he stepped on to the podium, I had evidence of his passion for art at a *Lohengrin* rehearsal conducted by Anton Seidl. It was to be the first production of my regime and I was directing it myself. Suddenly, in the second act wedding procession, I heard a voice from the stalls exclaim: 'Good God, I never believed it was possible to rehearse like that. That was divine!'

The day after the *Lohengrin* performance I conferred with Seidl and we decided to let the young hothead conduct Cherubini's *Les deux journées* on the Emperor's birthday.[4] The new conductor, who put every ounce of his energy into his task, seemed to us to move about too much on the podium, reminding us strongly of Hans von Bülow. Many people on all sides questioned our wisdom in letting him conduct before the Emperor, but we stuck to the decision.

His début went off well and as a result the young musician was given a year's contract at the Royal German Theatre. When I came to allocate roles for the rest of the season, I entrusted the young conductor with *Rheingold* and *Walküre*, which were to enter the repertoire for the first time, and not wishing to displace the first Kapellmeister, Slansky,[5] who had been twenty-five years at the theatre, assigned him a new production of *Don Giovanni*.

How astonished I was when after a few days of rehearsal, Kapellmeister Slansky showed up in my office

2. His later discoveries included Otto Klemperer, Franz Schalk and Leo Blech.
3. Seidl had given notice of his departure for America.
4. 18 August 1885 – also Neumann's birthday, his fifty-second.
5. Ludwig Slansky (1833–1905), orchestral director in Prague 1863–89.

to inquire: 'Herr Direktor, are you serious about performing *Don Giovanni*?' 'Obviously,' I replied. 'But look
here,' he explained, 'you have only just brought the
public back into the theatre. Surely you don't want to
drive them out again?' When I asked what he meant, he
replied: 'We have always had a failure in Prague with
Don Giovanni.' I said: 'Do you seriously think that the
German Theatre of Prague, the very house where Mozart
himself brought the opera into the world,[6] can have a
repertoire without *Don Giovanni*?' Whereupon Slansky
replied that people in Prague did not know what to make
of the opera. 'So it will be all right if I take *Don Giovanni*
away from you and replace it with another work?' 'Of
course,' he laughed.

That is how it came about that I gave *Don Giovanni* to
the new conductor who had been so successful in the
Cherubini opera. This young firebrand took on *Don
Giovanni* with great enthusiasm, I directed it, and the
public and critics were delighted.[7]

'Mahler in Prag', in Paul Stefan (ed.), *Gustav Mahler: Ein Bild seiner
Persönlichkeit in Widmungen*, Munich (Piper), 1910, pp. 7–9.

Max STEINITZER
(1864–1936)

Mahler was appointed second conductor to Artur Nikisch[1] at the
Neues Stadttheater in Leipzig in July 1886 and remained there just

---

6. Almost exactly a century earlier, on 29 October 1787.
7. Neumann's deputy, Heinrich Teweles, wrote: 'Mahler was immersed in his scores.
Even when not immersed, he disdained acquiring personal support at the Opera'.
(*Moderne Welt*, (1921), Mahler issue, 1921, p. 32.)

1. Artur Nikisch (1855–1922), Hungarian-born conductor who made his mark at
the Leipzig Opera in 1877 and was first conductor there 1882–9. He became the
outstanding orchestral director of his time, as permanent conductor of the Leipzig
Gewandhaus concerts and Berlin Philharmonic Orchestra and a formative influence
on the Boston and London symphony orchestras. Fond of cards and women, he had
little in common with Mahler but admired his early symphonies, premièring in Berlin
in November 1896 the opening movement of the Third.

under two years. During this time he completed and performed Weber's opera *Die drei Pintos*, finished his own First Symphony and wrote the opening movement of the Second. In Bach's town, Mahler became acquainted with venerable traditions and with the fast-rising Richard Strauss, who remembered that 'Max Steinitzer, my later biographer and friend of my youth, had sung the praises of Mahler'.[2]

Steinitzer, professor of music at the University of Freiburg, combined an academic and literary career with appearances as conductor and pianist. He was accompanist to the soprano Amalie Joachim and in 1892 introduced her to Mahler's Lieder. In the Nazi era, affected by the racial laws, Steinitzer committed suicide.

Among the soloists, choir and orchestra, and in musical and unmusical Leipzig society, many people got off to a bad start with the glowering young Austrian. Only a few companions felt the full impact of a personality whose every gesture and word was absolutely precise and individual. The young Mahler exemplified Man as expression, amid so many for whom Man exists only as a form. He did his best to be polite, but whenever anybody uttered a stupid remark or banality – even though it may have been apt for the occasion – his facial expression made his feelings all too clear. Before he could control himself and compose his features as conventional good manners demanded, everyone had read his thoughts.

Supporting every serious endeavour, he was a good friend of Karl Perron, followed Paul Knüpfer with interest and marvelled at the intuitive talents of Josephine Artner.[3] That was in Leipzig in the late eighties. Later, when I read in the Vienna newspapers of Mahler's authoritarianism, despotism, even satanism, I would smile and recall the affability, humour and good nature that characterized his private relations with us musicians. Pretensions, imperfections and dilettantism were what he so detested that one sensed his reactions instantly, for he was unable to disguise them.

---

2. GMRS, p. 107.
3. All three are singers. Karl Perron (1858–1928) was a baritone at the Leipzig Opera. Josephine von Artner (née Artanyi) (1867–1932) was a Czech-born soprano who followed Mahler to Hamburg and sang in the first performance of his Second Symphony. Knüpfer later joined the Kroll Opera in Berlin.

At one social gathering, an eminent musician who disagreed with Richard Wagner on a matter of interpretation asked politely for Mahler's opinion. Before he could arrange his features in the appropriate smile, Mahler blurted out: 'When Wagner has spoken, let others hold their tongues.'

At the same party, attended mainly by musicians, a young man sat down at the piano and played one of his compositions, 'In the Silent Valley', a salon piece so unsuited to the company that all were struck dumb with embarrassment. To end the painful silence, Mahler approached the offender with an irresistible smile. 'That's it exactly!' he said. 'I know that valley, at least I think I do. It's in Styria. Thank you so much.' And he shook the hand of the young man, who blushed with pleasure, while the host (a man much attached to formality) and all Mahler's friends relished his adroitness. Among those most grateful was the oldest musician present, Reinecke,[4] who would otherwise have had to force himself to say something complimentary. On such occasions, Mahler could be uncannily like [E. T. A.] Hoffmann's description of Kapellmeister Kreisler in *Kater Murr*, notably in the way he could appear official, yet at the same time be directly personal.

He would lunch daily at Baarmann's restaurant, usually with Karl Perron and myself. One day, he had just finished eating when a deputation of students turned up to seek his patronage for a new collegiate musical society with modernist tendencies. Mahler listened sympathetically to an embellished introduction speckled with serious North German courtesies. Finally, the leader came to the point: they wanted the support of the town's two most important musicians, Reinecke and Mahler. When he heard this, Mahler could no longer play along with the seriousness of the situation. Long after the deputation had taken itself off, he remained helpless with

---

4. Carl Heinrich Carsten Reinecke (1824–1910), conductor, prolific composer and pillar of conservatism in Leipzig where, as professor of composition, he taught Grieg and Albéniz.

laughter in the murky, underground tavern with the famously long menu.

In the orchestra and that section of the public close to its affairs, one often heard remarks like: 'As if we had to wait for Mahler to come here from Prague and teach us what a piano is. As if nothing would get done without these new ideas. If Nikisch had not recovered quickly,[5] the whole orchestra would have gone sick.'

The two other Leipzig conductors, Reinecke and Nikisch, ploughed separate furrows. Reinecke was at his best in Mozart and Schumann, Nikisch in the glittering ways of French and Italian music. One can well imagine the joy we youngsters felt at Mahler's unrestrained crescendos and ritenutos. It was a great event in our lives when, for example, he took the first four bars of [Beethoven's] Third *Leonore* Overture in a continuous ritenuto: thus, in the simplest manner, each of the descending octaves acquired tragic import until finally the low F sharp sounded in majestic, rigid stillness, like the waters over which God's spirit moved at the Creation.

In *Don Giovanni* he began the trio with the dying Commendatore at fairly quick tempo, slowing it down gradually to reach an enormous climax of which the final bars were an Adagio of deeply impressive effect. The Allegro of the same *Leonore* overture was begun with a real pianissimo, whose like few of us had ever heard. In short, when Mahler conducted every bar gained new interest.

The circle of his closest friends put up with the equally plastic style of his piano playing, shedding new light on Beethoven. It was astonishing how in even the most thankless pieces like Schubert's D major Sonata, one of his examination pieces at the Vienna Conservatory, he aroused unanimous admiration.

Despite his apparent tranquillity and coolness, one would occasionally surprise him at moments immersed in his own creativity and intoxicated with the beauty of his

5. Mahler stood in as first conductor for three months from February 1887, when Nikisch was laid low with an inflammation of the lungs.

sound-world. It was then no small matter to drag him away to a late dinner; one had to talk 'spiritually' to him and take him only to a tavern where he could not possibly meet people who might disrupt his exalted creative mood. And on the way we had to take good care that he did not collide with other pedestrians or vehicles.

His attention was occupied at the time with over-sweet melodies from a lost youthful composition that he was reworking into an orchestral piece. This, however, displeased him so much that he did not just burn the score but also destroyed the piano reduction I had made for him.

Of all the people I have ever known, Mahler was the most powerfully articulate . . . He could have been a highly original writer . . .

'Mahler in Leipzig', in Paul Stefan (ed.), *Gustav Mahler: Ein Bild seiner Pesönlichkeit in Widmungen*, Munich (Piper), 1910, pp. 10–14.

In a further recollection of Mahler nine years later, Steinitzer added:

As long as all I knew of Mahler's was *Das klagende Lied*, I never quite believed in his lasting artistic success. When, after completing the *Pintos* opera, he feverishly began to compose, I once said to him: 'It has never yet happened that real genius burst forth at the late age of twenty-eight. You seem to be temporarily uplifted, as at the time of *Das klagende Lied*. Far better, it seems to me, that you should write down the things you have expressed to me about artistic and human relationships and conditions. I know no one who, unburdened by accepted teachings, has such a sovereign command of words and so penetrating an insight into human psychology. In this, you have something almost like Goethe, and this should not be restricted to the handful of people who happen to know you. Composers, we have plenty.'

At that, Mahler laughed, saying: 'My dear Eckermann,[6] I can't help it. I just have to compose.' Later,

6. Johann Peter Eckermann (1792–1854) recorded and published his conversations with Goethe.

when I saw the draft of the First Symphony, I naturally changed my mind. Mahler also sang to me in his apartment, in a pricelessly vivid performance, the newly finished *Wunderhorn* Lieder.

Sometimes I accompanied him as far as his garden gate, where he would give a half-expectant, half-worried look and say 'Sdeinidhä' – he once heard a Czech pronounce my name like that and repeated it innumerable times – 'Perhaps the Devil will call on us today.' This was what he called the mood from which the first motive of the First Symphony finale and the *Totenfeier* of the Second Symphony originated, and which gave his features at that time their prevailing expression.

Musikblätter des Anbruch, vol. 2/7–8 (1920), p. 297.

Ethel SMYTH
(1858–1944)

In the course of completing *Die drei Pintos*, Mahler worked closely with Weber's grandson, a captain in the Leipzig Regiment, and fell in love with his Jewish wife, Marion. Their household was his 'escape-hatch from the world' and Marion's 'musical, radiant and aspiring nature gave my life new meaning'.[1] When he finished the first movement of his First Symphony, it was to the Webers that he ran at midnight to play it. He also wrote a song for their children.

The British composer and suffragette met Mahler while visiting friends in Leipzig, where she had studied. She reports the outcome of the illicit relationship.

The poor Webers' subsequent history was tragic. Gustav Mahler, who was then one of the conductors at the Leipzig Opera, fell in love with her and his passion was reciprocated – as well it might be, for in spite of his ugliness he had demoniacal charm. A scandal would mean leaving the army, and Weber shut his eyes as long

1. NBLe, p. 159.

as was possible, but Mahler, a tyrannical lover, never hesitated to compromise his mistresses. Things were getting critical, when one day, travelling to Dresden in the company of strangers, Weber suddenly burst out laughing, drew a revolver, and began taking William Tell-like shots at the head-rests between the seats. He was overpowered, the train brought to a standstill, and they took him to the police station raving mad – thence to an asylum. Always considered rather queer in the army, the Mahler business had broken down his brain. I afterwards heard he had lucid intervals, that his wife in an agony of remorse refused to see her lover again . . . and the rest is silence.

Mahler's life was full of incidents of this sort, and knowing him even as slightly as I did I can well believe it, not being able to conceive that any woman who loved and was beloved by him could resist him. I felt this even when I saw him last (it was at Vienna in 1907) worn out, exasperated, prematurely aged, wrestling with the Habsburgs as personified by the Intendant of the Opera House he had made the first in the world. He was far and away the finest conductor I ever knew, with the most all-embracing musical instinct, and it is one of the small tragedies of my life that just when he was considering the question of producing *The Wreckers*[2] at Vienna they drove him from office. When he was gone even his enemies regretted their action; but the ideal of art he set, his passionate refusal to abate one jot or tittle of his artistic demands, the magnitude and purity of his vision, these are things that start a tradition and linger after sun-set . . . At the time I am speaking of in Leipzig I saw but little of him, and we didn't get on; I was too young and raw then to appreciate this grim personality, intercourse with whom was like handling a bomb cased in razor-edges.

Impressions that Remained, London (Longmans, Green & Co.), vol. 2. (1923), pp. 173–4.

---

2. Smyth's third opera.

Richard STRAUSS
(1864–1949)

In a striking image drawn from Schopenhauer, Mahler likened himself and Strauss to 'two miners who dig a shaft from opposite sides and finally meet underground'.[1] His assumption that they shared identical musical goals was soon confounded. Their meetings, too, took place on the surface of musical activity rather than in the cerebral depths.

The uneven twenty-four-year friendship between the two leading Austro-German composers was founded on reciprocal aid and respect, rather than on a meeting of minds. Mahler described one encounter, their last, 'almost as between potentates',[2] suggesting the cordial atmosphere of a political summit with scant mutual comprehension.

When they were introduced in 1887, Strauss was visiting Leipzig to conduct his First Symphony and Mahler, the town's second conductor, had yet to compose one. Strauss reported excitedly to Hans von Bülow:

> I made a new, very delightful acquaintance in Herr Mahler, who seemed a highly intelligent musician and conductor; one of the few modern conductors who knows about tempo modification, and generally held excellent views especially on Wagner's tempos (in contrast to those of the currently acknowledged Wagner conductors). Mahler's arrangement of Weber's *Drei Pintos* seems to me a masterpiece; the first act, which Mahler played to me, I found quite delightful . . . I think you too will enjoy it![3]

Bülow, however, detested it, and Strauss rapidly recanted:

> At rehearsal yesterday I saw Acts 2 and 3 [of *Pintos*] and entirely understand your horror, they really are extremely mediocre and tiresome. Mahler has committed some terrible blunders in the instrumentation . . . I knew only the first act which Mahler played to me on the

1. Letter to Arthur Seidl, 17 February 1897 (GMB, p. 209).
2. GMRS, p. 99.
3. W. Schuh and F. Trenner, eds., 'Hans von Bülow/Richard Strauss Briefwechsel', *Richard Strauss Jahrbuch 1954,* Bonn, 1955, p. 54.

piano with great enthusiasm, some of which must have infected me, so I most deeply regret that you, esteemed master, have been the innocent victim of my youthful rashness.[4]

He remained in touch with Mahler, however, as each made efforts to arrange performances of the other's works. When Mahler conducted his Second Symphony in Berlin on 13 December 1895, he told Strauss 'there is no one in the world I would rather have in my audience.' Strauss was absent on the night Mahler won recognition as a composer.

In 1897, with Mahler about to assume real power in Vienna, Strauss grumbled half-jocularly that his friend 'had quite forgotten the first "Mahlerian"'.[5] He was wrong. Mahler remained his ardent advocate, so much so that he offered to quit when the Vienna censor outlawed *Salome*; Strauss pragmatically dissuaded him.

Their personal relations were complicated by a clash of wives. Alma's account of Pauline and Richard Strauss is uniformly hostile, but some of her sentiments were undoubtedly shared by Mahler. In particular, he complained of Strauss's coldness. Mahler, it would seem, was trying to be friends, while Strauss was content to be a colleague. Virtually all his recorded comments on Mahler are couched in strictly professional terms[6].

The epigrammatic contribution to Mahler's fiftieth-birthday tribute by 'the first Mahlerian' is almost offensively impersonal:

> Gustav Mahler's creative work is in my opinion among the most important and interesting in contemporary art history. Just as I was privileged to be one of the first to bring his symphonic works before the public, so I consider it one of my happiest duties to continue by word and deed to help his symphonies win the wide recognition they so deserve. The plasticity of his orchestration, in particular, is absolutely exemplary.[7]

He was shocked by Mahler's last illness and sent a warm and encouraging letter announcing that he planned to conduct the Third Symphony in Berlin that year – unless Mahler wanted to take the podium himself. On learning of his death, Strauss wrote:

---

4. op. cit., p. 60.
5. GMRS, pp. 44–5.
6. See GMRS, p. 144.
7. Strauss contribution to Paul Stefan (ed.), *Gustav Mahler: Ein Bild seiner Persönlichkeit in Widmungen*, Munich (Piper), 1910, p. 66.

Strauss conducting.
(Caricature by Hans Boehler)

Mahler conducting.
(Caricature by Hans Boehler)

The death of this aspiring, idealistic, and energetic artist is a heavy loss. [I] Read Wagner's memoirs with emotion. Read German history of the age of the Reformation, Leopold Ranke: this confirmed very clearly for me that all the elements that fostered culture at that time have been a spent force for centuries, just as all great political and religious movements can only have a truly fruitful influence for a limited period. The Jew Mahler could still find elevation in Christianity. The hero Richard Wagner came back to it as an old man through the influence of Schopenhauer.

It is absolutely clear to me that the German nation can only attain new vigour by freeing itself from Christianity.[8]

Two days later, he told Hofmannsthal:

Mahler's death has been a great shock to me. No doubt he will now become a great man in Vienna.[9]

That summer, he discussed Mahler with Otto Klemperer, reflecting that

Mahler had always sought 'redemption' but that he [Strauss] personally had no idea what Mahler meant by the expression. To quote his actual words: 'I don't know what I am supposed to be redeemed from. When I sit down at my desk in the morning and an idea comes into my head, I surely don't need redemption. What did Mahler mean?'[10]

With the passing of time, he grew increasingly remote from Mahler's music, perhaps uneasily aware of his own debts to it.[11] Twenty years later, in a remark to one of his favourite interpreters, Strauss gave an unequivocal verdict:

As for Mahler, he's not really a composer at all – he's simply a very great conductor.[12]

---

8. Diary entry quoted in GMRS. p. 153.
9. Franz Strauss (ed.), *Richard Strauss: Briefwechsel mit Hugo von Hofmannsthal*, Berlin, 1925 (London, 1928), letter of 20 May 1911.
10. *Klemperer on Music*, London (Toccata Press) 1986, pp. 147–8.
11. See particularly Norman Del Mar, *Richard Strauss*, London (Barrie and Rockliff), 1962–72; and Michael Kennedy, *Strauss*, London (J. M. Dent), 1976.
12. Fritz Busch, *Pages from a Musician's Life*. (J. M. Dent), 1953, p. 172.

Curiously, Mahler is said to have spoken of Strauss in almost identical terms:

> He regarded Strauss primarily as a fascinating conductor. A performance of *Salome* that we both heard Strauss conduct in Munich was a sheer delight for him.[13]

13. *Oskar Fried*, 'Erinnerungen an Mahler', *Musikblätter des Anbruch*, vol. 1 (1919), pp. 17–19. See p. 176.

II

Resurrection
(1889–97)

Mahler's first composing house, built to his instructions on a meadow beside the Attersee. The second and third symphonies were finished here.

Mahler's Life and Work

1889	18 Feb.	Death of his father, followed by
	27 Sept.	his married sister, Leopoldine, and most traumatically,
	4 Oct.	his mother.
	20 Nov.	Conducts his First Symphony unsuccessfully in Budapest.

| 1890 | May | Travels to Italy with Justi. |
| | | Takes responsibility for his younger sisters and brother. |

1891	14 Mar.	Quits Budapest after a quarrel with the new intendant.
	26 Mar.	Moves to Hamburg as chief opera conductor.
	summer	In Scandinavia. Stays at the hotel where Ibsen lives but is too shy to approach him.

| 1892 | | Starts composing the *Wunderhorn* Lieder. |
| | May–July | Conducts Wagner's *Ring* at Covent Garden. |

| 1893 | summer | Establishes his lifetime routine of composing during the long vacation, working on the Second Symphony at Steinbach am Attersee, Upper Austria. |

1894	12 Feb.	Hans von Bülow dies in Cairo.
	29 Mar.	At Bülow's Hamburg funeral, Mahler hears the *Auferstehen* chorale that inspires the ending of his Second Symphony.
	summer	Builds a composing-hut on a lakeside meadow at Steinbach.
	Sept.	Bruno Walter joins the Hamburg staff.
	18 Dec.	Completes Second Symphony.

1895	6 Feb.	Suicide of his younger brother, Otto.
	4 Mar.	Conducts three movements of the Second Symphony in Berlin.
	summer	Steinbach: composes three movements of the Third. Anna von Mildenburg joins the Hamburg company; Mahler falls in love with her.
	13 Dec.	Conducts the entire Second Symphony at his own expense in Berlin, announcing his arrival as a composer.

| 1896 | 16 Mar. | First Symphony performed in Berlin in revised four-movement form. |
| | 6 Aug. | Finishes Third Symphony, Steinbach. |

| 1897 | 23 Feb. | Converts to Roman Catholicism. |

Contemporary Events

1889   30 Jan. Crown Prince Rudolf, heir to the Austro–Hungarian throne, shoots his teenaged mistress and himself at Mayerling, in the Vienna Woods.
20 Apr. Adolf Hitler is born at Braunau, Austria.
Karl Kraus founds the satirical Viennese periodical, *Der Fackel*.

1890   Bismarck resigns as German Chancellor.
Ibsen, *Hedda Gabler*.

1892   Nietzsche publishes *Also Sprach Zarathustra*.
Edvard Munch's exhibition in Berlin creates a scandal and results in the formation of the first Secession.

1893   6 Nov. Tchaikovsky dies.
Electric street lighting arrives at the Kohlmarkt, Vienna.

1894   Alfred Dreyfus is falsely convicted of spying against France.
Theodor Herzl, reporting the Dreyfus affair, conceives political Zionism.
The first tram runs in Vienna.

1895   Röntgen discovers the X-ray.
Freud publishes *Studies on Hysteria*.
Karl Lueger wins the Vienna municipal elections on an anti-Semitic platform. Franz Joseph refuses to appoint him Mayor.
Marconi sends the first message by wireless telegraphy.

1896   10 Oct. Bruckner dies in Vienna.

Lilli LEHMANN
(1848-1929)

Mahler had been head of the Royal Hungarian Opera for two years when he asked the outstanding German soprano, a singer in the first Bayreuth *Ring*, to make a number of guest appearances in December 1890. 'You would', he told her, 'be doing a great favour to a German composer who has been transplanted on to foreign soil and yearns to set his eyes once more on the genuine Brünnhilde.'[1] Her acceptance launched a lifelong friendship that proved stronger than divergent musical attitudes and artistic disagreements.

> Gustav Mahler entered my artistic life as director of the National Opera at Budapest, a newcomer who had a strong will and understanding. He had informed me by letter that my terms went beyond his budget, but that he considered it absolutely necessary to engage me, so as to give his associates an artistic model after which they should strive. It was a delightful time that we spent there in a small select circle. There was Mahler, with his full devotion and freshness, steering towards his goal.
>
> I sang all my roles in Italian, and only that of Recha in *La Juive* in French, as the choice had been left to me, and I never suspected that Perotti, as the Jew, would sing in Italian. All the others' parts were sung in Hungarian, and one may imagine the cosmopolitan babel of tongues in these operatic performances, in which every foreigner who sang without a prompter had difficulty in keeping true to his language. The still young and fiery Mahler took the short men's trio of the first act of *Don Giovanni* in the fastest allegro, because it was marked *alla breve*, which here indicates not a quickened but a calm tempo. Mahler made the same mistake in the 'Mask' trio, without the *alla breve* sign, but there I promptly vetoed it, and I think he never again fell back, in that place, into his allegro madness. When I discussed it with Bülow, he was horrified, and said of that *alla breve* exactly what I have already written.

1. GMUL, p. 91.

I can still see Mahler kneeling before our stove, and brewing, in a tin spoon, some medicament for Hedwig H—, after a recipe of his grandmother's, for which he had brought everything with him. The missing coat buttons, which he had lost heaven knows where, were usually sewed on for him at Frau Taszai's. We often walked, rested, and leaped with him over hedges and ditches in the beautiful environs of Budapest, and had a jolly time. I was a friend to Mahler, and retained affection for him always.

My Path through Life, New York (Putnams), 1914, pp. 379–80.

The young Apponyi, reading to his mother.

Count Albert APPONYI
(1848–1933)

Hungarian politican who became minister of religious and cultural affairs and ambassador at the League of Nations. Apponyi was an ardent Wagnerian, friend of Liszt and one of Mahler's keenest supporters in Budapest. On learning early in 1897 that Mahler was a candidate for Director of the Opera in Vienna, Apponyi dashed off an unsolicited character reference.

This institution has to its detriment lost a leader who within two years succeeded in training a completely discredited company to achieve considerable artistic results; built up a rich and varied repertoire; and, while preserving the highest artistic ideals, ended his second season with a not inconsiderable financial surplus. Mahler is not merely – like some famous conductors I could name – an orchestral musician, but with all the works he produces he dominates the stage, the action, the expressions and movements of actors and chorus, with supreme control, so that a performance prepared and conducted by him attains artistic perfection in every dimension. His eye ranges over the entire production, the décor, the machinery, the lighting. I have never met such a well-balanced all-round artistic personality. I would beg Your Excellency by way of confirming this opinion to ask Brahms what he thought of the *Don Giovanni* performance conducted by Mahler which he watched in Budapest; please to ask Goldmark how *Lohengrin* under Mahler's direction struck him. Both will remember their impressions, for they were of the kind one remembers for a lifetime.

When I add that Mahler as a person, too, is a highly estimable, eminently respectable character, I shall have completed a portrait which, I trust, suggests that the Opera would be fortunate indeed to gain his services.

Letter dated 10 January 1897, in Kurt Blaukopf, *Gustav Mahler*, trans. Inge Goodwin, London (Allen Lane), 1973, p. 133.

Wilhelm KIENZL
(1857–1941)

Austrian composer, sweepingly successful in 1895 with his Wagnerian third opera, *Der Evangelimann (The Evangelist)*. He once vied with Mahler for a post at Kassel in 1883 and saw him again in Budapest, Hamburg, Vienna and Graz. Nine months after its world première in Berlin, Mahler conducted *Der Evangelimann* in Hamburg, though he came to dislike the opera as 'unserious' and 'a tear-jerker'.[1] After the First World War, Kienzl moved to Vienna and composed a short-lived anthem for the Austrian Republic.

I came to know Mahler when he was Director of the Budapest Opera.[2] He was already very nervous in his behaviour: he had the habits of repeatedly stamping his right foot and conspicuously nibbling at his moustache so that the ends were quite gnawed away.

Five years later I visited him in Hamburg where he worked for Pollini[3] as first conductor. Now moustacheless, he rehearsed and conducted my *Evangelimann*. When he was called to Vienna as Director of the Court Opera, appointed on merit and serving in the most exceptional manner, I came in contact with him more often. His was, so far as one can judge from brief encounters, a complicated nature with an infinitely fine and sensitive nervous system, fundamentally as kind and helpful as a child, but often suddenly, even terroristically, contentious.

The orchestral players feared him because in artistic matters he made no concessions whatever and, in his unwearying diligence at rehearsal, was as reckless with his musicians as he was with himself. He would not suffer sloppiness,[4] nor let the slightest fault pass.

---

1. KBD, p. 242.
2. In an earlier passage, Kienzl recalls that when dining with Mahler in Budapest 'he expressed most eloquently his unutterable longing for German singing.'
(*Lebenswanderung*, p. 135.)
3. Bernhard Pollini (1838–97), director of the municipal theatres of Hamburg and Altona, and commercial impresario.
4. *Schlamperei*.

So radical a personality naturally attracts enemies. All, however, apart from the most virulent anti-Semites, regarded him as an unmitigated idealist. He practised his art, in both its creative and recreative aspects, with total love and dedication to the point of self-annihilation. Tragically, he was consumed by the heat of his creative impulse, knowing he could never satisfy himself.

In his musical eclecticism, he suffered a thousand agonies as he strained relentlessly for the highest summit. Although his melodic inventions betray some unoriginal details, the whole bears the stamp of an imposing personality of Promethean magnitude, and leaves an inevitably deep impression on sensitive minds.

Can a Jew be an idealist?[5] In general, the Semite undoubtedly takes a materialist view of life. But a Semitic idealist, when one arises, surpasses most Christians in the way he leads his life. Or were Baruch Spinoza and Moses Mendelssohn not idealists? Mahler always acted against his own personal interests in the service of an art that was sacred to him. This warrants unbounded admiration, whether one considers his symphonies the highest form of revelation or merely musical monstrosities. (Mahler and Strauss – two polar opposites of contemporary art. Mahler worked against, Strauss for, his own time.)

In spite of his great, passionate nature, he was unprejudiced, demonstrating an objective attitude towards his contemporaries. As a conductor, he had something demonic about him. Just as E. T. A. Hoffmann might have imagined his Kapellmeister Kreisler, with all his quirks.

At a private reception in Vienna I had the rare pleasure of hearing the composer of the 'Symphony of a

5. Kienzl appears to relate to a vitriolic and racist review of Mahler's Second Symphony written by the Munich critic Rudolph Louis in 1900. Louis characterized Mahler as an eclectic who deceived audiences with cheap, ephemeral tricks, and lacked any 'sense of eternity'. In a book published in 1909, Louis wrote of Mahler: 'He speaks musical German with the accent, the cadence and above all the gestures of the all-too-oriental Jew.' (See HLG1, pp. 598, 936.)

Thousand' (as Mahler's Eighth Symphony has been
called since its sensational monster-performance in
Munich in 1910) play a waltz. Even in that, the man lived
up to his art.

Meine Lebenswanderung, Erlebtes und Erlauschtes, Stuttgart
(Engelhorn), 1926, pp. 150–51.

Hans von BÜLOW
(1830–94)

Pianist and conductor who served Wagner until 1870 and afterwards
devoted his efforts to young composers, among them Tchaikovsky,
Dvořák and Strauss. Mahler begged to become his pupil in 1884,[1]
but his supplication went unanswered. Three years later, Strauss[2]
urged Bülow to examine Mahler's completion of Weber's *Drei
Pintos*. Bülow replied:

On your recommendation I ordered the vocal score
(which, incidentally, is a monster of orthographical and
syntactical impurity) and with the best will in the world I
could find nothing worth praising. What is Weber's, what
is Mahler's,[3] it doesn't matter: the whole thing through
and through is a piece of infamous, antiquated rubbish.[4]

His abhorrence for Mahler as a composer was confirmed when they
became colleagues in Hamburg,[5] where Bülow had been active since
1887. But the senior musician was profoundly and generously taken
with his conducting and would embarrass Mahler by publicly
offering him the baton if he spied him in the concert audience. His
assessment of Mahler is given in a letter to his daughter Daniela,
dated 24 April 1891:

Hamburg has now secured a really excellent opera

1. GMBR, p. 28.
2. See p. 46.
3. Bülow was renowned for his musical puns, of which his 'three Bs' has attained
cliché status. The present phrase can also mean 'whether he is weaving or painting'.
4. W. Schuh and F. Trenner (eds.), 'Hans von Bülow/Richard Strauss Briefwechsel',
Richard Strauss Jahrbuch 1954, Bonn, 1955, p. 59.
5. See p. 77–8.

Bülow, wearing a laurel wreath, accepts the sacrifice of a rival conductor,
to the Kaiser's evident approval.

conductor in Herr Gustav Mahler (a serious, energetic
Jew from Budapest), who in my opinion equals the very
best: Mottl, Richter, and so on. I heard him do *Siegfried*
recently with Alvary[6] (who again struck me as ideal in the
title-role). I was filled with honest admiration for him,
for he made – no, forced – the orchestra to pipe to his
measure, without having had a rehearsal. In spite of
various drawbacks and my nervous condition I was able
to hold out until the last note. It lasted over four hours,
although the scene with S. and Wotan (a bad interpreter)
was reduced to a minimum. With all the mercantile spirit
that prevails in the theatre management here, we are, I
believe, better off than in the capital of the empire.

> *Letters of Hans von Bülow*, trans. Hannah Walter, ed. Scott
> Goddard, New York (Alfred Knopf Inc), 1931, p. 426.

6. Max Alvary (1856–98), German tenor, the first to play Wagner heroes without a
beard.

Sigismund STOJOWSKI
(1869–1946)

Polish-born pianist.

I remember having seen him for the first time years ago
in Hamburg in the house of Hans von Bülow, who would
comment upon his young colleague's rising fame in a
familiar but perspicacious manner, calling him 'ein
genialer Kerl' (a fellow of genius). Such as I saw him
then, in my student days, he appeared to me again at the
latest stage of his career in New York City. For in
essentials he had changed but little and rarely did an
appearance tell so much of a personality. He seemed a
fantastic figure cut out from some tale of E. T. A.
Hoffmann, the Romantic poet-musician: the pale, ema-
ciated face, the ascetic look behind the spectacles, a
supremely nervous demeanour – though his manner was
appealing in its directness and simplicity – bespoke a soul
of ardour and unrest, the noble and uncompromising
spirit of an artist-apostle, a rich inner life struggling for
its own existence and impatient of the world's cumber-
some obstacles – the whole pathos, in fact, of the modern
artist longing for solitude and self-expression in the midst
of the crowd to which he has to cater.

Gustav Mahler – The Composer, the Conductor, the Man;
Appreciations by Distinguished Contemporary Musicians, New York
(The Society of the Friends of Music), 9 April 1916, pp. 32–3.

Peter Ilich TCHAIKOVSKY
(1840–93)

The Russian composer came to Hamburg in January 1892 to
conduct *Eugene Onegin*. He acquitted himself feebly at rehearsal
and yielded the baton to Mahler, whom he described in a letter to his
nephew:

The conductor here is not a mediocrity but a versatile genius who keenly desires to conduct the first performance. Yesterday I heard a wonderful performance of *Tannhäuser* under his direction. The singers, the orchestra, Pollini, the stage-managers and the conductor – his name is Mahler – have all fallen in love with *Onegin* but I very much doubt whether the Hamburg public will share their enthusiasm.

The next day he added:

As far as the music goes, the performance was magnificent . . . a considerable success.

Tchaikovsky, Letters to Relatives, ed. V. A. Zhdanov, Moscow, 1955, p 507.

Herman KLEIN
(1856–1934)

Mahler paid his only visit to London in 1892, conducting Wagner's *Ring* in a production arranged between the Covent Garden manager, Sir Augustus Harris, and the Hamburg Intendant, Pollini. It was Britain's second *Ring* cycle; ten years had passed since Angelo Neumann's touring production, conducted by Anton Seidl. Hans Richter[1] was first choice as conductor, but he was committed to Vienna, and Harris, on Pollini's recommendation, settled for the unknown Mahler along with part of the Hamburg orchestra. Klein, a loyal Wagnerian, was music critic of the *Sunday Times*.

Mahler was now in his thirty-second year. He was rather short, of thin, spare build, with a dark complexion and small piercing eyes that stared at you with a not unkindly expression through large gold spectacles. I found him extraordinarily modest for a musician of his rare gifts and established reputation. He would never consent to talk

1. (1843–1916). Wagner associate and conductor of the First Bayreuth *Ring*, he was active at the Vienna Opera until 1899, when a clash of personal styles with Mahler provoked his departure.

about himself or his compositions. Indeed the latter might have been non-existent for all that one ever heard about them.

The second time I met him he invited me to a rehearsal of *Tristan* at Drury Lane Theatre (now thrown open exclusively for the German representations, which were in great demand); and then it was that I began to realize the remarkable magnetic power and technical mastery of Mahler's conducting. He reminded me in many ways of Richter; he used the same strong, decisive beat; there was the same absence of fussiness or superfluous action, the same clear, unmistakable definition of time and rhythm. His men, whom he rehearsed first of all in sections, soon understood him without difficulty. Hence the unity of idea and expression existing beween orchestra and singers that distinguished these performances of the *Ring* under Mahler as compared with any previously seen in London, apart from the enhanced excellence accruing from extra rehearsals, new scenery, and improved stage lighting.

The Golden Age of Opera, London (George Routledge & Sons), 1933, pp. 163–4.

For a man who knew so very little English, I never came across any one so bent on speaking that language and no other. I met Mahler frequently at Harris's office, but could never induce him to carry on a conversation in German. He would rather spend five minutes in an effort to find the English word he wanted than resort to his mother tongue or allow any one else to supply the equivalent. Consequently, a short chat with Mahler involved a liberal allowance of time. For the same reason, his orchestral rehearsals proved extremely lengthy and, to the spectator, vastly amusing.[2]

Thirty Years of Musical Life in London (1870–1900), London (Heinemann), 1903, p. 365.

---

2. When conducting in New York fifteen years later, he refused to speak English and obliged members of the orchestra to learn German.

Justine MAHLER
(1868–1938)

From the death of their parents in 1889 until they both married in 1902, Justi was Mahler's closest confidante, and from 1894 lived with him and managed his household affairs. He regarded her as 'a simple and completely defenceless human being' yet trusted her completely. Some of this faith evaporated when Mahler, himself falling in love with Alma, learned of Justi's secret romance with Arnold Rosé, leader of his orchestra at the Vienna Court Opera (Rosé's cellist brother, Eduard, had married their sister, Emma, in 1898). Yet despite obstacles interposed by the spouses, the relationship remained close.

Justi and Rosé had two children, both of whom became musicians. Their daughter, Alma, perished in Auschwitz; the son, Alfred, emigrated to Canada. In 1928, Justi took him on a nostalgic journey to Steinbach-am-Attersee to recapture the four summers she spent there with Mahler as he worked on his second and third symphonies. The reminiscences in this article are apparently hers; they were published first in the same year[1] and concur strikingly with Natalie Bauer-Lechner's account.[2]

Mahler was fully engaged during the season conducting operas and concerts. It was therefore of the greatest importance that his summer refuge should furnish solitude and quiet. Steinbach was chosen for this purpose by Justine Mahler, the older of the two sisters (and later my mother). Five rooms were spoken for at the inn for Mahler, Justine, the other sister Emma, and Natalie Bauer-Lechner, who was an old friend of the family. The rooms were poorly equipped and missing furniture had to be improvised in haste. The one luxury was a leather-upholstered couch which could be moved from one room to another as required. A Bösendorfer baby grand piano was placed at Mahler's disposal by the manufacturers in Vienna. A separate kitchen and a private guest-room

1. Alfred Rosé, 'Aus Gustav Mahlers Sturm- und Drangperiode: Wie die Zweite und Dritte Symphonie in Steinbach-am-Attersee entstanden sind', *Hamburger Fremdenblatt*, 5 October 1928.
2. See NBLe, pp. 29–73.

Mahler with his sister, Justi.

enabled Mahler and his companions to put up guests for any length of time.

Mahler arrived in Steinbach in June 1893, and the lovely meadow, resplendent in its abundance of colourful field blossoms, suggested to him the idea of building a little work-cabin at its end near the lake. This was done during the following year. It consisted of one square room with double windows on three sides and a glassed door facing the inn and the village. This door could be closed off at night by means of wooden shutters. There was a wood-burning stove for cooler days, and the other interior furnishings were a table, a few chairs, and of course the Bösendorfer baby grand in the place of honour. Mahler called his little workshop the 'Schnitzel-putzhäusel'.

From the first of June until the end of August Mahler worked there every morning. He rose very early, usually at six-thirty, and proceeded at once to the cabin. Soon after, his breakfast was brought to him, and he ate it with only the company of two kittens which he carried with him from the inn, one in each coat pocket. These same kittens he used to take along with him on his afternoon walks, until one day he found them gorging themselves with a captured fish, and became disenchanted with them.

All morning Mahler was busy in his study. The sisters watched from the inn for the door to open, this being their only signal that he was ready to come up for lunch. At the start of the summer he kept quite regular hours, but as the summer wore on the door would open later each day, and sometimes the deeply preoccupied composer would not join his hungry sisters for lunch until three o'clock in the afternoon. There was a rule that he was not under any circumstance to be disturbed so long as the door of the cabin was shut. Not even a telegram or an important visitor was allowed to interrupt.

It was most important to have absolute quiet around the little work-cabin, because the least hint of a noise disturbed the composer at his work. A scarecrow was put up in a meadow to chase away loud birds. The peasants were bribed with a gulden not to sharpen their scythes nearby. The village youngsters received pennies to stay away from 'Kapellmeister Mahler's' workshop. Once a famous comedian, who lived on the opposite shore of the lake, hired an organ-grinder to ply his trade a whole morning next to the 'Mahlerhäuschen'. He had been paid one gulden for the joke, and Mahler's sister had to fork out another to make him go away.

Mahler's diet had to be simple and light, because he was susceptible to migraine, and by this could be utterly incapacitated from work. His beverage was pure fresh spring water. He smoked cigarettes modestly, with the occasional cigar as an indulgence. Mahler had a friend in Hamburg, the famous actor Karl Wagner, who used to present him with a box of fine imported cigars on the occasion of Mahler's annual benefit performance. This box was taken along in the summer, and if Mahler was especially satisfied with his morning's work, he awarded himself one of these cigars. During lunch he would rise from the table, pick up a gold-wrapped cigar from the drawer, and with a pleased expression set it before him at the table. Everyone then knew that he was happy about something well done. This cigar was his ration for the day, however.

In the afternoon he had a nap and then read aloud to his sisters and friends. First he produced *Don Quixote*, which caused peals of laughter. Later he read Nietzsche's *Thus Spake Zarathustra*, from which he incorporated the 'Nachtlied' into his Third Symphony.

Later in the afternoon he took extensive walks with his companions, and he enjoyed the wild/life with a childlike enthusiasm. On these walks he would often stay behind or push ahead, always occupied with the music he was then writing. He carried little staff books with him, in which he jotted notes as they came into his mind. Once he had been long searching for a rhythmic motif needed for the last movement of the Second Symphony. As he walked, two crows suddenly flew up in front of him, screeching wildly. At this moment the desired motif came to him.

The evenings were spent on a veranda overlooking the meadow, chatting or reading. Often before his early retiring, he took another walk about the grounds of the inn.

Whenever Mahler completed an important section of his work, he organized an all-day excursion for the next day as a kind of reward. This hike usually led up into the Höllengebirge [the Mountain of Hell], into the 'Moos' or to the Langbathseen. A light meal, with black coffee in a thermos bottle, went along in a rucksack.

Mahler's birthday (7 July) was always celebrated in the 'Moosstuben', a lovely spot three to four hours' walk up in the mountains. The birthday dinner consisted of cold chicken and a special birthday cake made of three layers in black, white, and brown, with of course the indispensable black coffee.

In those years Mahler's works had not yet been published. The manuscripts of the First Symphony and the major part of the Second were kept in a special suitcase in his room at the inn. All inhabitants were told about the suitcase, and were instructed to rescue it first of all in the event of fire.

Alfred Rosé, 'From Gustav Mahler's Storm and Stress Period', *The Canadian Music Journal*, vol. 1/2 (winter 1957).

Franz LÖSCH

The builder who constructed Mahler's composing-hut at Steinbach in 1894 recalled the circumstances in an interview forty years later.

[Mahler] would always say: the lake had its own language, the lake talked to him. From up at the inn he couldn't hear it, so he needed to have a little house right by the shore. When he heard the lake, he composed more easily, and the compositions flowed fully formed from his head.

My father, who was still alive then, would say to me shaking his head, 'Strange, there's a man who talks to the lake.' He was a good man, my father, but he did not understand. I, however, who have spent my whole life by the Attersee, I understood very well.

Interview with Piero Rismondo in unidentified Viennese journal
(author's collection).

Josef Bohuslav FOERSTER
(1859–1951)

The gifted Czech composer was an utterly selfless man, quite the most undemanding of Mahler's friends, content to share his company without once exploiting it for personal gain. Born in Prague, Foerster succeeded Dvořák as organist of St Vojtech's and in 1888 married a nineteen-year-old soprano, Berta Lauterer.[1] In March 1893, just as his opera *Deborah* was about to be staged at the National Theatre in Prague, Berta was engaged at the Hamburg Opera. Foerster travelled with her but soon returned home, rejoining her at the end of the year once he had found work as a critic on the *Hamburger Nachrichten* and teacher at the local conservatory. By now, he knew the opera conductor well.

Director Pollini sent my wife the piano score of Wagner's *Mastersingers*[2] and asked her to learn the role of Eva as quickly as possible. We set to work without delay and devoted every free moment to it. Although my wife was intensely busy with repertoire, she was able to report for orchestral rehearsals within a few days. Gustav Mahler was conducting the *Mastersingers*. In the second act, quite unexpectedly, he interrupted the rehearsal and to the great astonishment of the soloists and orchestra demanded: 'My dear lady, with whom did you study Eva?'

1. Berta Foerster-Lauterer (1869–1936), daughter of a hairdresser, made a dazzling start in Prague, creating roles in two Dvořák operas. The rest of her career was spent in Hamburg (1893–1901) and Vienna (1901–13), where she was engaged by Mahler.
2. Produced in May 1893.

J. B. Foerster.

At her reply, 'with my husband', he turned to the orchestra and said: 'Gentlemen, this is how a musician studies.' And turning to my wife he continued loudly: 'Greet your husband from me, and tell him I would like to get to know him.'

My deepest secret wish was thus fulfilled. That same afternoon I hastened to the Fröbelstrasse, where Mahler then lived. The house faced a broad green expanse of moorland that today is completely built up. I went along to Mahler excited and fearful that I might not correspond to what the outstanding musician and unique conductor imagined.

I climbed up to the third floor and found the right door. I rang the bell. A friendly, courteous lady opened it. When she heard my name, she pointed to a door on the left at the far end of the passage.

I knocked a few times unanswered and finally ventured inside. The room was empty. I saw a bed, over which hung a half-withered laurel wreath. Its leaves were a greying olive-green, the colours matching the silk ribbon on which, in pale gold letters, I read: 'To the Pygmalion of the Hamburg Opera. Hans von Bülow.'

Although greatly excited, I immediately understood Bülow's words and was pleased that my impression of Mahler's personality had been confirmed by an artist of such magnitude.

But this was no time to stand in contemplation. I knocked at the second door and was promptly invited inside with a friendly 'Come in!' In this second, larger room I caught sight of Gustav Mahler. He looked at me, spoke my name and, ignoring my embarrassment, asked a few questions. It was not long before we understood one another; we had so many interests in common. I left with renewed proof of my conviction that all great men are simple and modest. To my great joy, I departed with an invitation to come again soon.

Back home, I assembled my impressions. . . . I saw myself again beside the simple bed and recalled the furnishing of his living-room, in which almost all the space was taken up by a piano, bookshelves and a writing table.[3] The piano stood in the middle and was covered with music; against the wall was the upright piano that Mahler mostly used. The score of a Bach cantata lay open on the stand.

On the walls, there was no sign of a beloved family portrait. Only a reproduction of Dürer's *Melancholy*, the photograph of a drawing unknown to me, *St Anthony's Sermon to the Fishes* and finally Giorgione's *Monk*, the one with his hand on a keyboard and an expression of indescribable beauty on his face. (Mahler once told me: 'That picture I could compose forever.')[4]

Not long after my first visit, I sought Mahler out again. We were getting to know one another. I picked days when he did not have to conduct in the evening and was delighted to see that I was welcome. Once, I no longer remember why, there was a long gap between visits. Then Gustav Mahler appeared at my house. We pledged true friendship.

Understandably, music was the beginning of our conversations; Johann Sebastian Bach was his hero. When I had seen the open score of a cantata on his piano top, I made some remark about the great Leipzig cantor. Mahler played a couple of marvellous pieces and voiced his amazement that Bach's cantatas were so seldom performed that they were almost unknown. We would occasionally take a score of the great polyphonist in hand, Mahler, it appeared, immersing himself particularly in studying those of Bach's works that enjoyed least popularity. He sought in them refreshment and purification from his theatrical activities, work that often forced him to tackle compositions of a kind that ran directly against his own inclinations.

'Here in this Castalian spring,[5] I rinse the grime of the theatre off me,' he remarked once after Pollini, though aware of Mahler's opinions, placed a new opera in his

3. There was also a chair in the room of which Mahler later confided to Foerster: 'On that chair, my good father used to work.'
4. See pp. 83, 91.
5. In mythology, the fountain of the Muses on Mount Parnassus.

hands, hands that touched it only with disgust.[6]

. . . After Bach, Mahler admired Beethoven and Wagner above all others. Among living composers, he was preoccupied with Bruckner and Strauss; Brahms he acknowledged but felt no sympathy for his music . . . Even at the outset of our friendly relations, I realized that Mahler saw Richard Strauss as his only rival. He got hold of each of his scores that were then being rushed out one after another by the Munich publisher Aibl.

He studied them, talked about them and appraised them critically, quietly and without emotional outbursts but with expert comments. Generally he concluded with a friendly question: 'Don't you think so? What's your opinion?'

We shared the same opinion of Strauss, saluting the young tearaway and foremost talent of the post-Wagner school, decadent in some respects but equally a riveting talent. Apart from the colourist of genius who had grasped an altogether individual type of orchestration and enriched the palette of the Classics and Romantics with a whole scale of charming tone mixtures, there was, if one might so express it, the Fortuny, Monticelli or Claude Monet of music.

It was not long until we knew one another heart and soul. Mahler's trust in me grew and he became talkative. Not infrequently he touched on intimate matters. But of his activity as a composer he did not say a word. One evening, however, as it started to get dark, he rose suddenly, took a manuscript from the drawer of his desk, and to my joyful surprise asked: 'Want to hear something?'

We took our places at the piano and Mahler played. I immediately recognized his handwriting in the score and had the premonition that a rare honour had been granted to me. From the impetuous and ecstatic opening theme, Mahler's unique ingenuity spoke to me. What followed deserved to be recognized as the highest level of artistic creation. My impression, powerful from the start, intensified into rapture. When Mahler, exhausted, illuminated

---

6. Mahler was obliged to conduct all manner of ephemera, among them *Runic Spell* by the Danish composer Emil Hartmann, *A Santa Lucia* by Pier Antonio Tasca and Ignaz Brüll's *Gloria*.

by a reflection of heavenly grace, brought to an end the colossal span of the successful movement, I was incapable of words. I shook his hand, mutely and warmly.

The intense look of gratitude that shone in Mahler's eyes sticks in my memory. He bowed his head as I, still lost in contemplation, sought words for my impression.

The piece I had heard was called *Totenfeier*:[7] I saw the title on the handwritten score. Today it is known to everyone as the first Allegro of Mahler's Second Symphony. It was initially intended as a symphonic poem, not as part of a cyclical work. At this first hearing and sight of the extraordinary dimension of the composition, I could not grasp at once the formal structure of the whole work, the novelty of it, the highly suggestive mood, the unexpected blending of themes and the hordes of remarkably unique details each pressing for attention.

We talked about the themes. Mahler assured me that he did not have a pure melodic shape in mind, but an elaborate, explicated theme, often intertwining with ideas that spring from it. We took up the score again and Mahler gave instances of what he meant. We were both convinced by the greatness and tonal beauty of his virtually unplayed work.

Meanwhile, the last rays of setting sun fell upon us . . . We sat silently – we understood each other well enough by now to share a silence – and after a while Mahler said quietly, as if awakened from a dream, 'You know Bülow . . .' I nodded, appreciating how highly Mahler valued the work of the severe and critical Bülow.

'Well,' he continued, 'I approached Bülow recently with this work and begged him to let me play it to him. When he saw the complications in the score he said he would be happy to let me play it: "At least I shall hear an authentic interpretation . . ."

'I played. It occurred to me to look at him and I saw Bülow holding both hands to his ears. I stopped playing. Standing beside the window, he noticed immediately and motioned me to continue.

7. Funeral rites.

'I played. After some time I looked up again. Bülow was sitting at the table with stopped-up ears. The scene was repeated; I carried on, various suggestions going through my head. Perhaps the virtuoso pianist Bülow did not like my way of playing or my touch, perhaps my forte was too passionate and crude. I remembered that Bülow is very nervous and often complains of headaches. But I played on without interruption or distraction, possibly even forgetting that he was present.

'When I finished, I waited quietly for the verdict. But my solitary listener remained at the table, silent and motionless. Suddenly, with a violent gesture of rejection, he said: "If that's music, I know nothing at all about music."[8]

'We parted friends. I was convinced that Bülow considered me a capable conductor but utterly hopeless as a composer.'

When I left Mahler that evening, I realized why he had been so pleased at my admiration. Undoubtedly for him, I was at that moment a spokesman for the younger generation and he had heard from my mouth that this generation would understand and follow him.

Der Pilger, Prague (Artia), 1955. pp. 350–7.

Within months of this incident, Bülow was dead. He collapsed on 12 February 1894 of a brain tumour while convalescing in Cairo. Foerster visited Mahler the day the sad news reached Hamburg and 'Mahler played through his *Totenfeier* in such a way that both of us felt as if he had depicted it in words: in memory of Bülow'.[9] At the funeral service on 29 March, Foerster saw Mahler discover the inspiration to complete his spurned Second Symphony.

Mahler and I were present at the moving farewell, but the church was overcrowded and we could not see each other . . . The strongest abiding impression was the children's voices, the innocence of their pure sounds in

---

8. 'Wenn das noch Musik ist, dann verstehe ich überhaupt nichts von Musik.' This quotation is taken from the German translation of Foerster's Czech autobiography. In an article Foerster wrote in German in 1921, Bülow's verdict reads slightly differently: 'Wenn das noch Musik ist, dann verstehe ich nichts mehr von Musik.'
9. *Der Pilger*, p. 404.

Klopstock's profound poem . . .

I could not find Mahler at the theatre, either. But by afternoon I was no longer able to contain my restlessness and hurried to his house as if in obedience to a command. I opened the door and saw him sitting at the writing-desk, his head sunk low and his hand holding a quill over music paper. As I stood in the doorway, Mahler swung round and said: 'Dear friend, I've got it!'

I understood. As if enlightened by a mysterious power, I retorted: 'Rise up, yea rise up from that brief sleep . . .'[10]

Mahler looked at me with an expression of extreme surprise. I had divined the secret that he had not yet divulged to anyone: the Klopstock poem we had heard that morning from the mouths of children was to be the foundation of the finale of his Second Symphony.

Der Pilger, pp. 404–5.

Gerhard STEHMANN[1]

Bass singer at Hamburg who followed Mahler to Vienna.

Hamburg. Rehearsal Room. Gustav Mahler, the conductor, is rehearsing the entire cast. A young man suddenly steps in. Mahler glances up from the piano score. 'Who are you?' 'Bruno Walter,[2] solo chorus coach,' he replies. 'How old?' 'Eighteen.' 'Can you play the piano?' 'Excellently, Herr Kapellmeister.'

Mahler purses his lips a little. 'Really excellently?' 'Yes sir,' affirms the self-confident new coach. 'Do you know

---

10. 'Auferstehen, ja auferstehen wirst du nach kurzem Schlaf . . .'

1. Dates unknown.

2. There are some inconsistencies between this and Walter's own account (Walter TV, p. 77). Walter at this stage was still known as Bruno Walter Schlesinger. It was Mahler who in February 1896 suggested that his identifiably Jewish surname would impede his career and he should adopt a neutral combination of his two personal names. (Bruno Walter, *Briefe 1894–1962*, Frankfurt am Main (Fischer), 1969, p. 15.) A year later Mahler advised: 'Above all, convert [to Christianity] and do your military service!' (GMBr, p. 223).

Hansel and Gretel?' 'No.' 'Good, then play it.' The
rehearsal proceeds to Mahler's satisfaction. 'Prepare the
[forest] echo for me please before the next stage rehearsal.' Bruno Walter bows. The echo goes well.

'Tomorrow morning at ten is the orchestral rehearsal,'
says Mahler. 'If I am not there in time, conduct it
yourself, Herr Walter.' 'Right, Herr Kapellmeister.'
Next morning Mahler is absent and Walter for the first
time has an orchestra under his hand.

Mahler, though, punctual as ever, is hidden in the
auditorium listening. When he knows what he wants to
know, he greets Walter amiably in front of the orchestra
and shakes his hand. 'Thank you, Herr Walter.' That was
Mahler's way of making certain. At the same time, it was
the start of a friendship that even Mahler's death could
not end. No one has tended so worthily or more nobly
repaid such friendship than Bruno Walter.

Mahler has meanwhile become Director of the Vienna
Court Opera. A unique, sharp-edged personality, not
easily approachable. Grounds enough for those who do
not understand him to become hostile, entrenched, and
to criticize his competence as Director. Members of the
company are not overjoyed. They all realize: with Mahler, it's not like a bowl of cherries. But the performances
go well. Some of the company, particularly the female
singers, predict that Mahler's regime will not last long.

Most interesting are Mahler's engagements. After a
few bars, if the auditioning singer is obviously inade-
quate, comes a 'thank you' from the Director in the
darkened auditorium. On the other hand, one beautifully
sung phrase or even a gesture can be significant. Once
Mahler finds something 'individual', he clings to it like a
limpet, demands more and more, seeks stronger proof,
examines, compares: in short, does everything possible
to get to the core. Mahler has an urge to idealize. But
disappoint him once, and his interest freezes over fast.

At ensemble rehearsals, Mahler has no need to ask for
silence. No one dares move, let alone whisper.

'Gustav Mahlers Proben', *Moderne Welt*, vol. 3/7
(Gustav Mahler Heft) (Vienna, 1921), pp. 17–18.

Bruno WALTER
(1876–1962)

Walter was not quite eighteen when he was taken on as chorus
répétiteur in Hamburg. He fell under Mahler's spell, a personal and
professional thrall that he had to resist by periods of physical
separation in order to acquire his own artistic identity. His rise in
Hamburg was meteoric. Within weeks, the coach became chorus
director; weeks later he conducted *Die Walküre*: 'Mahler took care
of that.' In 1898 he left Hamburg to conduct in Riga, rejoining
Mahler at the Court Opera in Vienna three years later.

He was closer to Mahler than any other musician, yet always kept
a position of worshipful deference. 'I came as near to him as the
difference of age made possible,' he reflected late in life. 'Mahler was
the greatest performing musician I ever met, without any exception.'[1]

In the year after Mahler's death Walter gave the first performances
of *Das Lied von der Erde* and the Ninth Symphony. This article
appeared between the two premières.

I came to know him in Hamburg in autumn 1894, soon
after reading a sneering criticism of his First Symphony
that imbued me with a passionate yearning for his work
and creations. He seemed to me then the very archetype
of a romantic. His appearance, his blazing, indeed
fanatical artistic zeal, his intensity, his grotesque humour, all struck me as the incarnation of one of E. T. A.
Hoffmann's fantasy figures. His incomparably passionate
concentration while rehearsing and conducting, forever
reminding me of his fantastical forerunner, Kreisler,
made such an impression that I wholly forgot that he
made room in his life for other activities and that his
name had first struck me as a composer.

I remember how surprised and oddly touched I was
when Mahler, taking a walk with me one afternoon, said
with one of his particular expressions of hidden sorrow:
'Do you not know that I am really a composer?' I urged
him to show me something of his works, and he invited
me to his home the next afternoon.

1. Bruno Walter, eightieth-birthday interview with Arnold Michaelis, issued on CBS
Records, BRG 72068/9.

I can still feel the tension with which I awaited my first
visit to Mahler, and my profound emotion upon leaving
his house. Entering his room, I caught my first sight of
Giorgione's *Concert*,[2] in a good reproduction hanging
above the upright piano; never before had I been so
impressed by a painting. The ascetic in the picture,
looking lost to the world, shook me deeply. Months
passed before I noticed that he was making music; until
then, I had thought the monk was being gently aroused
by friends from a religious ecstasy. In strange ways, this
monk appeared to me to throw new light on the essence
of Mahler.

Kapellmeister Kreisler faded into insignificance. Mahler seemed to me ever more like a man drawn towards
deepest suffering. An ascetic. A God-seeker,[3] so extreme
and radical an individual that an essentially vivacious
eighteen-year-old, as I then was, could perceive it.

Romantic or ascetic, demon-artist or moral genius, my
first impressions of the essence of Mahler swung between
these contradictions. Just as rich and contradictory were
the inspiring first impressions of his works. So far as I
understood them, the songs seemed romantic and somewhat 'kreislerisch' – I refer to 'The Heavenly Life'[4] or 'St
Anthony's Sermon to the Fishes'[5] – while the opening
movement of the Second Symphony, which in my view
at that time the monk in Giorgione's painting could also
have composed, was somehow classical.

In further contact with Mahler I was struck by the
explosiveness of his nature and a certain part wild, part
droll humour that contrasted with a touchingly deep and
clear tranquillity. With the triumphant closing move-

2. The portrait, now attributed to Titian and hanging in the Galleria Palatina,
Florence, shows a layman and a priest gazing with fond concern at an ascetic-looking
monk whose fingers are resting crookedly on a keyboard. The monk's features vaguely
resemble Mahler's.
3. Walter gives an over-simplified comparison between Mahler and Bruckner:
'Mahler, his whole life long, was seeking God. Bruckner had found God . . . For
Mahler, God was his whole life, *the* one dominating problem. And in each work
Mahler tried to find a new musical expression for a new way to God.' (CBS BRG
72068/9.)
4. Vocal final movement of the Fourth Symphony.
5. From *Des Knaben Wunderhorn*.

'Georgione's *Concert*', hanging above Mahler's piano.

ment of the Second Symphony it seemed to me, in my
inexperience, as if Mahler had expressed absolute belief
in immortality, as if he had conquered the wild torments
of his soul. The iridescent Kreisler had finally resolved
the savagely beautiful, if painful, dissonances of his inner
being in the harmony of the roaring E flat major in that
finale.

. . . In the Third Symphony, he raised his eyes from
the joy and pain in his own heart to the harmony and
disharmony of Nature. He related to it forever in the
most intimate ways, from gentle contemplation to a
shatteringly mystic unification. This feeling for Nature
provided the major source of all his works, at every level
of intensity.

It was not so much an appreciation of beautiful
landscapes as a profound intimacy with Nature. Obviously he took pleasure in her marvellous contours, but he
placed higher value on gazing into her eyes, into her soul.

Kapellmeister Kreisler, as drawn by his creator, Hoffmann.

Love and fear, rapture and horror, existed in that gaze.
He saw the *bellum omnium contra omnes*[6] in Nature and
sensed its self-destructive forces fighting within his own
inner being.

'Mahlers Weg, ein Erinnerungsblatt', *Der Merker*, vol. 3/5
(Mahler-Heft) (March 1912), pp. 166–71.

Ernestine SCHUMANN-HEINK (1861–1936)

The Czech soprano sang in Hamburg (1883–98) before pursuing an
international career in the United States. She was a sworn antagonist
of Mahler's. Yet even Mildenburg admitted[1] that she sang his *Lieder*
magnificently. Alma reports[2] that Schumann-Heink turned against
Mahler and spread the word that he was homosexual when he
resisted her advances. She was at the time between husbands and,
judging by her photographs, a formidable figure.

Gustav Mahler . . . was one of the men who played a big
part in my career, too; and it is all the more interesting
because, you see, Mahler didn't like me as a woman.
Gustav Mahler was a great conductor, but he was also
one of the most hated conductors . . . He was so anxious
for absolute perfection in every detail, and so sensitive,
that it was impossible for him to 'get along' with people,
as we say. Wherever he went there were fights and spites.
But you couldn't blame him, the man was so sensitive.
He wanted to be so just, so true to the masters –
Beethoven, Gluck, Bach, Wagner – in his interpre-

6. The war of all against all. This view is strikingly echoed by a living composer: 'We
look at Nature externally with mystic feelings. [But] when you get close you see that
it's incredibly violent. Everything's eating everything else. Nature is hell on earth.'
(Harrison Birtwistle, interview with the author, *Sunday Times* colour magazine,
18 May 1986.)

1. Anna Bahr-Mildenburg, *Erinnerungen*, Vienna and Berlin (Wiener Literarische
Anhalt), 1921, p. 111.
2. AMM, p. 109.

Schumann–Heink, in Hamburg and on stage at Bayreuth.

tations. But he often missed the very effects he longed to produce by over-anxiety.

He was the very opposite of Hans Richter. Richter, for instance, could sit there in his shirt sleeves at rehearsals and bring out of the orchestra a climax (still looking like a good, nice, family father), though by Jove, in his blue eyes and his conducting there was something that nothing in the world could beat! But even so, he was always quiet, easy, without any fuss or strain. This was Hans Richter.

But Mahler – poor Mahler! He was thin and nervous and sensitive, trembling to all music. It was always that he wanted and sought endlessly for perfection. He forgot that there is no perfection in this world. In his own mind and ideals, yes, but he forgot that when the orchestra was before him it was only eighty or a hundred men who were not geniuses like himself, but simply good workers. They often irritated him so terribly that he couldn't bear it; then he became a musical tyrant. And this people couldn't understand or forgive. They didn't see why he was so merciless, and so it was that he was misjudged wherever he went. It was a tragedy for him, this attitude, for deep in his heart he had charity, and he was the most lovable and kindest creature you could imagine – except when he was conducting. When the baton was in his hand, he was a despot! But he didn't bear malice. He was an idealist in every way. He enjoyed so every living thing. Why, the shining of the sun, a tree, even the smallest flower, could make ecstasy for him. But the people couldn't understand him, and so they condemned him. I tell you, loads and loads of my success in Wagner was due to Mahler. He would sit and bang and bang on one note at rehearsals (you know how you get careless) but he would have it perfect. He always insisted on perfection from me.

In Hamburg, when I was singing there, he helped me so much, and I repeat, it was the more interesting because he didn't like me as a woman.

Mary Lawton, *Schumann-Heink, the Last of the Titans*, New York (Macmillan), 1928, pp. 358-61.

Anna von MILDENBURG
(1872-1947)

The great soprano was Mahler's creation, developed by him almost
from scratch at rehearsals in Hamburg. She was also his lover.

Born in Vienna, she was taken to Hamburg in 1895 by her teacher
Rosa Papier[1] to replace Katharina Klafsky, who had broken her
contract and gone to sing in America. At her first piano rehearsal,

> the door was thrust open violently. A small man in a grey
> summer suit came in. He had a dark felt hat in his hand
> and, pressed under his arm, a badly rolled umbrella. His
> face was burnt almost black by the sun. He looked at us
> with bright grey-blue eyes[2] unhappily and moodily.
> When the *répétiteur* tried to greet him, he cut him short.
> 'Carry on,' he said irritably, slamming the door but
> without coming any nearer. He stood as if poised for
> flight, door-jamb in hand. The accompanist resumed
> playing but pressed his lips slightly together. I under-
> stood what he meant: M. So this was Mahler. I shut my
> eyes, my hands clenched together and my whole fervent
> will and wishes flooded into my singing . . . [Suddenly,]
> the man at the door stamped violently, scaring me. His
> hat flew on to the piano, then his umbrella, and the
> *répétiteur* was dismissed from his stool with, 'Thanks, I
> don't need you any more.'[3]

Mahler took over her rehearsal and promptly reduced her to tears.
The following month she made her début as Brünnhilde and before
the end of the year was deeply involved with him. The intensity of
his passion is conveyed in his letters to her[4] and in the creative
impetus he acquired to complete the Third Symphony. But Mildenburg was a garrulous young girl and gossiped about him so feverishly

---

1. (1858–1932). A former singer who played a pivotal role in bringing Mahler to
Vienna two years later.
2. His eyes were generally said to be dark.
3. Anna Bahr-Mildenburg, *Erinnerungen*, Vienna and Berlin (Wiener Literarische
Anstalt), 1921, pp. 12–13.
4. Most of the letters are deposited in the Austrian National Library and, for reasons
of copyright, have not been published.

that Mahler won a reputation for promiscuity, a slander that pursued him – with its author – to Vienna.

Her indiscretions undoubtedly hastened the end of the affair. Mahler, before leaving for Vienna, arranged Mildenburg's transfer to the Court Opera on condition that she 'renounce any private relationship and any form of favour from myself'.[5] She was the star of his company and an intermittent thorn in his unwilling flesh. She continued to pursue him, but no longer single-mindedly. Instead, she became the mistress of, among others, his Hamburg friend Hermann Behn and, evidently, of Siegfried Lipiner and Ludwig Karpath in Vienna. She made a last-ditch attempt to inveigle Mahler into marriage, on learning of his engagement to Alma in 1901. Eight years later, she finally married the distinguished writer Hermann Bahr, who had fallen in love with her stage persona.

Troubled by her past, she published selective sections of Mahler's letters to her in 1921 in her autobiography and in an article about him. Her book confines itself entirely to their professional contacts; the essay is rather more revealing:

Demonic, wildly grotesque, bizarre, comical, unique – that is how people regarded him. Many had an eerie feeling on seeing him at the podium. They sensed an extraordinary power and backed away as if from something threatening, or stood and stared at him inquisitively with a pleasurable thrill. And when one told them that this apparently ominous man could be as cheerful as a child, carefree and high-spirited like a boy on the first day of the summer holidays, they would smile incredulously and serve up examples of his terribleness. The victims of his sarcasm were the most unforgiving.

He hurt many unintentionally with his humour. Like most people when they talk in jest, he did not always weigh his words. For in the next moment he had quite forgotten about the individual who aroused his mirth and had forsaken the particular for the universal, for the deepest, most painful and self-denying introspection and the living truth.

It was not a common humour, avoiding cheap suggestiveness and preventing him from sharing ordinary conviviality, since 'they are all like that – scared of anything

5. Undated letter from the summer of 1897, quoted in KBD. p. 213.

that has depth – they are only happy when it is shallow.'

And they would look affronted and disgruntled, for-ever scenting a personal attack in his words. He noticed it and had to laugh at their darkened, suspicious, rejecting expressions. That really offended them, and they remain so even today – although since his death they have had to acknowledge his genius, his amazing abilities, and call him demonic, immense, and larger than life. But they saw him like the moon, seeing only one side and not the opposite.

He could say and do whatever he liked, but he always remained a stranger to them, stranger even in everyday life than when standing at the podium, compelling and dominant. What they saw as strange were his cheer-fulness, his love of nature, his humility in his own art, his religiosity, his faith and his love of God.

I see him now, suddenly standing still with mysterious gestures in the middle of a walk and, with bated breath and a quiet smile, avidly watching a small animal at work, listening to a bird singing. This serenity always gave way to reflection and serious, pensive contemp-lation, an awareness of God's wisdom, will and wonder. He always felt the miracle and the mystery, awestruck and with a touchingly childlike astonishment. He could not understand Man's indifference to these wondrous acts of nature. How joyful and happy, how grateful he could be, when he infected someone else with his enthusiasm, an enthusiasm for nature or for art, for all that was beautiful and genuine. But too often he wrestled in vain, squandering his best efforts.

In his study hung Giorgione's *Concert*.[6] The priest and the layman in the picture look at the musician with a kind of innate distance that I have seen so often in men's eyes as they were directed at Gustav Mahler.

'Aus Briefen Mahlers', *Moderne Welt*, vol. 3/7 (Gustav Mahler Heft)
(Vienna, 1921), p. 13

---

6. A copy of a painting now thought to be by Titian. See p. 82, note 2.

Ferdinand PFOHL
(1862–1949)

Music critic of the *Hamburger Nachrichten*, the Bohemian-born Pfohl was a keen supporter of Mahler's and regarded himself as his friend. Forgotten by Mahler when he moved to Vienna, Pfohl's affection soured into resentment. He became exceptionally aggrieved when Mahler's Viennese circle failed to approach him for a contribution to memorial issues of their magazines. Pfohl's reminiscences and wounded pride went into a notebook that came to light in the past decade.[1] In it he takes immediate issue with the sanctification of Mahler by his latter-day friends. 'Arnold Schoenberg said somewhere:[2] "Mahler was a saint",' begins Pfohl – and sets out promptly to disprove him.

One of my last encounters with Mahler was in spring 1897 in front of the Hamburg City Theatre, just after news came of his spectacular summons to the Vienna Court Opera. I expressed my warmest congratulations and asked him, more with my eyes than with words, how it had come about, since the strictly Catholic Kaiser appointed only Catholics as a matter of principle to his court. To become conductor at court, Mahler would have needed to submit to the ceremony of baptism. He understood my smile very well: 'The cloak has been changed . . .'[3] he said, with a peculiar devilish smile on his Lucifer-face.

This little scene made a fatal impression on me. A man's faith, even less than his religious affiliation, made no difference to me and is presumably of little consequence to God Himself. He would not ask: 'Did you believe in me as a Catholic, Jew, brahmin or Protestant?' Rather: 'Where are your works? Where is your heart?'

Mahler converted for material gain, forced by neither inner conflict nor inner need. A value we inherit from parents and forefathers is sacred in its own right, the

---

1. A revealing passage describing the revision of Mahler's First Symphony is translated by Donald Mitchell in DM2, pp. 264 and 372–3. See also KBD. p. 197.
2. Prague lecture, 1912. See p. 315.
3. 'Der Rock ist schon gewechselt . . .'

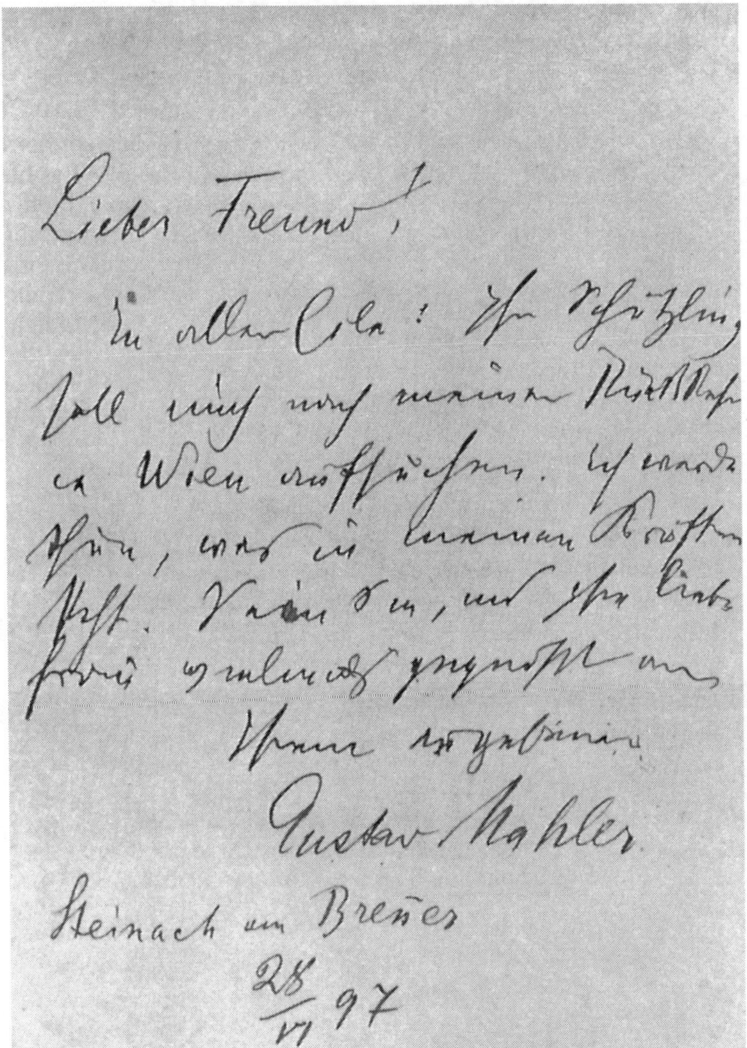

Lieber Freund!

In aller Eile: Ihr Schützling
soll mich nach meiner Rückkehr
in Wien aufsuchen. Ich werde
thun, was in meinen Kräften
steht. Seien Sie, und Ihre liebe
Frau aufs herzlichste gegrüsst von
Ihrem ergebenen

Gustav Mahler

Steinach am Brenner
28/VI 97

Mahler's farewell note to Foerster and his Hamburg circle.

value of a venerable tradition. *No, Gustav Mahler was no saint . . .*

Mahler was a mystic, a God-seeker. His imagination circled incessantly around these matters, around God and the world, around life and death, around spiritual matters and nature. Eternity and immortality were at the centre of his thoughts. Death and eternity are the great theme of his art. He wanted to believe, belief at any price.

He once asked me: 'Do you believe in God?'

I replied: 'Asking the question implies that you don't believe. Faith does not ask, as Love does not ask. Wagner constructed the Elsa problem[4] on the question of unconditional belief . . .'

Did Mahler really believe, in the deepest religious sense? I would have to say he did. Heaven, God's realm, was more to him than a beautiful dream. It was an essential need; his entire art is a cry for this belief. He drowns in it the scepticism that gnaws, pains and gives him no rest. Music, above all his own music, was simultaneously a narcotic, a trance and an act of asceticism. He tore his flesh with it as the saints once flagellated themselves. And it was a balsam to his wounds.

Gustav Mahler, Eindrücke und Erinnerungen aus den Hamburger Jahren, ed. Knud Martner, Hamburg (Verlag der Musikalienhandlung Karl Dieter Wagner), 1973, pp. 58–9.

---

4. In *Lohengrin*.

III

The heavenly life (1897–1902)

The Court Opera in Vienna.

Mahler's Life and Work

1897	4 Apr.	Mahler is appointed Kapellmeister at the Vienna Court Opera.
	11 May	Conducts *Lohengrin* triumphantly at the Court Opera.
	8 Oct.	Promoted to Director of the Court Opera.
1898	June	Undergoes major surgery for haemorrhoids.
	summer	Convalescence at Vahrn, south Tyrol.
	24 Sept.	Appointed conductor of the Vienna Philharmonic Orchestra in succession to Hans Richter.
1899		Buys lakeside strip and woodland to build a summer home and composing-hut at Maiernigg on the Wörthersee, just outside Klagenfurt.
	summer	Vacation at Alt-Aussee (Styria), begins Fourth Symphony.
1900	June	Gives concerts in Paris with Vienna Philharmonic.
	summer	Rents a villa at Maiernigg where on
	5 Aug.	he completes Fourth Symphony.
1901	17 Feb.	Conducts *Das klagende Lied* in Vienna.
	24 Feb.	Severe haemorrhoidal haemorrhage; further operations.
	1 Apr.	Ousted by the Vienna Philharmonic; replaced by Josef Hellmesberger.
		At Maiernigg, begins Fifth Symphony and composes Rückert Lieder and three *Kindertotenlieder*.
		Bruno Walter rejoins Mahler in Vienna.
	7 Nov.	Meets Alma Schindler over dinner at the Zuckerkandls.
	25 Nov.	Conducts première of his Fourth Symphony in Munich.

Contemporary Events

1897   3 Apr., Vienna: death of Brahms.
       Dissident Viennese artists led by Klimt form their own Secession.
       Karl Lueger is finally made Mayor of Vienna.
       Hugo Wolf is confined to an asylum after proclaiming himself
           Director of the Vienna Opera.
       Discovery of the electron, the first atomic particle.

1898   Emperor Franz Joseph's jubilee; Empress Elisabeth is assassinated.
       Chekhov, *The Seagull*.
       26 Mar. The Vienna Secession holds its inaugural exhibition.
       Spanish–American War: US forces invade Cuba, occupy the
           Philippines and annex the island of Hawaii.

1899   3 June, Vienna: death of Johann Strauss.
       19 June, London: Hans Richter revives English music, conducting
           Elgar's *Enigma Variations*.
       The first international automobile race takes place in Vienna.
       Boer War erupts in South Africa.

1900   Nietzsche dies.
       Freud, *The Interpretation of Dreams*.
       Joseph Conrad, *Lord Jim*.
       Blood groups are distinguished.
       Kodak introduce the Brownie box camera.
       Paris Métro opens.
       King Humbert I of Italy assassinated.

1901   27 Jan: Verdi dies.
       Thomas Mann, *Buddenbrooks*.
       Cellophane is invented.

Hermann BAHR
(1863–1934)

Prolific writer, among the founders of the *Jung Wien* artistic
renaissance, Bahr supported moderate progress in both cultural and
political spheres. He had mixed in the same student circles as the
young Mahler but, though their paths crossed often, theirs was little
more than a nodding acquaintance[1] and his memoir of Mahler uses
literary metaphors as a substitute for personal intimacy. In 1909
Bahr married Anna von Mildenburg, Mahler's Hamburg lover.

Pollini was in Vienna[2] – I had business with him – we
were sitting in his hotel, when something shot unseen
into the room, like a blast of wind forcing a window
open, like a jet of water from a pipe, like an element of
nature; he did not just enter, he burst in. He looked
familiar to me, as if I had seen him somewhere before,
perhaps in another guise, as if he had appeared to me in
another language that was not instantly recognizable in
its present translation.

It troubled me, but as I thought about it and caught
his name from Pollini, the unknown man shot around the
room, seemed disconcerted by my presence[3] and suddenly shot out again, stamping his feet; as a blast of wind
blows out, as a jet of water is switched off, suddenly gone
without a trace. 'A funny fellow, the conductor, eh?'
laughed Pollini.

At the word 'conductor' I realized with a start where I
knew him from: Wasn't this Hugo Wolf? Was there
another Hugo Wolf? A Hugo Wolf in black? But they did
not even look alike. They had no single feature in
common. Where did the idea come from? Summoning
up the image of Hugo Wolf in my mind's eye, I could not
grasp how this dark fiend could remind me of the
brightest man I had ever known. They were as different

1. Mahler's comments on Bahr suggest a lack of personal sympathy. See p. 253, and
HLG3, p.80.
2. Between 2 and 4 May 1897, when Mahler was in Vienna to prepare for taking office.
3. Presumably because he wanted to see Pollini alone.

as night and day. Nevertheless, I could not help feeling
that they were one and the same person, mysteriously
transformed. I remembered I had sometimes half-
jokingly called Hugo Wolf an animal, as in fairy-tales
where the handsome prince is trapped in the body of an
animal. The one who had just shot across the room was
like a stray, half-wild animal.

No, they had nothing in common, not a single feature,
did not resemble one another at all. But something, a
mark, as if they had been branded with the same sign,
belonged to the same herd, answered to the same master,
or perhaps laboured under the same curse. I once teased
Hugo Wolf that Kapellmeister Kreisler must have visited
Styria at some time. Now I realized that Kapellmeister
Kreisler may also have been in Bohemia, leaving a
Styrian and Bohemian line of Kreislers, in all of whom
the ancestor reappeared.

Cutting out the imagery, in both men the characteristics of the creative musician were stronger than any
personal trait. I had already half forgotten this, however,
and my first powerful impression of Mahler had gradually been weakened or obscured (we usually recognize
a man's nature at first sight: it can be obscured when we
know him better by the tiny details, the conversations
and the personal relationship) when quite unexpectedly I
experienced it again many years later.

I was then reading Romain Rolland's marvellous *Jean
Christophe*,[4] the supreme novel of our time . . . Hardly
had the impassioned fellow begun to speak than I cried
out: 'But that's Mahler, as he lives and breathes!'

It was peculiar. Did Rolland know Mahler?[5] It was
Mahler in every feature, spiritually and physically, even
metaphysically . . . as Greco painted the Grand Inquisi-
tor, as Dostoevsky portrayed himself as Count Mysh-
kin.[6] . . .

---

4. Rolland's *magnum opus*, a ten-volume fictional biography of a German composer,
issued 1904–12. Bahr had read the first three tomes in German.
5. Not until 1905, when the novel was well in progress. See p. 179.
6. In *The Idiot*.

There is a forgotten novel by Bulwer-Lytton called *Zanoni*.[7] It relates of a Neapolitan, Gaetano Pisani, a violinist at San Carlo and a composer,[8] but who was Bulwer describing? Mahler.

Externally in his 'strange contortion of visage'[9] and:

The features were noble and regular but worn and haggard, with a fixed, speculative, dreamy stare in his large and hollow eyes. All his movements were peculiar, sudden and abrupt, as the impulse seized him. But also in his music, of which we read: the style of the Neapolitan musicians was not on the whole pleasing to ears grown nice and euphuistic in the more dulcet melodies of the day; and faults and extravagances easily discernible, and often to appearance wilful, served the critics for an excuse for their distaste.

Yes, Mahler's entire relationship with humanity and the world is previously outlined here:

The affectations of Pisani were little visible on the surface. His mind and soul were so thoroughly in his art that domestic life glided by him, seemingly as if that were a dream, and the art the substantial form and body of existence. Everything that Mahler was, cannot be said better than in these words: he and his art seemed alone suited to each other – both quaint, primitive, unworldly, irregular. You could not separate the man from his music; it was himself.

Would you not think that the author must have known Mahler? The novel appeared in 1842.

Feuilleton in the *Neue Freie Presse*, 1 May 1914. Collected in Hermann Bahr, *Essays*, Vienna (Bauer-Verlag), 1962, pp. 275–8.

7. Edward Bulwer-Lytton, first Baron Lytton (1803–73), British politician (MP for St Ives and Lincoln, Colonial Secretary 1858–9) and a prolific author whose popularity spanned Europe. His historical novel *Rienzi* was the source of Wagner's first major opera, while *The Last Days of Pompeii* is a classic transformation of new archaeological discovery into accessible fiction. The work quoted here is among his slightest.
8. An altogether fictional creation, not to be confused with the Roman composer Pasquale Pisari (1725–78).
9. Quoted by Bahr in the original English.

Max GRAF
(1873–1958)

One of the youngest and brightest of Vienna's music critics, Graf havered uneasily between applauding Mahler's achievements and attacking his methods and appointments. As a boy in Prague, he had heard Mahler conduct Wagner and accounted it a formative experience,[1] but as critic of the *Neues Wiener Journal* and other periodicals he was cautious of a conservative readership. One of his early notices earned a written note from Mahler – 'Many thanks! *Vivat sequens!*'[2] – but he was never admitted to the inner circle and Mahler, despite his attraction to young musicians, apparently felt little personal sympathy for him.[3]

---

1. Max Graf, 'Begegnung mit Gustav Mahler', in *Jede Stunde war erfüllt: ein halbes Jahrhundert Musik und Theaterleben*. Vienna and Frankfurt (Forum-Verlag), 1957, pp. 23–5.
2. Long live the next!
3. See HLG3, p. 88.

Graf was active in various walks of Viennese life, was a friend of Freud's and father of his famous case 'Little Hans',[4] a sexually precocious little boy who grew up to be an opera producer.[5] He fled to the US when the Nazis came to power, returning to Austria after the war.

From the personality of Gustav Mahler, who was a demonic man, streams of nervous energy emanated, and pervaded stage, orchestra and audience at the Vienna Opera. Long before Mahler appeared in the orchestra pit, the audience became excited. When the house grew dark, the small man with sharply chiselled features, pale and ascetic-looking, literally rushed to the conductor's desk. His conducting was striking enough in his first years of activity in Vienna. He would let his baton shoot forward suddenly, like the tongue of a poisonous serpent. With his right hand, he seemed to pull the music out of the orchestra as out of the bottom of a chest of drawers. He would let his stinging glance loose upon a musician who was seated far away from him, and the man would quail. Giving a cue, he would look in one direction, at the same time pointing his baton in another. He would stare at the stage and make imploring gestures at the singers. He would leap from his conductor's chair as if he had been stung. Mahler was always in full movement like a blazing flame. Later he became calmer. Evidently he controlled himself, which only augmented his inner tension.

Mahler was conscious of the extreme tension which emanated from him into the theatre. He once told me, during one of our first talks, 'Believe me, people only realize what I am when I am gone. Then it is as if a storm had broken over the theatre.' The Viennese public, directly after Mahler's arrival, realized the additional artistic energy which had been bestowed on it in such a personality. In the first year of his direction, the operas of Mozart were performed ten times more often than in

4. 'Analysis of a Phobia in a Five-year-old Boy' in *The Standard Edition of the Complete Psychological Works of Sigmund Freud*, London (Hogarth Press and the Institute of Psycho-Analysis), 1953–74, vol. 10.
5. Herbert Graf (1904–73).

other seasons. Wagner had twenty evenings more than in the previous year. Even smaller-scale, lighter operas like Lortzing's *Zar und Zimmermann* played to sold-out houses. Mahler worked according to a broad programme, on the renovation of the ensemble and the repertory . . .

Rarely has any theatre operated according to a larger-scale plan, and in the first half of Mahler's directorship, what was accomplished corresponded exactly with the ideal picture set forth at the beginning. The intensity with which Mahler attacked the restudying of a classic work was unusual. Of every work which he prepared and performed, Mahler said: 'This is the greatest opera which has ever been written!' He was filled with solemn enthusiasm after he had brought out a new work. Stage and orchestra, décor and singing had to form a complete artistic unity according to his ideas. Each opera was a dramatic work of art. The Wagnerian conception of a comprehensive art work was applied by Mahler to every opera.

For this purpose, Mahler developed a new ensemble. The great Viennese heroic singers of the Wagner epoch had grown old. Winkelmann, Reichmann and Materna had to be replaced by younger forces, and Mahler found the noble tenor Schmedes and young Slezak. In Mildenburg, he had a modern Wagner tragedienne, in Weidemann and Demuth great baritones. He had Gutheil-Schoder as an interesting singer for lighter roles. Hers was a realistic talent of the first rank for tragic as well as comic parts. In Kurz he had found a new coloratura. All these singers blindly followed the dictates of the genial musician who had formed and trained them. Mahler clung to this ensemble with great love. I can remember how disturbed he was, when he had Gutheil-Schoder sing the Eva in *Meistersinger*, and read the unfavourable criticisms about her. He sat sunken down behind the mountain of newspapers, like a wicked dwarf, and nervously chewed his finger-nails – something which he was accustomed to do in moments of stress.

Legends of a Musical City, New York (The Philosophical Library), 1945, pp. 204–8.

Ludwig KARPATH
(1866–1936)

A nephew of the composer Karl Goldmark, Karpath was engaged by
Mahler in 1888 as a bass singer in Budapest and sacked a few days
later. He became a music critic, but operated more as an investiga-
tive journalist, reporting from the inside each twist and contortion of
musical politics in Vienna. He relished the intrigues of power-
mongering and played a minor intermediary role in the events that
brought Mahler to Vienna in 1897. As Director, Mahler soon
distanced himself from the indiscreet Karpath, to the writer's eternal
regret. He never understood why.

Bruno Walter once described Karpath as 'stupid but good-
natured, with a talent for publicity'.[1] He wrote for the *Neues Wiener
Tagblatt* (1894–1923) and for three years (1914–17) was editor of the
arts periodical *Der Merker*. His autobiography[2] provides a valuable,
generally accurate record of Mahler's road to Vienna and the
opposition he encountered there. The following anecdotal extract is
entitled 'Various characteristics of Mahler'.

One summer's day at noon I ran into Mahler on the
Ringstrasse. He always had a need to chat while walking.
So we strolled for about an hour, discussing in detail
various questions concerning the Court Opera.

When I, in various matters, did not share Mahler's
opinion he would invariably exclaim: 'Talk like that
could cost you your head!'[3] Any new objection raised
from my side was dismissed by Mahler with the same
exclamation: 'Talk like that could cost you your head!'
He was in the best of humour and smiled contentedly,
repeatedly saying I could lose my head. Finally I asked
him why I was in such danger. 'Because I was going to
take you to lunch as we're having *Marillenknödel* (apricot
dumplings),[4] but now I shan't take you, and you won't
have any.'

1. Letter to Hans Pfitzner, 25 September 1904, in Bruno Walter, *Briefe 1894–1962*,
Frankfurt am Main (Fischer), 1969.
2. *Begegnung mit dem Genius*, Vienna (Fiba-Verlag), 1934.
3. 'Sie reden sich um Ihren Kopf!'
4. For the recipe, see HLG3, p. 1050.

I replied that I was not at all fond of *Marillenknödel*, at which Mahler exclaimed histrionically: 'What! Is there a Viennese to whom *Marillenknödel* means nothing? Well, you know, that is so talentless that you will come with me right away to eat the heavenly dish compulsorily. My sister Justi has her own recipe for it, and we shall see whether you will remain indifferent.'

The dumplings were, as a matter of fact, outstanding and I have eaten them with relish many times since. On yet another occasion, Mahler took me to lunch in improvised circumstances. Once again we bumped into each other on the Ringstrasse[5] when Mahler was on the point of going to his home nearby on Auenbruggerstrasse 2. 'Accompany me,' said Mahler curtly.

I feared, as so often, the descent of a thunderstorm, but there was no trace of it: Mahler was altogether friendly and talked to me about the performance of one of his symphonies which had achieved success a few days earlier in one of the German towns. This then became a conversation about his works in general. That was really the subject that most interested Mahler. Apparently I said something that pleased him, for he thought no more of going home but was so engrossed in the subject under discussion that he kept approaching it from different angles and forgot about his lunch.

Finally I reminded him – it was already half-past two – so he took me by the arm and said: 'Now you must come along, as I have a few more things to say. Hopefully there is enough to eat. I know for certain we have a raw beefsteak, and nothing can go wrong with that.' A few moments later we were in his apartment and the conversation continued at table, winding down gradually until, pleasurably, we parted from one another. At such moments you knew that Mahler really liked you.

Occasionally at an improvised meal, we touched on the question of conductors at the Court Opera. 'I did have one young man,' said Mahler, his fork raised high, 'but I

---

5. The suspicion is that Karpath lay in wait for Mahler at lunch-time on his unvarying route from the opera house to his apartment.

can't engage him because he is a Jew. Admittedly by race
only, as he has long since been baptized a Protestant. But
unfortunately it is the race that matters.' 'A pity the
young man's a Protestant,' I said, 'if he had been Catholic
there would be no serious difficulties. Who is this man,
by the way, that you have in mind?' 'His name is Bruno
Walter, you know him as it happens. I had him under me
in Hamburg and he would be the right one for the job.'
'Try it then,' I replied, 'I'll have a word with the Chief
Court Steward [Prince Montenuovo] to see if it can be
done.' Soon afterwards, Walter, then twenty-four years
old, was engaged . . .

   Before that, when Humperdinck[6] sat once with Mahler
and me at the Café Imperial, Mahler asked him whether
he did not have a young conductor with lots of talent to

---

6. Engelbert Humperdinck (1854–1921), composer of *Hansel and Gretel*, which
Mahler conducted at Hamburg within a year of its world première. He was present at
the first performance of Mahler's Second Symphony in 1895 and attempted to bring
Mahler to Berlin after he left Vienna.

recommend. 'Certainly,' replied Humperdinck, 'one of my pupils who is now working at Aachen. Name of Leo Blech.[7] I can strongly recommend him.'

'Blech! Blech!' said Mahler, 'probably a Jew?' When Humperdinck nodded, Mahler continued. 'It won't work, unfortunately, even if he has been baptized as you say. For the anti-Semites, I still count as a Jew despite my baptism, and more than one Jew is more than the Vienna Court Opera can bear.'

Characteristic to Mahler was a certain sense of humour: not blatant, but pleasant and disarming. On the other hand, he could become very angry when he was not immediately understood. A now-deceased baritone blessed with a voice as big as his belly pestered me incessantly with demands to audition for Mahler and with his ambition to be engaged at the Court Opera. One fine August evening around six o'clock – Mahler even on such days and evenings sat in his hot office – I indicated to the bold singer that he should wait below at the porter's lodge and if Mahler came down in a good mood I would get him to agree to an audition. The matter was swiftly arranged. The good fellow sang out the praises of the lovely evening star, and Mahler himself accompanied at the piano.

'You have a very beautiful voice,' said Mahler, 'but I am afraid I can't engage you.' 'Why not?' demanded the talkative baritone. 'It just won't work,' replied Mahler. When the man absolutely refused to give way, Mahler shouted angrily at him: 'There is a big mirror. Look in it, and answer your question yourself.'

That same evening – I had remained with Mahler – he remarked with a sigh: 'Here is today's box-office report: almost sold out on a hot August day.' 'Well, that's excellent,' I replied. 'Yes, but it's *Fledermaus*,' said

---

7. (1871–1958). Blech twice approached Mahler for a position and in 1900 received an offer, but was unable to accept it as Angelo Neumann refused to cancel his contract in Prague. He conducted in Berlin from 1906 to 1937, when ousted by the Nazis, and spent the next twelve years in Riga and Stockholm before returning to end his career in Berlin.

Mahler, 'instead of *Walküre*, which I gave the night before last. I value *Fledermaus* and am very pleased that it brings in money, but it is none the less sad that *Fledermaus* packs the house, and not *Walküre*.'

Begegnung mit dem Genius, Vienna (Fiba-Verlag), 1934, pp. 176–80.

Franz SCHMIDT
(1874–1939)

Austrian composer and cellist, Schmidt was admitted to the Vienna Court Opera Orchestra (and the Vienna Philharmonic) in October 1896 and, despite impressing Mahler with his playing, soon came into conflict with the Director. Schmidt had nationalist tendencies and his First Symphony, which won the Philharmonic Society prize in 1900, was championed by Mahler's opponents.

Mahler burst over the Vienna Opera like an elemental catastrophe. An earthquake of unprecedented intensity and duration shook the entire building from the foundation pillars to the gables. Anything that wasn't very strong had to give way and perish.

In a short time the largest part of the singers fled (Van Dyck, Renard, Reichmann, Winkelmann), conductors (Hans Richter!), two-thirds of the orchestra. In the orchestra in particular Mahler dismissed and pensioned off so many people in his rage that although I was the youngest in 1897, in 1900 I was already the longest-serving active cellist. The principal cellists Hummer and Sulzer, although not formally pensioned off, played now only occasionally, and not at all when Mahler was conducting. Then I had to sit at the first desk, lead and play the solos. Mahler had earmarked me as Hummer's successor to the position of principal, but his intention was most doggedly resisted by his brother-in-law and friend Arnold Rosé. Rosé, as leader, was vested by

Mahler with special authority, his use of which was not exactly beyond reproach. He was seized with a sort of Caesar-like madness and ruled in the orchestra with brutal and narrow-minded arbitrariness. His unbearably arrogant behaviour led to the breach with Hummer, who left the Rosé Quartet and later left the opera altogether. Because I was an intimate friend of Hummer, Rosé's hatred and mistrust were transferred to me too. The result was next that, instead of appointing me a member of his quartet as Hummer's successor, as was generally expected, Rosé chose Buxbaum, whose playing in audition had previously been bettered by me . . .

The efforts to make me unpopular with Mahler (which was absolutely necessary to make room for Buxbaum) were aided by outside circumstances: by then (1901) I had already had my first success as a symphonist and at this same time Mahler himself was struggling to gain a foothold in Vienna with his symphonies. Since some of the Viennese critics now tactlessly played me off against Mahler, it was an easy matter to suggest to Mahler that I was conspiring against him with the press. But Mahler's estimation of my abilities at first remained unchanged – as usual, whenever he conducted, and without exception, I had to take the first desk. None the less clear signs of a 'fall from grace' could be noticed. Mahler's personal relations with me, in contrast to what they had earlier been, were icily cold. Rosé behaved more loutishly than ever; following the instructions of the almighty leader, the conductors Franz Schalk, Bruno Walter and others began to greet my solo performances with disapproving, disparaging and spiteful comments . . .

This intolerable state of affairs dragged on for some time until one day, while Mahler was away, Rosé made a direct attack. We were performing *Lohengrin*, an opera in which there is no cello solo. Before the performance began I was sitting, as usual, at the first desk when the orchestral attendant brought me orally (!) Rosé's order that I was to remove myself from the first desk, since from now on Messrs Buxbaum and Jeral were going to be sitting at the first desk and were to take it in turns to play the solos. I betook myself to Rosé, who was sitting in the orchestra's room, and asked him what the reasons for my sudden demotion were and whether I could not have been informed of it in a somewhat more dignified manner. Rosé answered me in his rude, provocative High German: 'I find myself forced to take this step, and you will have to be satisfied with that. I refuse to tolerate any further interrogation.' And in front of all those present he said to the orchestral attendant: 'My order stands. I cannot bear to listen to this man's playing any longer.' I spat in front of Rosé, turned my back on him and immediately reported sick; I was well aware that therewith I was risking dismissal but I was in no condition to play after this scene, which had upset me dreadfully.

After a few days, by which time my nerves had calmed down a little, I went back to the theatre and played at one of the back desks. Buxbaum and Jeral, Rosé's two favourites, were both significantly on in years but none the less considerably younger than I was in years of service. They found themselves in a very difficult position through their ponderousness and uncertainty, for when Mahler conducted, knowing that they had been forced upon him by Rosé, they were especially anxious and completely failed as leaders . . .

One morning, after repeated, thoroughly embarrassing accidents Mahler, who was to conduct *Die Walküre* that evening, notified me during rehearsal that I was to play the solos in the evening. I hurried to his office and had myself announced. I was admitted at once and explained that I was prepared to lead and play the solos in *Die Walküre* that evening if I was given the permanent contract for the position of principal there and then. I also complained about the unauthorized demotion Rosé had ordered. Mahler leapt up and shouted at me: 'What do you mean? Are you setting me conditions? Are you trying to play hard to get?' He continued in this tone; when I could get a word in, I pointed out that I could not see with what right the Opera should demand of me that for years I should do a more highly qualified job than I was contractually required to do without the slightest thought of compensating me in any way. Pale with rage, Mahler bellowed at me: 'You! I am at the end of my patience! You be careful! If you refuse to play for me, or say one more word, you can consider yourself dismissed! I'm warning you!'

I bowed and left. Mahler's warning rang in my ears all day long, but none the less I decided to push matters to the limit and not to give in whatever happened. That evening I went into the theatre earlier than usual and sat down at the last desk. Neither the official order brought to me by the orchestral attendant nor the brutal threats Rosé personally hurled at me could persuade me to exchange my seat for the principal's; and so, like it or not, Buxbaum had to sit at the first desk since Mahler could already be heard approaching and everybody had to be sitting in place when he stepped on the podium. Mahler surveyed the situation with a single glance; he didn't turn a hair. The performance began and came to an end. Mahler said nothing, but I wasn't dismissed.

After I had officially given up the fight for the position of principal through my 'refusal to play', I vegetated for fully ten years more in the Vienna Court Orchestra; as a *homo suspectus*[1] it wasn't exactly a bed of roses, but at a comfortable distance from the hotly contested post I was left in relative peace from now on . . .

'Autobiographical sketch', trans. Martin Anderson (© the Franz Schmidt Haus, Perchtoldsdorf, Austria), in Harold Truscott, *The Music of Franz Schmidt*, London (Toccata Press), 1984, vol. 1, pp. 175–79.

---

1. Suspected man.

Carl FLESCH
(1873–1944)

Hungarian violinist.

The post of orchestral leader at the Vienna Court Opera fell vacant, and I quickly decided to apply for it – by way of reinsurance. An invitation from the Director, Gustav Mahler, brought me one day to the opera-house, where Arnold Rosé, who for his part would have been very glad to see me next to him at the first desk, received me in the Director's office. He gave me a friendly explanation of the demands that Mahler, who did not know much about violin technique, used to make during auditions. He attached the greatest significance to the steadiest possible bowing in sustained notes and therefore considered the beginning of [Act 3, scene III of] *Siegfried* as a touchstone for the bowing technique of an orchestral violinist. Good old Rosé did not hesitate to cheat a little; he showed me the passage in question beforehand. Mahler came in a little later; he first asked me to play a Mozart adagio, and then – all unprepared as I was – set the *Siegfried* passage in front of me. But as my bow glided over the strings with the phlegmatic calm of a world-weary philosopher, he seemed greatly pleased, wanted to nail me down to the post of leader at once, and accompanied me himself to the administration building, where I was informed of the financial conditions attached to the post. The uncanny suddenness, however, with which the matter had developed went rather against my grain . . . and the question of my removal to Vienna fell to the ground . . . For the rest, Mahler seemed to me highly neurotic. An embarrassing tic made him frequently swing his right leg forward like a marionette, even when he was standing at ease. An angel and devil in one, he was regarded by the orchestra as a tyrant despite his undoubted idealism; it was certainly all to the greater glory of art. He was the kind of fine-nerved artist who reacts to a wrong note as if it were a box on the ear.

The Memoirs of Carl Flesch, trans. and ed. Hans Keller, New York (Macmillan), 1958, pp. 186–88.

Selma KURZ
(1874-1933)

One of the stars Mahler created in Vienna, an outstanding lyric-dramatic soprano in Wagner and eventually a superb coloratura in Italian roles. He may have been briefly in love with her, but there is no evidence to substantiate rumours of an affair.

Gustav Mahler first heard me in Frankfurt-on-Main shortly after he had arrived in Vienna. Some weeks later I was invited to audition at the Vienna Court Opera. I sang various pieces for Mahler, first in the rehearsal

room, then on stage, and after each he asked me: 'Why
are you so flustered?' And when I failed to reply he finally
shouted: 'You're engaged. How much do you want?'

I was so unsettled by this sudden stroke of luck, the
remote, long-enchanting dream of going to Vienna, to
the Court Opera, that I burst into tears and stammered,
'Pay me whatever you like'.

Mahler from the very first day took exceptional personal and artistic interest in me. He was crazy about my
voice and took over my development with typical intensity. It was only through Mahler that I found my
vocation. I had been trained as a mezzo-soprano, and he
first showed me the way to coloratura singing. In [Gold-
mark's] *Queen of Sheba*, my small role had a short trill
written in it. While I was trying it out at rehearsal,
Mahler gripped me violently by the arm. 'Carry on
trilling. More. As long as you can.' That is how I became
aware that I had the ability.[1]

Working with Mahler in rehearsal was marvellous. By
means of will-power and enthusiasm, he forced everyone
to give of their best and their last gasp, and he too was
totally exhausted and wrung dry after every rehearsal.

I was too young a girl to grasp Mahler's personality
properly. Only occasionally did I sense that something
utterly great lodged in that little man: when he fell into
philosophical contemplation that was rooted in a
strangely deep religiosity. In the last years of his activity
in Vienna we became, without real conflict, estranged.
But even from that distance he had my artistic development constantly in mind . . .

'Mein Entdecker, von Kammersängerin Selma Kurz', *Moderne
Welt*, vol. 3/7 (Gustav Mahler Heft) (Vienna, 1921), p. 15.

---

1. The 'Kurz trill' became world-famous: 'In the great aria in *Lucia di Lammermoor*,
she achieved such artistic unity with the flute that it was impossible to tell when the
flute and when the voice came in.' (Marcel Prawy, 'Gustav Mahler as Director of the
Vienna Opera', in Sigrid Wiesmann (ed.), *Gustav Mahler in Vienna*, London
(Thames and Hudson), 1976, p. 84.)

Marie GUTHEIL-SCHODER
(1874–1935)

Recruited from Weimar, where she had been coached by Strauss, Schoder made a triumphant Vienna début as Carmen on 26 May 1900. Mahler was thrilled to have found an artist of her quality. 'Schoder and Mildenburg,' he enthused, 'tower high above all the rest: they reassure one that there is still natural talent on the stage, not just affectation, grease-paint and pretence.'[1] Though doubts persisted about her vocal quality, she was a brilliant dramatic actress and one of the firmaments of Mahler's company. He was distraught when she took time off in 1902 to have a baby, 'regarding her happiness as a calamity for our opera house'.[2] She excelled in new music, was the first Viennese Elektra and Octavian, and sang in the historic première of Schoenberg's Second String Quartet, the work that broke the tonal monopoly.

Mahler never came to rehearsal with a finished, worked-out directorial concept. Possibly he pictured in his mind's eye one important scene that was the focal point of an entire act, but he would also leave room for individuality to find expression. 'Just do that! . . . Very pretty, I like that . . . That mood, I want to sustain.' That way, he intensified everyone's parallel or receptive inspiration, developing it further with his own original ideas.

When I came to Vienna, I was strongly inclined towards realistic portrayal of roles. Mahler showed me that every opera is a stylized work of art and everything must arrive at the style that the music and text demanded.

It would be rehearsed, of course, as often as was required. For that, Mahler always had time. He would reorganize a scene as many as twenty times, making changes even at the final orchestral rehearsal. That something 'stood', did not prevent him from altering it, even after the performance. That is exactly what made rehearsals so interesting and every performance a step

1. NBLe, p. 144.
2. GML, p. 264.

Gutheil-Schoder as Carmen.

upwards, whereas with others it usually went down. Nothing irritated him more than someone objecting: 'Herr Direktor, yesterday you wanted it like this, and today you want it done differently.' To which he would say: 'I had convinced myself yesterday that it could not possibly be done like that; you must go along with me!'[3]

When something was going well and he wanted to hold on to an impression, he might slow down the tempo; at other times, if it did not look right, he would take a rapid tempo to get us over the worst. His suggestive power was unbelievable. I became aware of it in seemingly minor details in recitatives in the new production of the Mozart cycle, which he accompanied from the harpsichord: when he struck a chord, one knew immediately how to sing and act what followed . . .

'Mahlers Opernregie' in Paul Stefan (ed.), *Gustav Mahler: Ein Bild seiner Persönlichkeit in Widmungen*, Munich (Piper), 1910, pp. 34–7.

Gutheil-Schoder added a further reflection eleven years later:

His formula for working, if one can call it that, was very simple: he did not impose a domineering conception on either the work or the artists, he left options open for individuals to develop without prejudice. His absolute authority was based not on childish tyranny but on personal, unconditional devotion to a work filled with suggestive power. He did not want his word to be overriding dogma. Often he would gratefully pick up someone else's apparently unimportant idea, which in his hands would begin to bloom and come together in a uniquely colourful impression. This respect of Mahler's for the individuality of each artist was virtually unbounded: it is the key to all the unorthodoxies that brought upon him the reproaches of the flock of outraged traditionalists.

'Mahleriana', *Moderne Welt*, vol. 3/7 (Gustav Mahler Heft) (Vienna, 1921), pp. 14–15.

---

3. In Kurt Blaukopf's expression: 'He claimed the right to be inconsistent.' (KBM, p. 204.)

Leo SLEZAK
(1873–1946)

One of the stalwarts of Mahler's operatic company, the Czech-born tenor made his début at Brünn (Brno) in 1896 and joined the Vienna Court Opera in 1901. He sang there until 1927, making almost 1,000 appearances and also singing at Covent Garden and the Metropolitan Opera. He had a repertory of sixty-six parts, among which his Lohengrin, Otello and Raoul (*Les Huguenots*) were outstanding. A famous wit, he coined the phrase 'What time's the next swan?' when his Lohengrin steed departed prematurely. His memoir of Mahler was written in March 1921.

Gustav Mahler

How I thank my lucky stars that I had the privilege of working under the direction of this man for seven full years in the *Sturm und Drang* period of my life as an artist.

It is true that as a director he was not easy to live with; indeed, often downright impossible. But when he worked with us in the rehearsal room or on stage, every grudge evaporated and was blown to the four winds. All the petty irritations of everyday life were immediately forgotten and you were proud of being in a position to go through thick and thin with such a genius.

He himself was a martyr to the consuming flames of work and he expected us to be the same. Concern with one's self, one's own self-interest, he regarded as a betrayal of artistic purpose. You were supposed to sacrifice yourself whole-heartedly to art, without a thought for yourself or your family.

If you asked for permission to make a guest appearance outside Vienna, that was a particular thorn in his flesh. I could only bring myself to ask for such leave of absence in the most pressing circumstances. The first step was to ascertain his mood from Hassinger, who had been assistant in the Director's office for many years; and the result was often that you went away and postponed the business until another day if Hassinger advised against it. But some day you had to get it over with.

With my heart thumping, I would step into the room. The Director would ask the reason for the call and take a negative attitude from the start.

'How can I be of service?'

'Herr Direktor, I should like to sing in Graz on two evenings so I am requesting four days' leave.'

'What, are you crazy? You've only just been away!'

'No, you are mistaken. It's weeks since I was away.'

On his desk there was a panel with roughly twenty-five or thirty buttons. Underneath there were little tabs with the names of the various members of the administrative staff, whom he could signal to appear at any time.

Mahler lunged irately at it and slammed down about twelve or fifteen buttons at once with the flat of his hand: he wanted Professor Wondra, who maintained a list of staff holidays so as pursue my claim to the point of absurdity.

Doors opened on all sides.

Lenerl Sgalitzer rushed in, out of breath, with her shorthand pad at the ready: 'Herr Direktor?'

'No, not you! Out!'

Linerl Ranninger arrived, white as a sheet, with a bunch of keys covering every music cabinet in the opera house. In seconds she too was back outside.

Secretary Schlader, stage-managers, people from props all rushed up, even the fire officer had got the signal and appeared in full regalia all set to man the pumps. The only one whose button had not been hit was Wondra!

One argument is countered by another, matters come to a head, my patience snaps and fuming I quit the scene of battle. I trample on Hassinger's toes and all the other staff members waiting outside for the Director with similar requests dissolve into their constituent parts and rapidly filter away. I go off home in a fury and swear to Elsa[1] by all the saints that I will put up with it no longer.

---

1. His wife.

But gradually, after a few hours, tempers begin to subside. We are in the auditorium, he is sitting at his desk and conducting and all the gall and irritation just disappear like the snows of March in the spring sunshine.

This scenario would be repeated several times a year, or a month, or a week. So things weren't exactly pleasant. Yet if I think of all the marvels that the man imparted to me along the way, and given the softening effects of memory, then all the irritations were a mere bagatelle compared with the treasures that were given to me.

Those Mozart cycles . . . *Fidelio*, *Les Huguenots*, *La Juive* and all the new productions – what a source of ideas the rehearsals were! Every single comment was a gift to be stored. It would never have occurred to any one of us to leave the rehearsal room if Mahler was rehearsing a few scenes in which we were not involved. His way of rehearsing brought everything out of a singer that he could possibly give.

However swimmingly and word-perfect everything went when Hesch, Demuth and I were on the stage, in Mozart with Mahler wielding the baton, everyone crept about full of anxiety that something wouldn't be perfect. If we did pull it off, Mahler would change beyond all recognition. He would come up to us on the stage and congratulate us and start handing out twenty-heller coins.

And *those* were the occasions I used to extract some holiday or other. I would describe to the Director in deeply moving terms my advanced state of impecuniousness, which could only be eased by a guest appearance in Brünn or Prague. He would laugh and say: 'All right then, for Heaven's sake go, but when you get back, give me a little peace for a while'.

I promised, and he would hurry off to the orchestra with a dancing rhythm in his step that you could hear from far away, to complete his celebration of the event.

I remember my very first encounter with Mahler. It was when I was still in Brünn but already under contract to go to the Royal Opera in Berlin. I got an invitation from the Director's office at the Vienna Court Opera to

Leo Slezak, self-portrait.

come for an audition. To every Austrian the Court Opera in Vienna was the highest he could wish for, and probably still is. So I hurried off to Vienna in delight . . .

I was to audition by myself just at the end of an orchestral rehearsal led by Hans Richter. All the big names in the house – Reichmann, Winkelmann, Greugg – were standing about in the wings. And there was I, up from Brünn, holding the stage with quaking knees and with Hans Richter at the desk.

Lohengrin: *'Heil, König Heinrich . . .'*

But before I began, a voice came at me from the dark recesses of the stalls: 'You, I'd just like to warn you, if you take it too slow for me I'll send you to the devil!'

It was the Director, Mahler, who was offering me such comfort and encouragement.

Everything went black in front of my eyes. How I managed to sing, I don't know. I was in a complete spin.

Afterwards I found myself in the chancellery in front of Mahler. He was very nice to me and said how sorry he was that I was already booked to go to Berlin. . . .

The very thought of that audition makes me break out in a cold sweat. It runs from every pore. And that was my first encounter with Gustav Mahler . . .

Magic Flute. I sang Tamino. In the big scene where he plays the flute there was a bit I never got right. I always made a nonsense of it. It annoyed Mahler every time but it was as if there was a jinx on it – whenever that bit came along, it somehow went wrong, if only because I was so nervous. That night when we reached that particular scene I spotted a lot of activity in the wings. Firemen were dashing back and forth and a young ballerina with a horrified expression on her face ran right across the open stage. There had been a short-circuit and the artificial cloud that carried the three little boys through the air had caught fire and was burning merrily.

All I could think of was: don't panic! And I sang on blindly to the end of the scene.

Suddenly someone in the audience shouted: 'Fire!'

At once, people began to leap up out of their seats and rush like mad for the exit, scrambling over one another.

With all my might I shouted: 'Stay in your seats! It's all over!' Mahler turned round as well. 'Stay in your seats!' he bellowed and went on conducting.

The audience calmed down, a tragedy had been averted.

Afterwards Mahler came up to me and said: 'Do you realize, Slezak, you sang that scene right for the first time?' And turning to the others he added: 'All you need to do if Slezak is to sing properly is to burn down the theatre.' . . .

Years later I met him in New York, a tired and ailing man. We were doing [Tchaikovsky's] *Pique Dame* – American première at the Metropolitan Opera House.

At the rehearsals it was usually he and I alone. The others did not turn up. He rarely had the whole company together. He sat there with me, resigned: a changed man. I looked in vain for the fiery genius of yester-year. He had become mild and sad.

He invited me several times to call on him at the Savoy Hotel. I felt he was only being polite and I was loath to trouble him. Once I did go but he could not see me. They told me it was angina, he was resting in bed.

Several weeks after that I met him in Central Park. He looked dreadful. We talked for a long time. It was the last time. He was like a shadow walking along. It made my heart sore.

In May, when I came back from America, I went to see him at the Loew Sanatorium in Vienna. It was too late, I wasn't allowed to see him. He died that very night.

I sincerely beg his pardon if I was unjust towards him. Now, in retrospect, I have only one feeling – of profoundest gratitude.

Meine sämtlichen Werke, Berlin (Rowohlt), 1937,[2] pp. 158–65.

Francis NEILSON
(1867–1956)

Anglo-American opera producer.

At the opera house in Vienna, I attended a performance of *Siegfried*, conducted by Gustav Mahler. We were walking across the Ringstrasse before the performance when he said to me: 'I do hope the scenery will know you are present and that it will behave with discretion.' Alas, the wretched cloths in the change in the third act went awry and completely spoiled the illusion of the ascent of Siegfried up the mountain, and a ragged piece of scenery hung swaying over the head of Siegfried while he gazed upon the sleeping Brünnhilde. When I saw Mahler the next day at lunch, he smiled rather sadly and said, 'It

2. First published in Berlin in 1922. It is interesting that Slezak's worshipful portrait of Mahler could still have been issued in Berlin in 1937, when Mahler's music had been officially outlawed by the Nazi authorities.

hurts me when anything happens that takes the attention away from the music. Nothing should break the spell.'

My Life in Two Worlds, Appleton, Wisconsin (C. C. Nelson Publishing Co.) 1952, vol. 1, p. 226.

Alfred SENDREY
(1884–1976)

Austro-American conductor and musicologist.

His face was that of a neurasthenic. Sharp eyes with his, with his glasses. His hair was disorderly almost, I would say, almost unkempt.

What was his rehearsal approach?

I would say one word: cruelty. He treated his musicians like a lion-tamer his animals. He was the best-loved and best-hated man in Vienna in musical circles. Those who understood his approach to music, his intentions, his enthusiasm, they adored him. The big portion of the public was absolutely averse to Mahler's intentions, Mahler's art and Mahler's way of treating audiences as well as musicians.

Mahlerthon

Ludwig SCHIEDERMAIR
(1876–1957)

After conducting his Second Symphony in Munich on 20 October 1900, Mahler was introduced to a young musicologist who was writing a monograph on him for the Leipzig *Moderne Musiker*

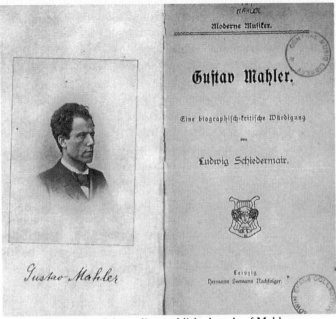

Title page of the earliest published study of Mahler.

series. He was pleased with the book when it appeared the following year, but told the author he had not understood two of the symphonies. 'The First has not yet been grasped by anyone who has not lived with me.'[1]

Mahler is, in the fullest meaning of the term, a tone-poet. His works do not therefore come into being entirely as those of an absolute musician but also from the experiences and arousal of his poetic nature. Mahler combines with his musical talent an equally powerful poetic aptitude. The poet and the musician are inseparable in him . . . But to think that his works merely describe limited events is to misunderstand the composer altogether. Mahler is a philosophically minded man and consequently vests in his creations universal thoughts that have affected him, thereby leading the symphony even further than Richard Strauss along the road to

1. MS letter cited in KBD, p. 225.

programme music.[2] Yet it appears that Mahler is an enemy of intricately analysed, elucidated programmes and printed concert programme notes.

The following episode illustrates his way of thinking. In October this year Mahler conducted a memorable concert for the Munich Hugo Wolf Society, and in it performed his Symphony in C minor.

After the concert, an illustrious company of leading artists, scholars and writers gathered to spend the rest of the evening with Mahler in convivial company. Someone brought up the subject of programme notes for concerts. It was as if a bright and sunny landscape had been struck by lightning.

Mahler's eyes shone ever brighter, his brow rose higher, he jumped up agitated from the table and shouted emotionally: 'Away with programmes, they give a false picture! Let the public form its own thoughts about the work being played, not be forced to read someone else's prejudgements while they are listening. If the composer forces listeners to feel the emotions that consume him, he has achieved his objective. The language of sound comes close to that of words, but expresses infinitely more than words can . . .' And with that Mahler seized his glass and emptied it, crying 'Perish all programmes!' And we looked at one another comprehendingly.

Gustav Mahler, Leipzig (Herrmann Seemann), 1901, pp. 13–14.

Half a century later, in his autobiography, Schiedermair reflected again upon Mahler:

Anyone who had the chance of a close personal acquaintance with Gustav Mahler would be struck by his tense, highly charged personality and captivated by his tremendous vitality. It is understandable that Mahler, in written remarks to me about himself, could say: 'Just as there is evolution in my physical life, so there is unbroken continuity in my works. When I am broaching a new

---

2. i.e. purely descriptive music.

symphony, having finished the previous one, I do not mean simply to tie a new thread on to the old yarn.'

Musikalische Begegnungen, Cologne (Staufen), 1948, pp. 43–4.

Bruno WALTER[1]

On 27 September 1901 Walter, now twenty-four, made his Vienna début conducting *Aida* and resumed his partnership with Mahler. It was to be less of an idyll than their Hamburg years, the critics deflecting much of their venom for Mahler on to a young conductor who bore the hallmarks of his intensity and high temper. Walter felt Mahler did not do enough to support or protect him and suffered a crisis of self-disbelief that almost provoked his summary departure.[2] Decades later, in his own brief tenure as music director in Vienna, Walter appreciated that the Director had no alternative but to let his protégés sink or swim.

Around the year 1900, not long before I moved to Vienna, I paid a visit to Mahler from Berlin and found him convalescing from a serious illness.[3] He had become older, milder and softer, and a deadly serious silence had spread across his nature. I told him years later how moved I had been by this change. 'Yes, I learnt something then,' he replied, 'but it belongs to those matters that one cannot talk about.'

I understood that he had felt the nearness of death and, if memory does not deceive, that he had already been touched by a ray of the wondrous glow of evening sun through which he saw the world in the last years of his life. 'You seemed to be enshrouded then in a serene view of the world,' I told him, alluding to this impression. 'I could only look at you with envy because I was

---

1. See p. 81.
2. See Walter TV, pp. 158–60.
3. A near-fatal intestinal haemorrhage provoked by haemorrhoids in February 1901 required two surgical operations in March and June of that year.

feeling the very opposite, the full unhappiness of my insecure station in the world. My experience and reflections painted the world unsparingly in the blackest, most hopeless hues. But in you, yearning, premonition and musical inspiration had brought peace, conciliation and a wonderful, all-encompassing sense of unity.'

'My dear friend,' replied Mahler, 'I used to possess certainty, but I lost it again. I will regain it tomorrow and lose it once more the day after.'

That is how he was. He wandered through life in seven-league boots and at every giant step had to change his entire image of the world. What could he gain from experience, even the most recent, when his particular strength was to embrace the present with an incomparable concentration that seemed to nullify almost all that had gone before?

Up to the end of his first creative period he was a true Romantic, relating to joys and sorrows, nature and God, in the most subjective possible manner. Now, he tried his hardest to be objective. What is peculiar about the Sixth Symphony is that its terrible, hopeless gloom is presented mercilessly without any human sound. The sounds are quasi-cosmic. They are sounds of the dark forces themselves; and no human soul sings of its suffering.

The man who fashioned this terrifying musical image of a world without God had begun searching for God in books. He had lost Him in the world, which appeared to him increasingly mysterious and gloomy. Where was this God whose gaze he had sometimes met? Previously he had searched for him in Spinoza, Plotinus,[4] and other philosophers and mystics. He now moved on to scientists, and to browsing among biological works, seeking in the cell that which eluded him in the universe.

He wrote his Seventh Symphony, like the Sixth an 'objective' work but richer and more colourful. The first

---

4. Baruch Spinoza (1632–77), pantheistic Dutch philosopher of Portuguese Jewish origins, who proclaimed the unity of God with Nature. Plotinus (c. 203–270), mystic philosopher who sought escape from the material world.

spirited and positive. The three central movements called 'Nachtstücke' are reminiscent more of his early Romanticism, but curiously charming because of their reminiscent effect. The third is perhaps the most beautiful piece of music Mahler ever wrote: a sweet and tender eroticism quivers within in it, the only erotic sound to be found, to my mind, in all of Mahler's works.[5]

And he searched on for his God: *accende lumen sensibus*[6] – that was the yearning in his soul, as it was the motivating force in Faust: *infunde amorem cordibus*[7] – this seemed to be the path to God, as taught in the final scene of *Faust*.

So he composed the hymn *Veni creator spiritus*, of which both parts are used as the first movement of his Eighth Symphony; and he took the final scene of *Faust* as the second part.[8] With unparalleled, elemental dedication Mahler plunged into composing these words. Nothing was closer to him than the appeal and prayer of mankind. And what joy it was to him that an answer existed to Goethe's promise. He could not tell me enough about it, his happiness at immersing himself fully in these Goethian words and absorbing them so deeply. Yet, this is his most 'objective' work.

It is not Mahler but mankind that intones the hymn and receives the consolation of the second section. This I consider to be the closing of the second period of his life. He could no longer liberate himself through art from the ever pressing, ever troubling metaphysical problems that overwhelmed him. The quest for God, for the meaning and aim of our existence and for the cause of the unspeakable sorrows of the entire Creation darkened his soul.

'Mahlers Weg, ein Erinnerungsblatt', *Der Merker*, vol. 3/5 (Mahler-Heft) (March 1912), pp. 166–71.

5. An ill-considered observation that vanishes from Walter's subsequent analyses of a work he rarely performed and never recorded.
6. Kindle light in our minds.
7. Pour love into our hearts.
8. The Eighth Symphony (1906–7) has two parts. The first is set to the ancient hymn *Veni creator spiritus*, the second to the closing scene of Goethe's *Faust*, Part II.

IV

*Songs on the death
of children
(1902–7)*

The picture above Mahler's desk.

Mahler's Life and Work

1902	9 Mar.	Marries Alma Schindler, 22.
	10 Mar.	His sister, Justine, marries Arnold Rosé, leader of Mahler's orchestra in Vienna.
	16–27 Mar.	Working honeymoon in St Petersburg, conducting three concerts.
	9 June	Performs Third Symphony at Crefeld.
	summer	Finishes Fifth Symphony at Maiernigg; trip to Toblach.
	3 Nov.	First daughter, Maria Anna, is born.
1903	21 Feb.	Forms partnership with stage-designer Alfred Roller in *Tristan and Isolde.*
	summer	Starts Sixth Symphony at Maiernigg after further excursion to Toblach for inspiration.
	Oct.	Conducts his Third Symphony in Amsterdam.
1904	15 June	Second daughter, Anna Justine, is born.
	summer	Finishes Rückert songs and begins Seventh Symphony.
	9 Sept.	Completes Sixth Symphony, Maiernigg.
	7 Oct.	Stages outstanding new *Fidelio* with Roller.
	19 Oct.	Premières Fifth Symphony at Cologne.
1905	29 Jan.	The *Kindertotenlieder* are sung in Vienna.
	20–22 May	Conducts at Alsace Festival of German and French music.
	summer	Finishes Seventh Symphony.
	21 Dec.	Roller's new staging of *Don Giovanni.*
1906	16 May	To Graz, to hear Strauss's *Salome*, prohibited in Vienna.
	27 May	Directs Sixth Symphony at Essen.
	summer	Composes Eighth Symphony, breaking his vacation to conduct Mozart at Salzburg.
1907	17 Mar.	After a vitriolic Press campaign against him, Mahler resigns from Vienna.
	5 June	Signs contract with Metropolitan Opera, New York.
	12 July	Elder daughter Maria, aged 4, dies of diphtheria. Alma collapses. Mahler is found to have a critical heart ailment. He spends remainder of summer at Toblach, reading poems translated from the Chinese.
	Oct.	Conducts in Helsinki and St Petersburg.
	24 Nov.	As a farewell to Vienna, he conducts his Second Symphony.
	9 Dec.	Leaves Vienna, bound for New York.

Contemporary Events

1902   8 Mar., Helsinki: Sibelius conducts his Second Symphony.
18 Mar., Vienna: Schoenberg, *Verklärte Nacht*.
28 Apr., Paris: Debussy, *Pelléas et Mélisande*.
Mahler is depicted as a knight in armour in Gustav Klimt's
Beethoven-frieze.
Hugo von Hofmannsthal, 28, abandons poetry.

1903   22 Feb., Hugo Wolf dies insane.
The Wright brothers fly their aeroplane.
Klimt completes the ceilings of Vienna University.

1904   Russo-Japanese war.
Janáček's *Jenůfa* is staged at Brno; Mahler asks to see a translation.
Otto Wagner's plain-faced Post Office building opens in Vienna.
Wedekind, *Pandora's Box*.
Excavation work begins on the Panama Canal.

1905   Abortive revolution in Russia; Jews are massacred in Kishinev
pogrom.
Einstein publishes his first theory of relativity.
Richard Strauss, *Salome*.

1907   Oskar Kokoschka, 21, writes a scandalous play, *Murder, Hope of
Women*.
Rilke, *New Poems*.
Britain, France and Russia form the Triple Entente.

Interlude:
Introducing Alma

On 7 November 1901, at a society dinner, Mahler met and fell in love with Alma Schindler, a young beauty courted by mature and famous men, among them Gustav Klimt and the Burgtheater Director Max Burckhard. She was at the time studying music and flirting with the composer Alexander von Zemlinsky.[1] Her engagement to Mahler was announced on 27 December 1901.

Mahler's friends were appalled, fearing for his fate with a wife barely half his age and for their own future role in his life. Alma rapidly alienated most of them. It was the end of Mahler's close ties with Lipiner, Adler, Karpath,[2] and most poignantly with Natalie Bauer-Lechner, who in January 1902 wrote:

> Mahler became engaged to Alma Schindler six weeks ago. If I were to discuss this event I would find myself in the position of a doctor obliged to treat, in life and death, the person he loves most in the world. May the outcome rest with the Supreme and Eternal Master.[3]

Bruno Walter, alone in his immediate circle, won Alma's approval. Walter gave an account of her in a letter to his parents on 30 December.

> Well, folks, what do you say to Mahler's engagement? That's a surprise, what? Justi's engagement with our concert-master Rosé is an old story. But they would have abstained from marriage if Mahler had remained unattached; Justi would not have left her brother on his own.
>
> He has surprised everyone with his engagement. The Lipiners and Spieglers[4] had to find out about it from the newspapers; so did we, of course. Even Justi only

---

1. (1871–1942) Rising Viennese composer whose third opera, *Es war einmal*, Mahler commissioned and conducted at the Court Opera. He was brought into the inner circle, with his brother-in-law Arnold Schoenberg, after Mahler's marriage to Alma.
2. HLG1, pp. 697–8
3. Final paragraph of Natalie Bauer-Lechner's memoir; manuscript in the possesion of Henry-Louis de La Grange, Paris.
4. Albert Spiegler's friendship with Mahler dated from their student days together. His sister was married to Lipiner.

Alma Mahler with her daughters, c. 1906.

learned of it by chance two days beforehand when they met his future father-in-law on the street and, expressing surprise at his familiarity with this man, got the reply: 'Well, I'll tell you, it's because I am engaged to his daughter.'

His fiancée, Alma Schindler, daughter of the late and famous landscape artist[5] (her mother made a second marriage with the painter Moll, so the father-in-law is actually a stepfather), is twenty-two years old, tall and slim and a dazzling beauty, the most beautiful girl in Vienna; from a very good family and very rich.

But we, his friends, are terribly anxious about all this. He is forty-one and she twenty-two, she a celebrated beauty accustomed to a brilliant social life, and he so other-worldly and solitude-loving. One could count any number of misgivings. He feels very uncomfortable and embarrassed about it, and is furious if one congratulates him. He received me with the words: 'What do you say, the newspapers have got me engaged! In other words, it's true, I am really engaged, but please do not congratulate me – or congratulate me very quickly, like that – now let's talk about something else.' A comical bridegroom, what?

Their love must be very great. The wedding is planned for the end of March; [6] Justi will marry in four weeks' time – those two have waited long enough, they go splendidly together. You know her, and I can only add that he is a rare person, a marvellous artist of lovable and noble character.

Bruno Walter, *Briefe 1894–1962*, Frankfurt am Main (Fischer), 1969, pp. 52–3.

---

5. Emil Jakob Schindler (1842–92), a favourite of Crown Prince Rudolf, died when Alma was thirteen.
6. This refutes any suggestion that Alma became pregnant in order to entrap Mahler. The wedding date had been set well before January 1902, when their union was physically consummated.

Carl MOLL
(1861–1945)

Alma's stepfather was a former pupil of her father, Emil Jakob Schindler, and a leading figure among the Secession artists. Although he opposed Alma's marriage to a man of his own age – his account of their romance forms a subdued counterpoint to hers (AMM, pp. 3–6) – Moll grew deeply fond of Mahler. In later years, under the influence of his daughter and son-in-law, he became an ardent National Socialist, committing suicide with his family when the Russians entered Vienna. In this previously unpublished extract from his manuscript autobiography, he struggles to reconcile his affection for Mahler with the creed of racial supremacy.

We had been invited over to lunch with friends[1] – Zuckerkandl the anatomist – the occasion being a visit from Mrs Zuckerkandl's sister, who was married to the engineer Paul Clemenceau and lived in Paris. The other

Carl Moll, 1909.

1. 7 November 1901; the invitation was to dinner, not lunch.

people present were Burckhard, Kolo Moser, Max
Klimt, Roller and Gustav Mahler. Mahler sat next to
Mrs Clemenceau at one end of the table and Alma was
between Klimt and Burckhard at the other end. My wife
was unwell and had not come along. Alma's table
companions were ribbing her about the 'handsomeness'
of her tutor Zemlinsky, who was really remarkably ugly
but was very much respected as a musician by his pupil.
Mahler's attention became fixed on Alma, and in spite of
the distance separating them he followed the lively talk at
the lower end of the table with his uncannily sensitive
hearing. At the end of the meal he went straight up to
Alma and took up with her the conversation about
Zemlinsky. It was obvious that he was infatuated with
Alma. A few days later, my wife was at the Opera with
her daughter. During the interval they were on the way
to the buffet and as they were passing the door of the
Director's office they ran into Mahler. He immediately
came over to Alma and she introduced her mother. 'Ah,'
he said, 'you were about to take tea in the foyer: do please
come into my office instead and I will have everything
brought in.'

The interval had been going on for a considerable time
when the conversation turned to the Hohe Warte.[2]
Mahler said he knew our house from the outside since he
often liked to go for walks in Heiligenstadt. To which my
wife responded politely: 'Well, Herr Direktor, if you
should chance to come past again, do please come in and
see our house from the inside too.'

Next day[3] at five in the afternoon the bell rang, and
there stood Mahler at the door. He willingly accepted an
invitation to tea and was soon engrossed in warm and
entertaining conversation with mother and daughter.
Our neighbour Kolo Moser turned up and Mahler looked
at the clock: he was supposed to be back at the Opera that
evening as a visitor was expected, but he was loath to

2. A district on the northern fringe of Vienna where the Molls had recently moved.
Their address was Steinfeldgasse, 8.
3. Not immediately, but some days later, on 27 November.

abandon our company: 'May I use the telephone?' We were not on the telephone: the only solution was to go to Döbling post office. 'Very well, show me the way and perhaps I can make my excuses.' Mahler and Alma went ahead; Moser and I accompanied them, following on behind. Afterwards, Mahler came back with us and stayed for dinner. The day after, Alma told her mother that on the way Mahler had asked for her hand and had said that she should give herself time for consideration!

If my Schindler experience was what shaped my life, the second equally huge influence on me, both from an artistic and from a personal point of view, was Gustav Mahler. He too enriched my life over a period of ten years of very intimate contact. Mahler was the offspring of Jewish parents. St Paul says: 'A Jew is not he who is outwardly a Jew, but he who is inwardly a Jew.'

Mahler had none of the typical Jewish characteristics: no false intellectual pretentions and certainly no craving for financial gain. Although he eschewed the former in the pursuance of art, he was able to respect all genuine effort – even if it might be misguided; but he thoroughly despised the latter.

Mahler was both highly intellectual and deeply, mystically instinctive. *Veni creator spiritus*. 'All the passing things of this world are no more than tokens.'[4]

Filled with a creative urge of his own, he devoted himself to the creative work of others to the point of total self-sacrifice; thanks to this sacrifice, the Vienna Court Opera enjoyed ten years of what amounted to a golden age.

Mahler had already announced his retirement as Director when he postponed it for a few more months to work on Richard Strauss's *Feuersnot*, and Strauss came to Vienna for its production.[5] After the dress rehearsal I picked Mahler up at the Opera for lunch at Hartmann's Restaurant next door to the opera house. Strauss decided

---

4. From the closing lines of Goethe's *Faust*, quoted in Mahler's Eighth Symphony.
5. Moll is confused here. *Feuersnot* was premièred by Mahler on 29 January 1902 and had eleven performances until 1905, when it was dropped.

to join us and the conversation turned to America: Mahler had already concluded his agreement to conduct at the Metropolitan Opera House in New York during the coming winter. 'Isn't it foolish of me', Mahler said to Strauss, 'to want to work in New York where actually none of the basic conditions are right for what I hope to achieve?' And Strauss smiled and said: 'Really, Mahler, you'll never grow up. Over there, all you do is walk on to the platform and do this' – he pretended to beat time – 'and then you toddle off to collect your cash' – he pretended to count money.

To Mahler, the faithful reproduction of a work of genius was an act of religion, so he was deeply hurt by Strauss's suggestion and sat through the rest of the meal in silence. Clash of temperament between two men of great generosity of character . . .

Mahler sacrificed himself to the point of destruction. And who was there to thank him? The composers of the great works were long dead and he was not thinking of the audience: his only reward was his own inner satisfaction.

He demanded the same sacrifice from the people who worked with him. As with artists everywhere, many were called but few were chosen, and only the latter understood his purpose and his talents and were delighted to follow him. The others saw him only as a taskmaster and responded only to the whip and to the demon within him.

The Vienna Court Opera boasted a glorious past, but it lived on a tradition that was often mere hollow convention.

Mahler's predecessor was Otto Jahn, dignified as a musician and rather easygoing as a person – something that conveyed itself in his appearance. He exercised his authority as Director fairly loosely and saw nothing wrong in living on the most intimate terms with the leading soprano and leaving it to her to choose her roles – which cannot have been exactly good for discipline among the staff.

His first conductor, Hans Richter, was a product of the

Bayreuth academy but in his everyday work was more inclined to set a comfortable Viennese pace. As a matter of principle, he never rehearsed beyond twelve noon – so as not to miss the first round of drinks at the bar nearest to the opera house, where his circle of friends used to assemble.

It was into this cosy atmosphere that Mahler, with all his asceticism and restless energy, suddenly burst. One of his first experiences was that in a performance of *Götterdämmerung*,[6] which is extremely long and to which he had devoted an exceptional amount of preparatory work, there was an important entrance of the kettledrum in the final act – but when he gave the nod, all he got was the empty pause signifying kettledrum missing. His control sufficed to hold the orchestra together, but after the performance was over the storm broke. The stage-manager who had been called to book explained by way of excuse that the man on the kettledrum lived in Klosterneuburg: his last train left before the end of the performance and the stand-in had let him down.

The next day there was an inquest with the whole orchestra. He would no longer tolerate this wretched practice of substitutes. At a performance, the man sitting at the music-stand had to be the one with whom he had rehearsed. A request from members of the orchestra that in view of their low salaries they should not be deprived of the right to earn a little on the side by taking part in occasional concerts was countered by an invitation for them to put in claims for a salary increase. In due course these claims were submitted and supported by Mahler at the Chief Steward's office with an indication that his ability to work and his continuation as Director depended on their acceptance. The rise in salaries was approved.

But the opposition of those who were called but not chosen was stilled only for a time.

When illness[7] forced Mahler to resign as Conductor of

6. The incident occurred in *Das Rheingold*, Mahler's first Wagner performance in Vienna, on 24 August 1897. See p. 262, and NBL, pp. 98–100.
7. A euphemism for anti-Semitic political intrigues.

the Philharmonic Orchestra, the man the majority chose as his replacement was a colleague Pepi Hellmesberger, the Conductor of Ballet Music: and at his very first concert they welcomed him with a laurel wreath.

And Mahler? When he returned from America years later suffering from his final illness, among the countless bunches of flowers that were sent to him at the sanatorium was a basket of roses from all the members of the Philharmonic who had worked with him. He gazed at it for a long time in silence. The nurse dried the tears that were streaming down his cheeks.

Mahler's achievements, and his memory, are currently the victims of the great revolution,[8] of the fight against the worshippers of the golden calf. In the past, the Jews themselves used to crucify and stone to death the men of exception that they produced: now these men are martyrs to their race in a different sense.

When the revolution is over and the air has cleared, there will be a time to separate the wheat from the chaff. Intellectual worth will never be totally suppressed. – 'Thou shalt rise up and live again.'[9]

If Mahler was to be admired both as an artist and as a man, at least a part of this admiration is due to his young wife, Schindler's elder daughter, Alma. She was nearly twenty years younger than her husband, charming to behold, highly talented and with an advanced musical education. She was made for the pleasures of life and much sought after. Mahler on the other hand was ascetic and a demon for hard labour, living only for his work: and his wife gave up her youth for him, abandoning many of the pleasures of life. Luckily, she had the capacity to find full compensation in her husband's intellectual career. The laughter of two delightful children – I am reminded of my first visit to the Schindlers' house[10] – added the lighter notes to the harmonies of their sheltered home.

8. National Socialism.
9. A quotation from Mahler's Second Symphony.
10. When Alma and her sister were small children.

The elder daughter, her father's favourite, succumbed before the age of five to scarlet fever complicated by diphtheria. Mahler never went back to the house on the Wörthersee, the scene of the tragedy. I spent two summers with my own family by the Wörthersee not far from Mahler's remote lodge, and in the course of evening walks came to understand Mahler's love of nature. It was a love which did not – as with painters like myself – fix itself upon detail: it was directed instead towards distant horizons or upwards towards great heights.

Mahler's intense love for his wife also extended to his mother-in-law, whom he worshipped in the full sense of the word. As a relaxation from his extremely concentrated work he used to set aside the early afternoon for a daily walk, usually into the Prater. But when his wife's mother was ill with pneumonia he would give up this relaxation every single day and sit at her bedside to divert her and cheer her up.

'Mein Leben', Vienna, c. 1940–45. German typescript in the possession of Henry-Louis de La Grange, Paris.

Alma Maria MAHLER (1879–1964)

Alma's account of marriage to Gustav Mahler is one of the outstanding literary documents of musical history, a book that has introduced innumerable readers[1] to the complexities of Mahler and his music. The researches and discoveries of recent years have undermined sections of her narrative and exposed deliberate falsehoods, but there can be no doubt of her love for Mahler or her desire to describe him as dispassionately as she could. In charting the course of their relationship, she is the only witness.

[*27 November 1901:*]
We [the Moll family] had just moved into a new house

---

1. Including the present writer.

and my books were still waiting to be installed. Some lay
flat, some stood on end, some were on the shelves, some
in heaps all round the room. Mahler walked to and fro,
inspecting them. My taste appeared to please him, except
for a complete edition of Nietzsche, at which his eye-
brows went up in horror. He demanded abruptly that it
should be cast then and there into the fire. I refused and said
that if his abhorrence had any justification it would be
easy enough to convince me; and it would be more to his
glory if Nietzsche stayed where he was and I refrained
from reading him than if I consigned him to the flames
and yet yearned for him ever after. He was put out, but
not for long. He proposed that we should go for a walk. We
met my mother in the hall, and in that unruffled way which
was her peculiar charm she invited him to stay to dinner.

'There's *Paprikahendl*[2] and – Burckhard.[3] Do stay —'

'I'm not very fond of either. But I'll stay all the same.'

And then we walked over the crunching snow, side by
side – so near and yet apart – down to Döbling, and there
he wanted to telephone to his flat to say that he would be
out that evening. Every other minute his shoe-laces came
undone and he selected the highest point of vantage to
put his foot upon and tie them up. His childlike help-
lessness went to my heart. In Döbling we went to the
post office, but he did not know his own number; and so
he had to ring up the Opera. His message gave no
explanation of his absence, a thing unexampled in all the
nine years Justine and he had lived together. Then we
climbed the hill again in silence.

Suddenly he burst out: 'It's not so simple to marry a
person like me. I am free and must be free. I cannot be
bound, or tied to one spot. My job at the Opera is simply
from one day to the next.'

A feeling of suffocation came over me. He laid down
the law without thinking of consulting my feelings. After
a moment's silence I said:

'Of course. Don't forget that I am the child of artists

---

2. Chicken in pepper sauce.
3. Dr Max Burckhard (1854–1912), Director of the Burgtheater, 1890–8.

The Hohe Warte in Winter, woodcut by Carl Moll.

and have always lived among artists and, also, I'm one myself. What you say seems to me obvious.'

I can still see the sparkle on the snow as we passed each lamppost. I can recall how we both without a word drew attention to its fairy-tale beauty. We did not speak another word all the way home. He seemed cheerful and reassured. We went by tacit agreement straight up to my room. There he kissed me and went on to talk of a speedy marriage, as though it went without saying . . . We were married on 9 March 1902, and on the 10th, the day after we had left for our honeymoon, Justine and Arnold Rosé followed suit.

Mahler went to the church on foot in galoshes, as it was raining hard; my mother, Justine and I drove. There was no one in the Karlskirche[4] except ourselves and the witnesses, Moll and Rosé. It was early in the day. When it came to kneeling down, Mahler misjudged the hassock and found himself on the stone flags; he was so small that he had to stand up again and make a fresh start. We all smiled, including the priest. There were six of us at the wedding breakfast, a rather silent occasion, and our guests took their departure immediately afterwards, leaving us alone to pack and drive to the station. As the wedding had been publicly announced to take place in the evening, a crowd of inquisitive people must have come to the church in vain.

Once in the train for St Petersburg we breathed again. His clouded spirits cleared as though by magic; and I too, alone at last, was no longer oppressed by the need to conceal my condition. He had been invited to conduct three concerts in St Petersburg and so we had decided to make this trip our honeymoon. Unfortunately, Mahler caught a severe feverish chill on the journey, induced in this case by the overheated compartment of a Russian train. He suffered all his life from these infections and his fatal illness was partly due to one of them. I was aghast as

4. Green-domed Church of St Charles Borromeo in the Karlsplatz, a few minutes' walk from the Opera. It was commissioned by Emperor Charles VI in 1713 in thanksgiving for the end of a plague, designed by Johann Bernhard Fischer von Erlach and completed in 1739.

I saw him rushing up and down the corridor – his face as white as a sheet, incapable of uttering a syllable. He jumped out at every station and walked about the platform, in thirty degrees of frost without hat, coat or gloves. The Russians, who kept out the cold with huge fur caps and gloves, were greatly amused.

I sat in our compartment, waiting anxiously for his martyrdom to end, as I was often to do during these onsets of his . . .

During the early years of our married life I felt very uncertain of myself in my relations with him. After I had conquered him by my audacity before I knew what I was about, all my self-assurance was undermined by the psychological effects of becoming pregnant before being married. From the moment of his spiritual triumph, too, he looked down on me and did not recover his love of me until I had broken his tyranny. Sometimes he played the part of a schoolmaster, relentlessly strict and unjust. He soured my enjoyment of life and made it an abomination. That is, he tried to. Money – rubbish! Clothes – rubbish! Beauty – rubbish! Travelling – rubbish! Only the spirit was to count. I know today that he was afraid of my youth and beauty. He wanted to make them safe for himself by simply taking from me any atom of life in which he himself played no part. I was a young thing he had desired and whose education he now took in hand . . .

The summer [of 1904] was beautiful, serene and happy. Before the holidays came to an end he played me the completed Sixth Symphony. I had first to get everything done in the house, so as to have all my time free. Once more we walked arm in arm up to his [composing-] house in the wood, where nothing could disturb us. These occasions were always very solemn ones.

After he had drafted the first movement he came down from the wood to tell me he had tried to express me in a theme. 'Whether I've succeeded, I don't know; but you'll have to put up with it.'

This is the great soaring theme[5] of the first movement

---

5. The movement's second subject.

of the Sixth Symphony. In the third movement he
represented the arhythmic games of the two little children, tottering in zigzags over the sand. Ominously, the
childish voices became more and more tragic, and at the
end died out in a whimper. In the last movement he
described himself and his downfall or, as he later said,
that of his hero: 'It is the hero, on whom fall three blows
of fate, the last of which fells him as a tree is felled.'
Those were his words.

Not one of his works came so directly from his inmost
heart as this. We both wept that day. The music and
what it foretold touched us so deeply. The Sixth is the
most completely personal of his works, and a prophetic
one also. In the *Kindertotenlieder*, as also in the Sixth, he
anticipated his own life in music. On him too fell three
blows of fate, and the last felled him. But at the time he
was serene; he was conscious of the greatness of his work.
He was a tree in full leaf and flower.

One more word about his playing the work through to
me: he always said he would never play an unfinished
work, and he never did. It would, he said, be an
immodesty. An artist could no more show unfinished
work than a mother her child in the womb.

I remarked to him once during a walk: 'All I love in a
man is his achievement. The greater his achievement the
more I have to love him.'

'That's a real danger. You mean if anyone came along
who could do more than I —'

'I'd have to love him,' I said.

He smiled: 'Well, I won't worry for the time being. I
don't know anybody who can do more than I can.'

All the same, each of us was jealous of the other,
though we belied it. He often used to say: 'If you were
suddenly disfigured by some illness, smallpox, for
example, then at last, when you were pleasing in the sight
of nobody else – then at last I could show how I loved
you.'

AMM, pp. 18–19, 33, 43, 70–71.

Alfred ROLLER
(1864–1935)

Mahler met Roller in Alma's circle of artist friends in 1902 and listened intently to his criticism of operatic stage design. Although the painter lacked theatrical experience, Mahler promptly commissioned him to create a new *Tristan and Isolde*, and subsequently had him appointed director of design at the Opera. Their collaboration there, effectively as joint producers, reached its summits in *Fidelio* and *Don Giovanni*. They became close friends and continued to correspond and see each other after Mahler's departure from Vienna.

Roller saw Mahler with an artist's eye and his physical description is the most acute and accurate in existence. It was written in 1921 as the introduction to a book of Mahler photographs that Alma was having published.

. . . 'Unattractive, puny, ugly, a fidgeting bundle of nerves' – these are the expressions commonly used to describe Mahler's outward appearance. They are inaccurate and only occasionally derive from the man himself.

To begin with the outer shell: Mahler dressed carelessly. In his prime he owned some very good clothes but took poor care of them. His overcoat had only the top button fastened, his fists were crammed into the pockets; his tie had been wound in three seconds into a crooked knot: the newest hat, jammed down over his ears with both fists, soon looked as shapeless as an old one.

If he was taken to task over this, he would listen with an indulgent smile, as if to the prattlings of a little child, then perhaps to show willing he would correct the offending habit for a while – only to resume his old ways almost immediately. Thus, by his indifference to any impression he was making, he contributed to the assumption that he was a poor physical specimen . . .

The low priority he gave to his clothing was not devoid of the playfulness that was so characteristic of him. It sometimes gave him childish pleasure, with people who laid great stress on outward form, to throw them into confusion with his sartorial delapidation. At one period

the silk lining of his coat was torn and Mahler, who was far from troubling his head with anything so trivial, did not bother to have it mended; before long, it was in a pitiful state. It became so bad that it inspired him to perpetrate a practical joke. 'It would be fascinating', he said, 'to see what that immaculately ceremonious door-keeper of the [Imperial] Chief Steward thinks as he helps me on and off with this coat whenever I call on official duty. He looks so proud in his uniform and keeps his face so straight – not a flicker, I assure you – when he helps me into it, and it really is in tatters. Imagine how the social order must be all drawn up inside a head like that, and which rung of the ladder I have been assigned to! What a thought! My, what a thought!' I did not have the heart to spoil this state of delight (which went on for weeks) by mentioning the torn lining in the right quarters, namely to Frau Alma.

If I mention recollections such as these, they may seem to have very little to do with describing Mahler's outward appearance. But there was nothing about this very real human being that was merely what it seemed on the surface, and a description of his visible traits leads inevitably to anecdotes that illustrate what lay beneath them.

One set of clothing that really was new and impeccably maintained was Mahler's tails. Since he wore them for conducting, he always called them his 'working clothes'. Anything else connected with his work was also regarded as worthy of attention. When people saw him on the podium, upright, elegant and full of explosive energy, and noted the difference between this Mahler and their everyday impression of him, they tried to resolve their confusion by describing him as 'a man of sudden moods'. By a process of auto-suggestion they invented a kind of half-savage or three-quarter madman as 'their' Mahler, adding all kinds of distortion and elaboration.

When the masses turn their gaze on to a great man, the first things they look for are signs of their own baseness and weaknesses. For example, the finest items of Mahler's daily attire were always his magnificent shoes. So at once the legend sprang up that he was vain about his slender feet! It was simply that he was a keen walker and like all such enthusiasts was conscious of the value and importance of a good pair of shoes.

Mahler's pleasure in walking arose from his great love of the outdoors. This love did not stem from a desire to see anything special or reach any special objective. Any spot among the fields where he could while away a few untroubled moments delighted him and seemed to him 'just perfect'. I remember reclining with him on a small slope in the forest one late summer afternoon. It was in a thinned-out patch of the woods, dotted with rough left-over stacks of half-grown pines that had come under the axe. The forest floor was strewn with mouldering woodchips and covered with matted bilberry bushes. Anonymous tree-covered slopes. Nothing out of the ordinary. Just peace and pleasant sunshine. But Mahler, lying on his back, wormed his shoulders deep into the carpet of bilberries as if he were snuggling up to the earth as close as he possibly could. 'Isn't this wonderful spot!' he kept saying over and over, 'Isn't this marvellous!' and soon he was in such a good mood that he told me all about the plot of his abandoned opera *Rübezahl*.

At his summer homes each year, when he indulged his passion for rambling, Mahler wore a grey walking-suit. He liked to hang the jacket over his shoulder on a cord and his cap would be pinned to the front of his coarse linen shirt. The black pleated belt would be pushed down well below the waist. His feet sported yellow lace-up boots and above them thin black knee-length socks. Fawn woollen socks or spats were standard garb with this sort of outfit, but he never seemed to use them. Another unusual feature of Mahler's clothing was that he always had his night-shirts cut to the length of riding-shirts. He said he hated long night-shirts and that anyway he slept a lot better when he felt slightly chilly.

Some people might find such details ridiculous or unnecessary to mention. Perhaps they are, but the job of a collector, including an assembler of observations, is simply to collect and set down without distortion. The evaluation and sorting of the material is up to others. In any case, I feel that the way a man chooses to dress can say more about him than many a hair-splitting psychological analysis.

No sketch of Mahler's outward appearance is complete without taking into account his much-discussed 'jerking foot' [or tic]. As a child, he was afflicted by involuntary movements of the extremities. These are commonly found in mentally advanced children and, if neglected, can develop into St Vitus's dance. That ailment, however, disappears when the child's mind and body grow and are properly occupied. With Mahler, unfortunately, an involuntary twitch persisted in his right leg throughout his life. He never mentioned it to me, and I gathered he was rather ashamed of it.

When he was walking, one noticed that anything from one to three steps would sometimes fall out of the regular rhythm. Standing still, one foot would tap lightly on the ground, kicking the spot.

With his incomparably powerful will, he usually managed to control the impulse. But if his will was otherwise occupied or relaxed, the right foot would resume its unusual habit. Whatever made his will relax, whether something surprising, or comic or unpleasant, the effect was the same. It is incorrect, as is often said, that the stamping reflected Mahler's impatience or annoyance. It would occur just as often and even more vigorously when he laughed. And Mahler laughed readily and heartily like a child, tears streaming from his eyes. He would then take off his glasses to wipe the lenses dry, and give a little dance of joy on the spot where he stood.

That this stamping has been construed as a sign of impatience or anger shows that Mahler had more dealings with people who irritated or bored him than with those who made him laugh . . .

In conversation, peacefully expounding his thoughts, the tic was never seen. Nor did it appear when he exerted his will as, for example, while conducting. But when walking alone, working out a musical idea before he

entered it in his sketch-book, he regularly started striding
along with one or two paces that were too short.

I have seen him sometimes standing motionless in the
middle of a room, poised on one leg, one hand on a hip
and the index finger of the other stuck against a cheek,
his head bowed, the back of his other foot hooked in the
hollow of his knee, eyes fixed on the floor. He could stand
like that for several minutes, lost in his thoughts.

Was this odd pose an exercise he had developed to
counteract the inadvertent movements of his leg? It is
possible. For he was not gentle with his body, that body
that was regarded as delicate but was really nothing of the
kind.

Among southern Germans like ourselves, Mahler was
bound to be considered small in stature. Unfortunately, I
never took his measurements. I would say that he was not
above 1 m 60 cm in height. His thick hair, allowed to
grow fairly long at Frau Alma's wish, made his head
appear too large. While Mahler was sunbathing, which he
was very keen on, I had the opportunity to study his
naked body closely. It was very tidily formed and very
masculine in its proportions. His shoulders were broader
than one would imagine from seeing him in clothes, and
perfectly symmetrical. His hips were very narrow and his
legs, which were by no means too short, had beautifully
formed and regularly spaced axes, firm, clearly
developed muscles and just a light covering of hair.
There was no sign of any prominent veins. His feet were
small with a high instep and short regularly shaped toes,
without a blemish.

His chest stood out strongly with very little hair and
well-defined musculature. His belly, like the rest of his
body, bore no trace of excess fat, the central line of
muscle was plainly visible and the outline of the other
muscles as clear as on an anatomical model. In the course
of my profession, I have seen a great many naked bodies
of all types and can testify that at the age of forty Mahler
had the perfect male torso strong, slim, beautifully made,
although the total body length was probably not quite
seven and a half times the vertical head diameter. The

first time I saw him without clothes, I could not refrain from expressing my surprise at such a fine display of muscle. Mahler laughed in amusement because he realized that I too had been misled by the general talk about his poor physical shape. The most beautifully developed part of him, quite an outstanding sight because it was so well delineated, was the musculature of his back. I could never set eyes on this superbly modelled, sun-tanned back without being reminded of a racehorse in peak condition.

His hands were real workman's hands, short and broad and with unmanicured fingers ending as if they had been chopped off. The nails – it must be said – were mostly bitten short, often right down to the skin, and only gradually did Frau Alma have any success in her campaign against this bad habit. His arms were thin, at least in proportion to their great strength – because contrary to general opinion, Mahler was muscularly powerful. Many people saw him from time to time vault up on to the stage out of the orchestra pit via the ramp. He was also capable without great strain of carrying his sick sister all the way from the street up to their flat on the third floor. Standing for long periods in the restricted space of the conductor's podium, often with no railing and high above the heads of the audience in the stalls, was probably also quite a feat of strength.

At a rehearsal for the first performance of *Lohengrin* in 1904, Mahler, as producer, worked hard to create the necessary amount of movement among the assembled 'nobles' on the arrival of the Swan Knight. He manhandled the hefty singers around as if they were balls, to set them in the right places. Leaving the stage at the end of the scene, he suddenly came to a halt on the wooden steps leading down to the stalls and stood there for a moment with his hand reaching up to his heart. That was the first time I was struck by a feeling that something dreadful might happen. However, Mahler did not die from the strain on his heart: it is established that it was a streptococcal infection of the blood resulting from repeated bouts of angina that proved fatal.

Villa Mahler am Wörther See

The house that Mahler built beside the Wörthersee;
postcard commissioned by Mahler.

So long as he believed his heart was sound (that is, up
to 1907), he was not only an avid walker but an
outstanding swimmer, a powerful oarsman and an agile
cyclist. At Maiernigg by the Wörthersee, his summer
residence for seven years, he would rise at 5.30, take his
first swim alone, then hasten through secret paths to his
small composing-house deep in the woods, where his
breakfast awaited. Then followed around seven hours of
uninterrupted work.

Before lunch he would take another swim, make music
with his wife or play with the children. Afterwards he
had a short rest – something he never allowed himself in
town, no matter how tired he became at morning rehearsal. If one tried there to persuade him to rest, he would
refuse saying, 'It's just ordinary physical tiredness.'

His short afternoon rest in the country was followed
around four o'clock by a long daily walk, Frau Alma
usually accompanying him. It was often not easy. He

could walk at a brisk march tempo, not feeling the pace. Walking slowly, he put one foot daintily before the other, stretching his legs straight out at the knee. He was a narrow-gauge walker.

Walking fast, however, as on these long walks, he would lean forward, his chin stretched out, and tread firmly, almost stamping. This gait had something stormy, almost triumphant, about it. Mahler was incapable of strolling. His body had bearing, if not always a conventional one. Uphill he would go far too fast: I could barely keep up with him.

His swim usually began with a high dive. Then he swam under water and did not reappear until he was far out in the lake, bobbing about comfortably like a seal. Rowing a boat with Mahler was no pleasure. He had a very powerful stroke, and pulled too fast; his strength enabled him to keep going for a long time.

Evenings in the country he usually spent in his wife's company. She often read aloud to him, he sometimes to her. She reports that in the summer months – the time of his real work – he was always more approachable, human and devoted than in town. He even overcame his great inhibition and played her his half-finished works.

Mahler at that time gave the impression of being utterly healthy. He slept splendidly, relished his cigar and in the evening enjoyed a glass of beer. Spirits he abstained from completely. Wine he drank only on special occasions, preferring Mosel, Chianti or Asti. One or two glasses sufficed to make him light-hearted and he would then invent puns which, in Frau Alma's expression, fabulously entertained their inventor.

But for all his sensual pleasures, including those of the table, he was a man of great moderation. You never saw him do anything in excess. He abhorred drunkenness, as much as obscenity or indecency. The strict cleanliness that he kept about his person was observed, without prudishness, in his speech and doubtless also in his thoughts.

In middle life, Mahler underwent a serious intestinal operation that left him with extensive internal scarring.

This obliged him to be particularly careful about his food and to follow a strict diet. But he ate well and derived much pleasure from food. Lots of fruit, especially apples and oranges, plenty of butter, plain vegetables and pasta, very little meat and only from farm animals. He avoided game and anything that came from the wild. Since anything outside his careful diet made him too unwell to work, he was exaggeratedly cautious, even finicky, at table, particularly if he was just completing a composition and had only a few more days of vacation left. In general he was very good at enduring aches and pains. Sometimes he would enter the podium with a terrible migraine; at the final rehearsal of the Eighth Symphony in Munich he conducted with severe rheumatic pains in the back of his neck and shoulders. It was only the constant anxiety not to have his working schedule disrupted that sometimes made him hypochondriacal, and frustrated over small annoyances such as a wasp sting or a cut from a knife. He was haunted by the secret fear, shared by all creative artists, that he might die too young and leave his work unfinished.

In the summer of 1907, after he had resigned as Director of the Court Opera in Vienna and scarlet fever had robbed him of his eldest child in Maiernigg, Mahler was told that his heart was not in order. The announcement was entirely unexpected and was accompanied by a strict set of rules. Its effect on Mahler was severe and disabling. That summer yielded no artistic fruit. He abandoned Maiernigg forever after the death of little Maria Anna and rented a place in Schluderbach. His mood was one of silent resignation. The long, happy rambles had been replaced by careful little strolls. An old friend succeeded in restoring his shattered confidence in his physical powers. Mahler tried taking longer walks and ignored the doctor who had sent him so much into his shell. But there were to be no more route marches, mountaineering, rowing or swimming. And after that time I often saw him set aside the one cigar a day that the doctor had allowed him after dinner: he would smoke it only half through, then stare at it thoughtfully and quietly stub it out. The trip to America that followed during that autumn was a valuable diversion, and in the summer of 1908, when he had found rooms at the Altschluderbach farmhouse near Toblach, his creativity also came back. Much to his own astonishment, it seemed, because as I was arriving there he called out to me from a distance: 'Imagine, I'm actually writing again!' It was *Das Lied von der Erde* . . .

From his first visit to America he had returned not exactly aged but nevertheless very much changed. I was taken aback when he stood there before me in the dim light of the station forecourt. The easier work-load over there and the reduced amount of exercise had thickened him up. His clothes were smarter too. He was still not a stout man but everything about him, his figure, the way he moved, his face, had become less taut. Even his voice seemed different, though that was merely an illusion.

In fact, Mahler's voice functioned in two separate registers, one directly above the other. A very sonorous baritone when he was speaking in a relaxed manner and a ringing tenor that came into play when his excitement began to grow. His voice could be raised to a very high volume without losing its deeper tones. This was demonstrated, for example, during his celebrated theatrical storms. 'Please don't think I was really angry,' he told me after I was taken aback the first time, 'but being fierce is the only weapon I have for keeping the sort of order you need.' Subsequently I learned to recognize by the sound of his voice whether he was putting it on or whether he was really becoming heated. In the latter case his voice would suddenly soar into the higher register with a kind of break: it would happen whether his excitement was of joy or anger, or whether it sprang from intense involvement in a subject of conversation. After 1907 his higher voice was to be heard less and less. His increasing melancholy caused the lower register to predominate more and more, and that is why it could seem that his voice had actually altered. – Incidentally, Mahler was an exceptionally gripping and entertaining speaker. He spoke a fine, pure form of German that was completely free of any foreign intonation, and he uttered clear, rounded sentences that did not sound at all bombastic. His delivery was very masculine. His 'r's were quite strongly emphasized and rather guttural . . .

Mahler had a quite unusually short skull from front to back: you could say it had absolutely no rear segment. The impetuousness of his nature expressed itself in the bulging curve of his temples and the older he grew, the more this dominated his features. The structure of the skull, together with the thrusting lower jaw and the way the wavy locks of his naturally curled hair – which was dark all over – stood up over his forehead, gave his head its striking similarity to an antique mask of tragedy.

From his thirtieth year, Mahler wore no beard. Only in the summer months, to save himself the trouble of shaving, he sometimes had a short-trimmed moustache. One summer when I met him he also had a magnificent beard, thick, dark grey overall but with two fiery streaks of lighter grey extending down from the corners of his mouth. But bowing good-humouredly to the general protests, he soon emerged beardless again. That way his strong, healthy teeth showed up better. They were white and regular. No dentist got any employment from them until the last few years of his life, and not much then either. On either side of his face between his mouth and the strong chewing muscles there were three vertical folds. A zigzag one with a rounded outer edge at the corners of his mouth. A second one, the fold of cares, running from the nostrils down to just above the corners of the mouth. And a third one that started round about the yoke-bone extension of the upper jaw and slanted down to the horizontal components of the lower jaw. This last fold is characteristic of people with unusually strong determination and in Mahler's case it was deep and well defined, as if carved in stone by a knife. Next to this groove, directly over the eye-teeth, there was also a slight hollow. The fine hooked nose was not as prominent in life as on his death-mask, where the general wasting of the face tends to exaggerate it . . .

His ears were small and close to the head, with

particularly intricate and delicately modelled folding and completely free-standing lobes. His lips were classically shaped, and their immediate area had that multiplicity of detail which is produced by the habit of very carefully articulated speech. They were thin, and, when he was wearing his customary sober expression, usually closed. It was only when he was listening intently that they stood slightly open. But if Mahler was disgruntled, angry or out of sorts, he would pull his mouth out of shape, taking half his lower lip between his teeth, wrinkling his brow and tightening the folds of his nose. Pulled about like this, his face took on such a distorted grimace that he really did become the 'nasty Mahler' . . .

It was not entirely Mahler's fault that this was the only face that many people saw and that they never really got to know any but the 'nasty Mahler'. He was short-sighted and, as the pictures show, wore glasses from boyhood. Sometimes spectacles, sometimes a pince-nez. By the end of his life they were usually rimless spectacles with oval lenses and gold frames. They made the area surrounding the eyes look bigger than the eyes themselves. His irises were dark and speckled, mainly a deep shade of brown. All round his eye sockets, the features jutted well forward. His tear sacs were small and flat. There had been an energetic lift to his upper eyelids ever since he attained maturity, giving him a very wide-awake appearance. If they drooped a little, that was a sign that he was beginning to grow tired. They were a pair of eyes that registered intelligence, honesty and an ability to hold their own.

This spare visage was a true mirror of every internal emotion of its owner, which is why different people have described it so differently, depending on their relationship with Mahler. The mask-like quality is referred to almost universally. But whereas some individuals denote earnestness, severity or ascetic coldness as its dominant expression, others use the words 'liveliness', 'nervousness', 'impatience' and 'quixotic'. Others still talk about hardness, lack of emotion, unapproachability and pride. Yet anyone who was sufficiently close to Mahler could not help recognizing that every movement of a great and impassioned human spirit was capable of finding expression in these features; but that the principal moving force within this strong personality was a combination of robust goodwill and triumph over adversity.

Mahler must have experienced much inner turmoil and suffered an enormous amount. His music resounds with all that his lips were too modest to express. On the evening after the final rehearsal of the Sixth Symphony, he asked a friend who was not a musician what sort of impression he had gained. This friend, still reeling from the effects of the work, could only manage to gasp: 'How can such a kind person as you manage to express so much cruelty and lack of pity?' And Mahler replied very seriously and pointedly: 'These are the cruelties that have been inflicted on me and the sufferings I have had to endure.'

Mahler's profound kindness was experienced by many people. These experiences are usually shrouded in discretion. What tend to be recalled in fullest detail are those unavoidable occasions encountered by everyone in a position of authority when one has to do things that are bound to hurt others.

How marvellous he was with children and how quickly they learned to love him. In his dealings with even the humblest of creatures, his great awe for the mystery of life was always evident. Yet he was fond of saying 'there is a huge difference between being gentle and being weak, and between being sweet and being sugary.' Once in his large Vienna living-room he was pacing back and forth in pursuance of a train of thought when his flow of speech was interrupted by a troublesome fly. To keep it away, he kept waving his hand at it until eventually by chance he caught it such a blow that it fell to the floor twitching and dying beside him. In order to put it out of its misery, he trod on it. But he raised his foot so inordinately high, and held it in the air for so long, that you could see how immensely difficult the decision was. He gazed in distress at the crushed little corpse at his feet and with a spontaneous movement of the hand towards it, as if to calm and console it, he murmured: 'There, there, don't fret: you too are immortal!' He turned away, wandered aimlessly about the room and did not go on with what he had been saying. Apart from myself, another visitor, a well-known musician of Jewish descent, had witnessed this odd little incident. 'Why worry your head so much over treading on a fly?' he asked. He got no answer. The man who put this question belongs to the circle which says that in order to understand Mahler properly, you have to be a Jew.

Mahler never hid his Jewish origins. But he had no joy from them. They were a spur and a goad towards ever higher and more lofty achievement. He once explained to me the effect of his background on his creative works. 'You know,' he said, 'it's like a man who comes into the world with one arm shorter than the other. The other arm has to cope with so much more, and in the end perhaps manages to do things that two sound arms would never have achieved.' People who were trying to be pleasant to him would often say that because of the way he had developed, he was really no longer a Jew. That made him sad. 'People should listen to my work,' he said, 'and see if it means anything to them, then either accept or reject it. But as for their prejudices for or against a Jew, they should leave those at home. That much I demand as my right.'

The main thing that bound him to Judaism was compassion. The reasons for this he had apparently sensed often enough within himself, though he seldom talked about the subject and when he did, it was only to utter a statement of fact, never in embittered or sentimental tones. But: 'Among the poorest men, there is always one who is poorer than them all and who also happens to be a Jew.' Yet Jewish blood, in his eyes, gave not the slightest excuse for corruption, heartlessness or even bad behaviour. He was not a card-carrying Jew and at times was more attacked for not being so than he was from the other side. 'It's a funny thing,' he often said with amusement during his final period as Director in Vienna, 'but it seems to me that the anti-Semitic papers

are the only ones who still have any respect for me.' . . .
On the whole, his Jewish ancestry was less of a help than
a hindrance in the reception he got. He certainly never
sought advantage from his Jewishness. His feeling of
being one of the chosen had other, personal, roots, not
racial ones.

Ernst Bloch describes Mahler among other things as 'a
human hymnal' and that is probably the most apt
summing-up of Mahler's essential nature. He was deeply
religious. His faith was that of a child. God is love and
love is God. This idea came up a thousand times in his
conversation. I once asked him why he did not write a
mass, and he seemed taken aback. 'Do you think I could
take that upon myself? Well, why not? But no, there's the
credo in it.' And he began to recite the credo in Latin.
'No, I couldn't do it.'

But after a rehearsal of the Eighth in Munich he called
cheerfully across to me, referring to this conversation:
'There you are, that's my mass.'

I never heard a word of blasphemy from him. But he
needed no intermediary to God. He spoke with Him face
to face. God lived easily within him. How else can one
define the state of complete transcendency in which he
wrote? He was once sitting at work in his composing-hut
in Altschluderbach with its double ring of fencing. A
jackdaw that was being chased by a hawk mistook his
dark window-pane for a place to hide and flew straight
into the hut, crashing through the glass and shattering it
right next to Mahler's table. The hawk flew in behind it
and the whole of the tiny room was filled with screeching
and fluttering. But Mahler had no idea all this was
happening around him in the real world. It was only
when the hawk flew out again and brushed his head with
its wings that he came back to reality. The jackdaw
cowering in a corner and the broken window enabled him
to put together what had happened. So are we not
entitled to refer to this complete transportation of the
artist as 'being with God'? . . .

When, on the morning after the night he died, I took
my leave of Mahler's mortal remains, his features still

bore the agony of his long struggle with death. Klimt, who saw him several hours later, told me what regal calm and unworldly beauty they had then taken on. This indeed is the way they appear in the splendid death mask taken by Moll.

Die Bildnisse von Gustav Mahler, Alfred Roller (ed.), Leipzig and Vienna (E. P. Tal & Co.), 1922, pp. 9–28.

Alfred Roller's monogram.

Willibald KÄHLER
(1866-1938)

At the beginning of February 1904 Mahler conducted his Third Symphony on successive nights at Heidelberg and Mannheim. Both concerts were sold out (which, gloated Mahler, did not even happen to Strauss)[1] and he was pleased with the performances. Kähler, the Mannheim opera conductor, prepared the orchestra and chorus and observed Mahler at rehearsal.

At the first rehearsal the orchestra naturally had to get used to Mahler's way of conducting. In the first half-hour

---

1. AMM. p. 232.

the general nervousness reached such a pitch that no one was capable of blowing an untroubled note or of drawing the bow in a relaxed manner. Soon, however, he had the orchestra under control: the sharp instinct of good orchestral players told them that here was someone for whom the matter in hand was all that counted. Mahler rehearsed with incredible precision, fascinating each player with his glance. He did not rest until each phrase corresponded entirely with his intentions. He repeatedly called to the wind players: 'In the long-held notes breathe where you like, but never at any price on a downbeat!' . . .

There was a small incident with the first oboist L., an artist of distinction. Mahler demanded that he should play a certain passage 'with the bell pointing upwards'. L. declared this impossible. Irritated, Mahler burst out: 'And I tell you, in ten years' time no one will play passages like this any other way! Just try it!' And lo! it worked, and the effect Mahler intended came across extremely well. Whereas Mahler's stick technique in the rehearsals had been somewhat violent and often excessively vivacious, in the performance the great moderation of his gestures was surprising. It struck me that while conducting he almost continually gripped the left lapel of his dress-coat with his left hand. When asked the reason for this, he said that this was his means of compelling himself to relax as much as possible.

*150 Jahre Musikalische Akademie des Nationaltheater Orchesters
Mannheim 1779–1929*, Mannheim, 1929, pp. 63–4,
trans. in DM2, p. 299.

Arnold SCHOENBERG
(1874–1951)

Mahler first heard Schoenberg's music more than two years before he met his future protégé. Given a score of *Verklärte Nacht*, he asked his concert-master, Arnold Rosé, to run through the sextet in his office, exclaiming when it was finished: 'You must play that!'[1] Both he and Schoenberg missed the Rosé Quartet's première on 18 March 1902. Mahler, who had married a week earlier, was conducting in St Petersburg;[2] Schoenberg was living in Berlin.

Despite catcalls at the first performance, Rosé decided to repeat the work on 1 March 1904. It was at his rehearsal in one of the practice rooms at the opera house that Mahler ran into Schoenberg.[3]

They became connected in other ways. With his brother-in-law, Alexander von Zemlinsky, Schoenberg formed an Associaton of Creative Musicians – 'to give modern music a permanent home in Vienna' – with Mahler as its president. Zemlinsky worshipped Mahler, composed an opera to his commission and ultimately joined him at the Court Opera. He had also been a teacher and pre-marital lover of Alma, who drew him and Schoenberg into Mahler's social ambit.

Schoenberg's initial attitude to Mahler was characteristically rebellious. 'How can Mahler do anything with his Fourth [Symphony] when he has already failed to do anything with his First?' he mocked. Alma recalled furious rows over the piano at their apartment, ending in Schoenberg storming out and Mahler ordering his wife never to readmit 'that conceited puppy'. But their rifts healed swiftly. Mahler conceded that he did not understand Schoenberg's music, 'but he is young and perhaps he is right.'[4] He attended Schoenberg's concerts, lent him money, even bought one of his paintings anonymously when the impecunious atonalist exhibited in Vienna in 1910. In his dying months he worried about Schoenberg: 'Who will look after him when I am gone?'[5]

1. Max Graf, *Legends of a Musical City*, New York (The Philosophical Library), 1945, pp. 218–19.
2. Rosé himself had married Mahler's sister Justine on 10 March 1902.
3. H. H. Stuckenschmidt, *Arnold Schoenberg: His Life, World and Work*, London (John Calder), 1977, p. 78. Dika Newlin, one of Schoenberg's last pupils, recounts: 'I was interested to learn how S. had met Mahler for the first time: Mahler just wandered in on a rehearsal of *Verklärte Nacht* one day, completely unannounced and a stranger to Schoenberg.' (Dika Newlin, *Schoenberg Remembered*, New York (Pendragon Press), 1980, p. 290.)
4. AMM, pp. 77–8, 112.
5. *Klemperer on Music: Shavings from a Musician's Workbench*, ed. Martin Anderson, London (Toccata Press), 1986, p. 140; Specht, p. 43.

Self-portrait by Schoenberg, 1909.

Born of Jewish parents in Vienna and intended for commerce, Schoenberg was entirely self-taught in music, with the exception of tips picked up from Zemlinsky. By 1907 he was hovering on the fringes of tonality and arousing uproar in conservative audiences. The following year, he abandoned key structures altogether.

It was in that year that his conversion to Mahler's music was completed.[6] Schoenberg had come to love both the man[7] and his symphonies. He had long since recognized 'the most uncompromising truthfulness'[8] in the Third; now he found 'perfect repose'[9] in the Seventh. Yet later in life, between 1925 and 1935, he 'did not dare to read or listen to Mahler's music: I was afraid that my aversion to it . . . might return.'[10]

His emotions at Mahler's death were a mixture of grief and guilt more appropriate to a parental bereavement than to the loss of a friend and supporter. Two months afterwards he 'consecrated' his *Treatise on Harmony* to Mahler's memory, 'this martyr, this saint.'[11]

An unpublished autobiographical fragment, written some twenty years later, conveys similar sentiments:

> I do not have a great deal to say about Gustav Mahler. Only this: he is one of the greatest men there could possibly be.
>
> Whether he is a good or bad composer is not in question here. Great people do everything in one and the same way: greatly. And that is a different matter from good or bad.
>
> Why he does not appeal immediately to most musicians is easily explained. They are unintelligent (so was I, in this respect, for a short while) and convinced of their own aesthetic opinions. However, music does not exist just for musicians.

> 'Kleine Manuscript', MS 11, p. 30, deposited at the Arnold Schoenberg Institute, University of Southern California, Los Angeles. Reproduced by kind permission of the Institute.

---

6. In a combative 1948 letter to the critic Olin Downes, Schoenberg confesses to disparaging Mahler between 1898 and 1908. 'For that I made good subsequently by adoration.' See Erwin Stein (ed.), *Arnold Schoenberg Letters*, London (Faber and Faber), 1964, p. 264.
7. AMM, p. 182.
8. AMM, p. 257.
9. AMM, p. 325.
10. Stein, *Letters*, p. 264.
11. *Harmonienlehre*, Vienna (Universal Edition), 1911, frontispiece.

A further private jotting of the same period[12] frets over Mahler's recommendation to the Viennese Academy of Music to accept Schoenberg as a private tutor:

> People are bound to find Mahler's assessment of me rather cool. But what's the point of muttering 'Hothead' when the whole haystack is on fire? And what use is all my enthusiasm if my compositions are no good? And if he doesn't like them, how can he like me? – Yet, it must be universally clear that what I was doing was either complete nonsense, or warranted people going on their knees before it.
>
> Anyway, I do not believe Mahler was so cool as his assessment of me. Merely that as former Director of the Opera he knew that petty bureaucrats are not best motivated by an enthusiastic tone; he expected a cooler, more prosaic tone to be more effective. He kept quiet about his possible respect for my work to avoid suspicion that he was acting as cheer-leader for a colleague.

A more personal reminiscence of Mahler is contained in another fragment, dated 21 July 1932:

> Around 1903 to 1909 I lived in the Liechtensteinstrasse in Vienna and had a view from my study window over the Thury – the Liechten Valley – with a church right in the middle. The many lessons I gave at that time were usually fixed for the afternoon. But sometimes I had an afternoon free, and spent it composing. Well, from two o'clock onwards there was an unbroken succession of funerals in the church, so that the bells did not stop ringing for hours on end.
>
> At the outset, absorbed in work, I hardly noticed them. After a while a certain fatigue, a depletion of imaginative reserves, set in and in the end I had to give up working.
>
> I told this to Mahler and complained about it. It is strange how indifferent people can be if they have not

---

12. Bio 111, p. 19, dated 30 August 1932, Arnold Schoenberg Institute.

experienced something themselves. One cannot really appreciate the sufferings of others.

That is why Mahler's answer was: 'Surely it doesn't disturb you. Just compose the bells in!' (I would call that pretty rich, as I have committed the same fault hundreds of times.)

But even stranger – and again I have experienced it myself many times – is that one is *punished* for this sort of arrogance. (I grow fat when I mock fat people; I am treated unjustly after abusing others . . .). Mahler had a composing-house, built specially for him, a quarter of an hour up through the woods from his villa (at Maiernigg). In the stillness of this spot, the birds' singing disturbed him so much that he declared he could no longer compose there.

Did he remember then that he had advised me to include the bells in my composition?[13]

'Glocken am Thury', Bio. III, p.29, deposited at the Arnold Schoenberg Institute, University of Southern California, Los Angeles. Reproduced by kind permission of the Institute.

Anton von WEBERN
(1883–1945)

Like his teacher Schoenberg, Webern was attracted by Mahler the man before he began to appreciate the composer. His enthusiasm grew upon hearing Mahler conduct four of his symphonies. By 1907 Webern's name was at the head of the circular summoning admirers to bid Mahler farewell from Vienna. In September 1910 Webern

---

13. Repeating this story near the end of his life to students in California, Schoenberg added that he had then told Mahler: 'Don't worry, you can put the [birds'] songs into your next symphony.' (Newlin, *Schoenberg Remembered*, p. 197.)

travelled to Munich to assist at the rehearsals of the Eighth
Symphony; he was rewarded with the manuscript of a Mahler
song.

Webern's earliest meeting with Mahler took place after a concert
of Mahler Lieder on 3 February 1905. So overwhelmed was the
young composer that he resolved to record in his diary every word
that fell from the Master's lips:

> These hours spent in his presence will always remain in
> my memory as exceedingly happy ones, since it was the
> first time that I received the immediate impression of a
> truly great personality. Almost all his words that I could
> hear are embedded in my memory, and so I want to note
> them down in this book that is so dear to me. At first
> there was a discussion of Rückert's lyric poetry. Mahler
> said: 'After *Des Knaben Wunderhorn* I could not com-
> pose anything but Rückert – this is lyric poetry from the
> source, all else is lyric poetry of a derivative sort.' He also
> mentioned that he did not understand everything in the
> *Wunderhorn* texts. The discussion turned to counter-
> point, since Schoenberg said that only the Germans
> knew how to handle counterpoint. Mahler pointed out
> the old French composers, Rameau, and so on, and
> admitted only Bach, Brahms and Wagner as the greatest
> contrapuntists among Germans. 'Nature is for us the
> model in this realm. Just as in nature the entire universe
> has developed from the primeval cell, from plants,
> animals, and men beyond to God, the Supreme Being, so
> also in music should a larger structure develop from a
> single motif in which is contained the germ of everything
> that is yet to be.' With Beethoven, he said, one almost
> always finds a new motif in the development. The entire
> development should, however, be carried out from a
> single motif; in that sense Beethoven was simply not to
> be considered a great contrapuntist. Variation is the most
> important factor in a musical work, he stated. A theme
> would have to be really especially beautiful, as some by
> Schubert are, in order to make its unaltered return
> refreshing. For him, Mozart's string quartets were over
> at the double bar (of the exposition). The task of
> contemporary creative musicians would be to combine

the contrapuntal skill of Bach with the melodiousness of Haydn and Mozart.

Hans Moldenhauer; *Anton von Webern, A Chronicle of his Life and Work*, London (Gollancz), 1978, pp. 75–6.

Oskar FRIED
(1871–1941)

In Vienna for a performance of his ephemerally successful choral work *Das trunkene Lied*,[1] Fried was told that Mahler wanted to see him. New to musical summits – he had been making his living as a dog-breeder in Berlin – he was surprised first by the invitation, then by the intense attention Mahler directed at him.

He showed a very strong interest in me. I spent the rest of the day in the Director's office. What I saw before me, this unjustly feared and notorious master in his own house, can only be described as wonderfully beautiful. Above all, on a human level. This man looking at me through stern and aloof spectacles, yet with childlike curiosity and an unadulterated openness intent upon discovering and penetrating the essential humanity in others, this man with his childlike yet entirely masculine head seemed to me simply beautiful to look at.

His gaze, which cut through everything and laid bare the innermost, his deep bell-like voice, his mouth whose fine shape hinted at unshakeable energy while its almost feminine line spoke of goodness and inner warmth, and last but not least the intensity of his gestures and whole being – all these together made him irresistible.

And I confess I liked him immediately. Apart from anything else, he was exceptionally pleasant to me and unexpectedly warm from the moment we began to talk.

---

1. *The Drunken Song*, a setting of texts from Nietzsche's *Thus Spake Zarathustra*, performed at the Gesellschaft der Musikfreunde on 6 March 1905.

We took to one another instantly, talking like two old friends to whom nothing is worse and more banal than wasting time on showing-off and self-indulgent courtesies designed to ingratiate. Thus our first conversation was a serious discussion of each other's artistic plans.

'Erinnerungen an Mahler', *Musikblätter des Anbruch*, vol 1/0 (1919), pp. 17–19

Discovering they were both about to conduct Liszt's *Legend of Saint Elizabeth*, they exchanged ideas on the work. Mahler found Fried's approach so compatible that he announced: 'You will conduct my Second Symphony in Berlin. I shall come to hear it myself. You will do it splendidly.'[2]

Fried subsequently conducted the symphony many times, making the première recording in 1924.[3] Alma reports that Mahler in the last summer of his life cooled towards Fried, who was unable to share his intellectual and spiritual obsessions. 'Philistine though he was, he had a streak of genius: but now suddenly Mahler could not put up with him.'[4]

From the time of his summons to Mahler,[5] Fried's creativity declined. He became primarily a conductor, one of few who persisted in performing new music in Berlin. With Hitler's advent in 1933, he fled to Russia, became a Soviet citizen and died there during the war.

What I adored and valued in Mahler beyond measure was not so much his strengths. It was his weaknesses. And they took on the fascination of tragedy by being essentially so very human. He was a God-seeker. With incredible fanaticism, with unparalleled dedication and with unshakeable love he pursued a constant search for the divine, both in the individual and in man as a whole. He saw himself bearing a sacred trust; it suffused his whole being. His nature was religious through and through in a mystical, not a dogmatic, sense. He talked of this to me time and again on our walks in Toblach and he would be filled suddenly with earthly rapture as if he had just come from heaven.

2. For an account of the performance, see p. 204.
3. Polydor 66290–300.
4. AMM, pp. 176–7.
5. See Rudolph Stephan, 'Gustav Mahler and Oskar Fried', GMUL, pp. 47–8. He ceased composing altogether in 1913.

But from time to time he would doubt this heavenly mission and worry momentarily whether he had the ability to carry it through, even though he was convinced of nothing so firmly as his faith in himself. In such moments of inner conflict, he needed, so as not to perish in the mortal wilderness, some earthly support to cling on to: to recover from outside himself an echo of the credo he bore within him in his reverence for the divine. A servant, a disciple on whom he could test the reality and validity of his religious mission. His unconscious was always on the look-out for someone around him whose degree of enlightenment and salvation he could use as a measure of the security and implications of his religious powers. And if he received no answer, no echo from my direction, if I was not immediately ready and willing to follow him wherever he desired to go, his face would become remarkably set and he would retreat into his impenetrable spiritual shell, a child enduring mortal disappointments and bewailing his divine origins. Such moments shook me greatly. They weighed heavily on my heart. How I would have loved to say something, to have lied a little and feigned sympathy: all this for the love of this tremendous human being, in recognition of the colossal workings of his soul. But it was just not possible. We would proceed in silence side by side; he perhaps recognizing that it was after all not his mission in life to set a religious example to mankind but rather to bear witness and fulfil himself through his art. Thus he was always a fighter and a wrestler. Perhaps more than any other he had to wage a titanic struggle to wrest the smallest victory from himself. And he, the notorious despot, needed in his art to find comfort and recognition and love as much as any other spurned and lonely soul. That is how vulnerable he was, and how love-starved. Yet he did not receive the slightest recognition or the faintest degree of understanding merited by the meticulous and unblemished way he exercised his high office. He was really superhumanly pure. A redeemer in his profession.

This remoteness from the world, added to the burdens

of running the opera house, gave him little time and
scope for deep involvement in other people's problems.
Moreover, he was so immersed in his own creative work
that he kept himself at arm's length from other people's
productions. Yet not a single thing happened in music
that he was not aware of. Emotionally, he stood aside
from anything that did not conform with his own
outlook. That is why his views on contemporary musicians are very sparse. Schoenberg was one of few whose
prominent personality and enormous ability commanded
huge respect from him. And he never begrudged him
recognition, even when he was vainly struggling to follow
compositional idiosyncrasies from his own utterly different standpoint. Schoenberg was the only contemporary
composer on whom Mahler worked intensively to the end
of his life . . .

The last time I saw him was six months before he died.
He was on the point of returning to America. On the way
there, between Berlin and Hamburg, he came to visit me
in Nikolassee. We did not exchange a word about future
plans, his or mine. He just played in the garden with my
child.

'Erinnerungen an Mahler', *Musikblätter des Anbruch*, vol. 1 (1919),
pp. 17–19.

1. *The Drunken Song*, a setting of texts from Nietzsche's *Thus Spake Zarathustra*,
performed at the Gesellschaft der Musikfreunde on 6 March 1905.

Ida DEHMEL

Wife of Richard Dehmel (1863–1920), post-Romantic poet whose texts were set to music by, among others, Strauss and Schoenberg. This diary extract of 22 March 1905, written apparently for her husband's eyes, appears in Alma's memoirs.

He was delighted by the reception his symphony had had in Hamburg.[1] The warmth of the applause after the rehearsal alone was a great satisfaction to him, and on the way to Berlin he told me more of what he felt about it. Travelling and particularly stopping in hotels was a martyrdom. 'But you travel all the same – for the sake of your children, no doubt,' I put in.

'Do you mean my real children or my musical children?'

I had meant only his musical ones.

'I have to think of both. Actually, I should like best to live only for my compositions, and, to tell the truth, I am beginning to neglect my operatic duties, but if I gave up my salary as Director of the Opera I should have to make it good in some other way, as a guest conductor perhaps. I doubt whether I shall ever make a penny from performances of my own works. So that's one reason for my travels. The other is this: my Fifth Symphony was performed the other day in Prague and Berlin, each time to little effect. So I thought to myself: Is it the fault of the symphony or the conductor? Now Hamburg has given the answer. We musicians are worse off than writers in that respect. Anyone can read a book, but a musical score is a book with seven seals. Even the conductors who can decipher it, present it to the public soaked in their own interpretations. For that reason there must be a tradition, and no one can create it but I.'

He asked my opinion of the settings of Dehmel's

---

1. Mahler conducted his Fifth Symphony at Hamburg on 13 March 1905. It was the second performance (the première was at Cologne on 19 October 1904), and in the course of the year he conducted it again at Strasburg, Trieste, Vienna and Breslau (Poland).

poems,[2] and was obviously delighted when I said we found Fried promising. That was his own opinion. We agreed too about Pfitzner. Only the way composers search for librettos seems to him ludicrous (in Pfitzner's case too). Music, he said, was superfluous for a completed drama; no professional playwright would leave his work uncompleted, so that a composer could bring out what he himself had passed over; and no music, however inspired, could make a great work of a bad play. No one, therefore, who had not both gifts, as Wagner had, should attempt it. It even seemed to him a profanity when composers ventured to set perfect poems to music; it was as if a sculptor chiselled a statue from marble and a painter came along and coloured it. He himself had only appropriated some few bits from the *Wunderhorn* – from earliest childhood his relationship to the book had been particularly close. The poems were not complete in themselves, but blocks of marble which anyone might make his own.

If you ask me when he seemed to me human, all too human, my answer is when he spoke of Strauss and the Strauss and Hauptmann[3] marriages. He only spoke of Strauss's music very cursorily, but stressed Strauss's way of making a business of it. Strauss was the businessman first and foremost and an artist only in the second place: when the two came into collision it was the businessman who won. In this I detected a little envy of Strauss's success, in terms of money, that is. Of Strauss's marriage he spoke with contempt, even with disgust. He thought it verged on masochism . . .

I had already mentioned Mahler's wife and said what a wonderful impression her sunny disposition had made on us. This was accepted with pleasure, but in reply he gave as an instance of her merits that she made all the piano scores of his symphonies. That might have sounded

2. Fried, Pfitzner and Reger were among several composers then working on Dehmel verses.
3. Gerhart Hauptmann (1862–1946), dramatist, poet and novelist, was among Mahler's admirers.

marvellous but for the hint of making good use of her. In short, the man whom I call a genius behaves as if he were a delicate instrument to be fenced round by the barbed wire entanglement of egoism. To pass to quite another matter, he is the first Jew, except my father, to impress me as a man – one who doesn't, to put it crudely, strike me as impotent. I am glad that such a beautiful, proud, strong Christian girl has married him.

AMM, pp. 91–5.

Romain ROLLAND (1866–1944)

French novelist, dramatist and writer on music, winner of the 1915 Nobel Prize for Literature. His perceptive essay on Mahler was written after the Alsace Franco-German Music Festival of May 1905 and appeared two months later.

Gustav Mahler is forty-six years old. He is a kind of legendary type of German musician, rather like Schubert, and half-way between a schoolmaster and a clergyman. He has a long, clean-shaven face, a pointed skull covered with untidy hair, a bald forehead, a prominent nose, eyes that blink behind his glasses, a large mouth and thin lips, hollow cheeks, a rather tired and sarcastic expression, and a general air of asceticism. He is excessively nervous, and silhouette caricatures of him, representing him as a cat in convulsions in the conductor's desk, are very popular in Germany . . . He is second only to Strauss as a composer in Germany, and the principal musician of South Germany.

His most important work is a suite of symphonies; and it was the Fifth Symphony of this suite that he conducted at the Strasburg Festival . . . The chief characteristic of these symphonies is, generally speaking, the use of choral singing with the orchestra. 'When I conceive a great

musical painting (*ein grosses musikalisches Gemälde*),'
says Mahler, 'there always comes a moment when I feel
forced to employ speech (*das Wort*) as an aid to the
realization of my musical conception.' . . .

In spite of appearances, Mahler refuses to connect
these choral symphonies with programme music. Without doubt he is right, if he means that his music has its
own value outside any sort of programme; but there is no
doubt that it is always the expression of a definite
Stimmung, of a conscious mood; and the fact is, whether
he likes it or not, that *Stimmung* gives an interest to his
music far beyond that of the music itself. His personality
seems to me far more interesting than his art.

This is often the case with artists in Germany; Hugo
Wolf is another example of it. Mahler's case is really
rather curious. When one studies his works one feels
convinced that he is one of those rare types in modern
Germany – an egoist who feels with sincerity. Perhaps
his emotions and his ideas do not succeed in expressing
themselves in a really sincere and personal way; for they
reach us through a cloud of reminiscences and an
atmosphere of classicism. I cannot help thinking that
Mahler's position as Director of the Opera, and his
consequent saturation in the music that his calling
condemns him to study, is the cause of this. There is
nothing more fatal to a creative spirit than too much
reading, above all when it does not read of its own free
will, but is forced to absorb an excessive amount of
nourishment, the larger part of which is indigestible. In
vain may Mahler try to defend the sanctuary of his mind:
it is violated by foreign ideas coming from all parts, and
instead of being able to drive them away, his conscience,
as conductor of the orchestra, obliges him to receive
them and almost embrace them. With his feverish activity, and burdened as he is with heavy tasks, he works
unceasingly and has no time to dream. Mahler will only
be Mahler when he is able to leave his administrative
work, shut up his scores, retire within himself, and wait
patiently until he has become himself again – if it is not
too late.

His Fifth Symphony, which he conducted at Strasburg, convinced me, more than all his other works, of the
urgent necessity of adopting this course. In this composition he has not allowed himself the use of the choruses,
which were one of the chief attractions of his preceding
symphonies. He wished to prove that he could write pure
music, and to make his claim surer he refused to have any
explanation of his composition published in the concert
programme, as the other composers in the festival had
done; he wished it, therefore, to be judged from a strictly
musical point of view. It was a dangerous ordeal for him.

Though I wished very much to admire the work of a
composer whom I held in such esteem, I felt it did not
come out very well from the test. To begin with, this
symphony is excessively long – it lasts an hour and a half
– though there is no apparent justification for its proportions. It aims at being colossal, and mainly achieves
emptiness . . .

Above all, I fear Mahler has been sadly hypnotized by
ideas about power – ideas that are getting to the head of
all German artists today. He seems to have an undecided
mind, and to combine sadness and irony with weakness
and impatience, to be a Viennese musician striving after
Wagnerian grandeur. No one expresses the grace of
ländler and dainty waltzes and mournful reveries better
than he; and perhaps no one is nearer the secret of
Schubert's moving and voluptuous melancholy; and it is
Schubert he recalls at times, both in his good qualities
and certain of his faults. But he wants to be Beethoven or
Wagner. And he is wrong; for he lacks their balance and
gigantic force. One saw that only too well when he was
conducting the 'Choral' symphony.

But whatever he may be, or whatever disappointment
he may have brought me at Strasburg, I will never allow
myself to speak lightly or scoffingly of him. I am
confident that a musician with so lofty an aim will one
day create a work worthy of himself.

Richard Strauss is a complete contrast to Mahler. He has
always the air of a heedless and discontented child. Tall

and slim, rather elegant and supercilious, he seems to be of a more refined race than most other German artists of today. Scornful, blasé with success and very exacting, his bearing towards other musicians has nothing of Mahler's winning modesty. He is not less nervous than Mahler, and while he is conducting the orchestra he seems to indulge in a frenzied dance which follows the smallest details of his music – music that is as agitated as limpid water into which a stone has been flung. But he has a great advantage over Mahler; he knows how to rest after his labours.

Musicians of Today, Trans. Mary Blaiklock, London (Kegan Paul, Trench, Trübner & Co.), 1915, pp. 219–26.

Richard SPECHT
(1870–1932)

The music critic of *Die Zeit* was unwaveringly loyal to Mahler, wrote a short book about him in 1905, and two years after his death produced a study that became the standard German work on Mahler. 'Burn all the others,' wrote Schoenberg, 'but preserve Specht's Mahler biography. His spirit is preserved within it.'[1]

A would-be architect who took up writing when his eyesight failed, Specht had made a name for himself as a poet when he met Mahler at Steinbach in the summer of 1895. In Vienna he enjoyed Mahler's confidence and, more remarkably, that of Alma, to whom he later dedicated his biography of Puccini[2] and who helped sharpen his perceptions of Mahler.

He was really a great child. This often uncannily brilliant man could surprise others in conversation with uninhibitedly natural powers of argument, disarming the most dazzling paradoxes, acute antitheses and biting ironies.

1. Unpublished notes on Mahler's Ninth Symphony; copy at the Arnold Schoenberg Institute, University of Southern California, Los Angeles.
2. 'To Alma Mahler: incomparable as both woman and friend.'

He surprised people even more with the pure, untouched childliness of his nature.

He was spontaneously trusting or suspicious, like a child. Easily aroused by a casual word of malevolence, even by an unintended smile or glance, his suspicions could hardly ever be undone. They did great harm to him and to others. Above all, he craved love as a child does. He needed love, understanding, tenderness as few others do. But his abruptness, his moodiness and volatility, swatted people away from him and rarely permitted him these experiences. If he had only had the courage to say, 'No, no, I will not let myself be rejected!' – feelings that his wounded, yearning heart was able to express in unforgettable, steadfast and moving sounds.

In daily matters, he gladly let others make decisions for him and influence him. Totally withdrawn into his own dream and his own world, he would leave others to deal with the practicalities of everyday life, including his financial affairs, not always selflessly and with his best interests at heart. He was often exploited and short-changed, but it is premature to talk of such matters . . .

If one wanted to experience his untouched purity and simple honesty, one had to see him with children. Above all with his own . . . Seeing him playing with his children, you did not need the evidence of his music to sense the deepest, cosmic elements within his genius . . .

That he was a genius was felt by everyone who encountered him. He was not one of those great artists who pass their lives virtually incognito, like Schubert or Anton Bruckner. Anyone who heard him say a couple of words, or looked at his pale, spiritual nervosity, his face lined with sublime and anguished thoughts and feelings, would invariably be certain of his genius and his demon . . .

I don't believe anybody truly knew Gustav Mahler. Equally, I don't believe he truly knew any other person. He could have dealings with people for years, offer them friendship and help, and still know nothing of their real way of life, of their sorrows and aspirations. If one took them to him, he would help out of the kindness of his egocentricity that did not want to see another's pain – and then forget all about it. He had to forget it. He had his work to do; and when from time to time (and more often than other people) he would give help, he did not want to be reminded of it, as it would distract him from his own affairs.

Even in ordinary relationships most people only meant to him as much as they could give him: in information, spiritual stimulation, advice on his bodily well-being, admiration, promotion, parcels of certain favourite foods and fruits, lively conversations on particular topics.

I often sensed that he was irritated if this scheme of things was somehow disrupted, as when a friend in whose house he liked to stay because he could live there peacefully and undisturbed suddenly broke into a conversation with another person with whom he enjoyed philosophizing. Or when someone from whom he had been accustomed only to receiving good apples shocked him with a remark about music. I realize this may sound exaggerated and might be misunderstood because it appears selfish. But it was a kind of economy in his use of people . . .

Mahler's best friend was one with whom he never met or exchanged a word and who, in so far as it was possible to influence his nature, had a decisive impact on it. This was Dostoevsky. The encounter with his books had been for Mahler an experience of determining force . . .

Mahler (and equally his music) was a Jew: Jewish in the impact of his spirituality, in the fevered restlessness of his search for the purpose and order of the world, in his passionately dark glow, in his innate inconsistencies and hair-splitting. He was a Christian: Christian in his faith, his trust in Heaven, his humility before all that is divine, his belief in the afterworld, his yearning for disciples and his healthy regard for instinctive, childlike, genuine and uncorrupted ordinary people who, untroubled by greed and not yet dulled by the questionable civilization of the great city, still live in Nature, facing God in their daily lives. He got on best with farmers, shepherds, fishermen and children.

And he was entirely German: in his spiritual culture, in his objectivity and self-discipline, his submission to the order he accepted, in doing nothing for himself but for the chosen cause – as Richard Wagner described the Germans.

If, however, one wanted to call this mixture Jewish, then Jewishness has found in Mahler its most powerful expression and we have for the first time what could be called 'Jewish music' (not just music with Jewish traits, that we have heard before). Not to mention the elements that are rooted in the German land, in the mother soil, in the indigenous folk-songs that permeate his symphonies. But these are matters for the psychologist; they are too involved for us here.

That Mahler was devout and religious to the core is certain, but he related to each religion merely as legend and belonged to no community, not even to the Buddhists or pantheists. When I once asked him about it and wanted to know his religious confession, he looked at me seriously and said: 'I am a musician. All else is contained in that.'

. . . Sickness horrified him. Even in others. He would even get irritated and angry with anyone who felt indisposed. 'Sickness is talentlessness,' he used to say. He regarded it as a dereliction of duty. But he was a terrible hypochondriac, anxiously avoiding anything that might impair his health and agility.

Specht, pp. 26–8, 31, 37, 53–6.

Klaus PRINGSHEIM
(1883–1972)

Twin brother of Thomas Mann's wife, Katia, and son of an eminent Munich mathematician and Wagnerian,[1] Pringsheim was entranced by Mahler as an adolescent and sought a musical apprenticeship with him as a *répétiteur* at the Vienna Opera. He later served as Music Director of the Reinhardt theatres in Berlin and, from 1931, as conductor and teacher at the Imperial Conservatory, Tokyo, finally emigrating to Canada. His centenary recollection of Mahler is late but lucid.

As a fifteen-year-old high school student in Munich I saw and heard him for the first time. This early encounter with Mahler became decisive for my life. He appeared as a guest conductor of a concert of the Kaim orchestra at the Tonhalle in Munich.[2] The programme contained only one Mahler item, the Andante from his Second Symphony: there had not been enough rehearsal time for more. In addition there were two movements, the second and third, from the *Symphonie Fantastique* by Berlioz and, finally, Beethoven's Fifth. It was like a revelation. Never had I – and never again did I – experience such an overwhelming impression of the works. From that day on I dreamed – or might say that I considered it to be my destiny to come some day under the guidance of this conductor, who, as he stood before the orchestra, seemed to exude magical powers. My future as a professional musician was then already a firm resolve in my mind, but another seven years were to elapse before my dream became true.

He came again to Munich with his Fourth Symphony shortly after its première in Vienna, but had little chance of success in Munich. The musical bigwigs of the Bavarian capital who attended the dress rehearsal sat

---

1. Katia Mann (1883–1980), studied physics with Röntgen before marrying Thomas Mann in 1905. Alfred Pringsheim (1850–1941) was professor of mathematics at the University of Munich.
2. 24 March 1897. See pp. 196–7.

GUSTAV MAHLER
Karikatur von Oscar Garvens

around shaking their heads, contemptuously shrugging their shoulders, and exchanging addled glances. They were numbly uncomprehending and sullenly unwilling to comprehend, an attitude he met almost everywhere in those days; yet, in no other city had he to face such a wall of non-receptivity as he did here in the very city in which to his own surprise ten years later he was to experience (in 1910) the unique triumph of his Eighth Symphony . . .

A similarly triumphant affair was the performance of the Second Symphony at the conclusion of the musical festival in Basle, Switzerland, in 1903. On the first evening all eyes were focused on Mahler's box where he sat with his beautiful young wife. It was a long, excessively long, programme with new works, mostly by composers whose names were as yet unknown. A song for baritone and orchestra, 'Venedig' (Venice), was my contribution to this programme, and it was scheduled to be played towards the end. After every number I anxiously looked towards Mahler's box, hoping that he would stay long enough to hear my composition, but precisely when the time came for my song I saw with great dismay how he and his wife arose and vanished. Years later I told him of this. 'But why,' said he, 'why did you not simply come to me and say a word?' Why not? How could I have dared! 'Then I would gladly have stayed.' And, sure, he would really have stayed. He could never say 'No', when a young beginner appealed to his benevolence.

My big hour came when, in February of 1906, I received a telegram from Vienna. Director Mahler expects me next Friday between four and five in his office at the Imperial Opera. This meant that he was prepared to fulfil my wish and to accept me as his singing coach. I had been recommended to him by my teacher, Bernard Stavenhagen,[3] who, as director of the Academy Concert in Munich, was one of the few German conductors actively promoting Mahler's works. Thus I now sat

3. (1862–1914), Court Kapellmeister in Weimar from 1895 and in Munich from 1901.

facing him and could not believe it, for it was truly like the awakening into a dream. But, within five minutes, without any formality there developed a conversation in which he naturally asked the questions and I supplied the answers. How were things in Munich? What was going on there? He wanted to hear about Felix Mottl, the music director of the Bavarian Court Orchestra, and Mottl's Wagner festivals in the Prinzregenten theatre. Mottl, with Mahler who was four years Mottl's junior, had as a student of the Vienna Conservatoire, fought for radical progress in the academic Wagner association in Vienna. He also wanted to hear about Max Reger, about whom much fuss was being made in certain circles as being the man to watch. Max Reger's name was mentioned three or four times, and I sensed that Mahler was not eager to hear that I shared the admiration of my fellow citizens of Munich for this name. No, I did not share it, and could say so sincerely from the bottom of my heart – I never liked him.

Frequently I accompanied Mahler on his concert tours from Vienna. On one of these trips,[4] on the way to Linz (a small town about one hour from Vienna) I was alone with him in a railway compartment. Then it happened, and it was a great moment in my life: he almost solemnly offered me his friendship. Yes, so it was. From this moment on I could call him, Mahler, my friend, and could call myself a friend of Mahler's. I have often asked myself what might have moved him thus to honour the young apprentice conductor. It is possible that he, who resented superficial compliments and who was insulted by flattery, was receptive to the deep and sincere admiration which I, without realizing it, had for him. I had nothing else to offer him and I have no other explanation but this which he himself then indirectly and in negative form gave to me. I don't recall how we came to discuss the matter, but he called the ingratitude between human beings a basic evil of human society. Mahler was a grateful person – it was part of his nature. He could not

4. Probably 20 January 1907.

receive without returning that which he had received in a spirit of gratitude. I had many opportunities to observe this even when it was not obvious to the casual observer.

As a composer, and this is well known, Mahler, until the last year of his life, was subject to malicious attacks; found enemies on all sides to an extent perhaps unparalleled for a creative artist. However, where he, the famous conductor, appeared in person as an interpreter of his symphonies he was received with cheers by the audience, but ever again he complained that he considered it to be humiliating that he was obliged thus to travel round the world to bear witness for his own works. Naturally, above all else, it was the reviewers – not all, there were exceptions – whose stubborn resistance made life miserable for him. I often hear it said that he must have hated them. No, I do not believe that . . . When Mahler hated he did not waste his hate upon those who harmed him, but he was capable of boundless contempt. The presumption of the ignorant, the inflation of those without talent, the self-sufficiency and self-complacency of the eternally mediocre – all that, he despised. He despised all careerists and opportunists, but he liked to speak, and his voice had a warm tone at such times, of the effort of other conductors to help him prevail. There were not many at that time. Among them was Oskar Fried, whose ready wit and relaxed manner Mahler also liked personally. But in the first place there was Mengelberg who, in Amsterdam with the Concertgebouw Orchestra, had created a European Mahler cult centre . . . The fulfilment, however, of his prophetic phrase, 'My time will come through Bruno Walter', this work of love on behalf of Mahler's work by the most intimately initiated among the initiates, this Mahler did not live to see.

If the word 'self-discontent' does not exist, it would have to be coined for Mahler, to explain the peculiarity of his working method when he sat at the conductor's stand during orchestral rehearsals. Often it was a testing rather than simply a rehearsing in the conventional sense. Until the last rehearsal before a première performance he used to change, correct, try over and over again. Sometimes it

was almost like an inner insecurity, or actually not-yet-
decidedness in regard to his own work. He gladly, on
those occasions, listened to the opinions of a few who
were close to him in the rehearsal hall. I still remember
how I was sitting with other musicians, among them the
pianist Ossip Gabrilowitsch, at that time not yet active as
a conductor, in the rehearsal for the Sixth Symphony.[5] It
was at a music festival in Essen, in 1906, and I could still
point to this or that spot in the score which was changed
on the advice of the twenty-year-old voice coach who had
come along from Vienna. He also performed it at other
functions; an important one – at least it seemed important to himself – he was allowed to conduct the cowbells
behind the scenes. Mostly such changes were matters of
tonal balance, be it to establish it, or only tiny details of
instrumentation. The conductor, Mahler, and here the
conductor of his own works, was above all concerned
with the achievement of maximum clarity. This was
more important to him than colour and tonal appeal.
During a rehearsal of the Sixth Symphony, at one place
in the finale he stopped the music, and called to the
trumpets, 'Can't you blow that more strongly?' In the
empty auditorium it already sounded like uncontrolled
noise – but the trumpets still stronger? He interrupted
for a second time, and again, addressing the trumpets,
now with a gesture of the left hand, the commanding
power of which was irresistible, 'Can't you blow that still
stronger?' They played still louder, obliterating all other
sound, and what had earlier been mere noise only now
acquired the musical meaning which it had concealed.
After the final rehearsal Richard Strauss, who was
present, remarked casually that he considered the
symphony to be partly over-instrumented. Over-
instrumented! The Fifth really had been in its orchestral
proportions. After Mahler's own experience at the première in Cologne he had later extensively retouched the
score, that is, on some pages had considerably thinned

5. Premièred on 27 May 1906.

out the orchestra. Not so much, however, with the score of the Sixth, with its still larger section of brass and woodwind. Over-instrumented! The word, since it was uttered by Strauss – the occasion of the *Salome* première in Dresden was half a year ago – long worried him. In this connection I have never forgotten it. Mahler made a remark which indicated more than it seemed to say. 'Isn't it remarkable', he said, 'that Strauss could manage with a few rehearsals, and yet it always sounded good?' He on the other hand plagued himself in countless rehearsals with the orchestra to bring out everything as he wanted it, yet, when could he say, after a performance, that he really did not find anything wrong with it? . . .

The first opera in which I participated in a new production under Mahler was the Shakespeare opera *The Taming of the Shrew*, by Hermann Goetz – who knows it today? He let the last act end without a musically weak finale, and wanted as an ending of the opera only a short postlude for orchestra. It would have to be newly composed, and he gave me the task of writing it. The next day I came with a complete composition – three pages of score. No, that was not what he meant. He wanted eight bars at most. For the next rehearsal I brought my eight bars. They were copied into the orchestra parts and played twice to try out how it would work, together with a slowly dropping curtain. Mahler seemed satisfied, but then he again changed his mind. The scene now was to close without an appended postlude. 'But', he added jokingly, 'now you can tell people that you have been played at the Vienna Opera.'

On the Saturday evening after the première of *Walküre*, with rather famous settings, we ate, as was frequently the case after Mahler premières, in a small group at the Hoffmann Restaurant in the Ring. Arnold Rosé sat next to Mahler . . .

In the circle of his close friends he spoke about all things but the theatre. I recall how a short newspaper notice of a suicide on the railroad tracks long haunted him and caused him to ponder what might have been in the mind of the unfortunate one who was capable at night to lie down at the place which he had chosen for his end, then to wait for hours for the early train which he wanted to kill him and which punctually did just that. Once he asked me if I had already read *The Brothers Karamazov* by Dostoevsky, which had just appeared in a new German translation. When I replied in the negative he said that a significant experience was awaiting me. The greatest psychologist of world literature had far more to convey to him than some theoretical dissertation in the field of psychology. Abstract theory was alien to him. The most convincing argument to him remained the parable.

He was standing in his overcoat at noon one day when I entered his office after the rehearsal. 'Come with me, I'm going home,' he said. He did not drive. No vehicle waited downstairs; he walked all the way. It was not a great distance from the Opera, just far enough to be comfortably manageable by foot. When I parted from him at his house he suggested that the next day at the same time I should come to pick him up again; and the next day again, and thus it became a habit and for him a daily occasion. He spoke of musical matters. I walked next to him and listened with the receptivity of the astonished learner. But I too was permitted to ask questions. There was no question he was unwilling to discuss, no problem that I brought up that he would not discuss with me in detail. Often inadvertently those walks became extended excursions almost, and it sometimes happened, that, illustrating his remarks by a gesture, he remained standing, not precisely in the Ringstrasse, the main thoroughfare, but in the Belvedere Park which he liked to frequent, or in some other place where there were not so many people. I have not recorded these innumerable conversations which he had with me, but I know that more of them have remained with me than could have been recorded. These were not lessons. This was not instruction given by a teacher. It was much more. Time and again it was a spontaneous part of valid communication of Mahler the musician. It is to him that I owe what I have been able to acquire in higher appreciation and deeper insight into matters of

music beyond mere technical ability and factual knowledge. In the informal intimacy of improvised walks there
were revealed the most likeable aspects, the gentlest traits
of his character, and this happened in the most unpreten-
tious manner which is ever the most eloquent. At noon
one day we were walking up the Kärntnerstrasse when it
occurred to him that he could bring his wife some
pastries, or was it some special kind of candies, with
which he would give her some pleasure. He stepped into
a shop and made his purchase. When he re-emerged I
wanted to carry the package for him, but he would not
hear of it. 'Why,' . . . he explained, 'if it slips from my
hand and falls into the dirt – ' and he pointed to the road
which had the appearance with which the Viennese are so
familiar, 'then this is no catastrophe, but if the same
thing would happen to you, you would feel terribly
embarrassed.'

On my last evening at the Mahlers', in the late summer
of 1907, one conversation remains vivid in my memory,
in the course of which the name Freud was mentioned, or
to be precise, it was I who, in the given context,
mentioned it. Mahler's reaction was immediate silence.
The subject of psychoanalysis did not interest him, and
he made only a concluding remark, accompanied by a
deprecatory gesture. 'Freud, he tries to cure or solve
everything from a certain aspect.' From a certain aspect.
He did not name it. Apparently he was reluctant, in the
presence of his wife, to use the appropriate word. He did
not speak from personal experience. This was three years
before his only encounter with Professor Freud in Leiden
in August 1910.[6] . . .

I saw him again at the première of the Seventh
Symphony in Prague in 1908,[7] and again in 1910, in the
great days of the Eighth in Munich. At that time a group
of sad people were gathered around the music author and
critic, Dr Rudolph Louis,[8] of the *Münchner Neuesten*

6. See pp. 280–84.
7. 19 September 1908.
8. (1870–1914), anti-modernist, anti-Semite.

richten. These people were attempting in advance to discredit the occasion of the première before it even took place. Two such uneven halves as the old church hymn, *Veni creator spiritus*, and the final scene from Goethe's *Faust*, both set to music, could never, under any circumstances, become a symphonic whole – not a whole, and not a symphony! Their objection lay close at hand, and that is precisely where it is today, because who could have bothered to clear it away? No objection can survive in the face of the categorical imperative of the creative genius.

At our last encounter, two days later, at the Munich main railway station he did not refer with one word to the incomparable triumph he had scored in the city which until that day had been most opposed to Mahler. He spoke of two new works, the scores of which lay in a drawer of his desk in Vienna, the Ninth Symphony and *Das Lied von der Erde*.

'Erinnerung an Gustav Mahler', *Neue Zürcher Zeitung*, 7 July 1960.

William RITTER
(1867–1955)

One of the most intriguing and least known of Mahler's friends, Ritter was a Swiss writer, painter and critic, a homosexual who lived in quasi-marital circumstances with a Czech, Janko Càdra. Mahler, often considered a puritan, was aware of their relationship, regularly sending regards 'to your friend, Janko'.[1]

Ritter served in Munich for fourteen years as reader in French to Crown Prince Ruprecht of Bavaria,[2] arriving there in October 1900 just as Mahler was performing his Second Symphony. In November 1901 Mahler returned to première his Fourth and Ritter, as reaction-

---

1. For some of the letters see GMUL, pp. 139-49. For Janko's background see HLG1, p. 944.
2. (1869-1955) son of King Ludwig III, dethroned when the monarchy ended in 1918.

ary an anti-Semite as he was artistically progressive, went with mixed emotions to the general rehearsal.

Weingartner[3] is rehearsing his part of the programme when Mahler, accompanied by his friends the Pringsheims[4], enters the stalls and sits down in the front row of black seats covered in red velvet. A thin, bespectacled little man, swarthy, frizzy-haired, yellow, with a very pointed cranium, all in black in a frock-coat, with the air of a clergyman, very absorbed. Weingartner is finished and leaves the podium. Mahler marches straight up and instantly inspires us with confidence. Great calm, absolute simplicity, utterly self-assured and without charlatanism. The same could not have been said then of Weingartner. The orchestra has not budged, but one senses that habit of passivity when musicians have no intention of committing themselves . . . Evidently, there is some danger in this symphony.

Ritter is appalled by the work: 'Such improper music', says one of his friends. He hears the poet Karl Wolfskehl[5] call it 'Viennese corruption, cabaret music'. Standing to boo at the concert ('all of Munich's Israelites were there'), Ritter feels as if he has participated in a musical Black Mass. But 'this music will not let us sleep'.

Profoundly disturbed, he wrote to Mahler, who sent him proofs of the score. In 1904, while visiting Prague – Ritter was an authority on Czech art and a biographer of Smetana – he heard Mahler conduct the Third Symphony. This time he was completely won over by the music, though 'the man is of another clan, another party; the man will mean nothing to me.' He began to write impassioned articles about Mahler[6] but still avoided meeting him.

The fatal, inevitable meeting took place on 6 November 1906 at 10 a.m. in the Kaim-Saal in Munich. I shall

3. Felix Weingartner (1863–1942) was regular conductor of the Kaim Concerts. He had known Mahler since 1885, premièred three movements of his Third Symphony in Berlin in 1897, and succeeded him at the Vienna Court Opera ten years later.
4. Alfred Pringsheim (1850–1941) was professor of mathematics at the University of Munich and a keen Wagnerite. His son Klaus became a conductor under Mahler, another son, Heinz (1882–1974), was a music critic, while his daughter Katia married the author Thomas Mann.
5. (1869–1948), a Jewish adherent of the Stefan George circle.
6. See his fascinating collection *Études d'art étranger*, Paris (Mercure de France), 1911.

never forget the look he shot at me, from below to above
(he was much shorter than me) when, presented to the
master with Marcel Montandon[7] and Janko Càdra, I
stated my name. From that moment I stopped trying to
fight the fascination exercised upon us by this prestigious
and in some respects absolutely fantastic being. We heard
four rehearsals full of tiny episodes that gave us an even
more captivating impression of the Master. On the
evening of 8 November the concert took place (repeated a
week later by Stavenhagen). But hardly had he bowed to
the audience than Mahler hurled himself into his automobile and returned that night to Vienna.

Two years later Ritter and his friend went to Prague to follow the
Czech Philharmonic throughout its preparation of Mahler's
Seventh.

The rehearsals were very chaotic. The festival hall was
also a banqueting hall, where waiters were laying the
tables while on the stage the Master and orchestra gave of
their utmost . . . On Wednesday, 15 September, when
Madame Mahler arrived from Vienna and the orchestra
had worked excessively on the first movement, Mahler
suddenly realized that neither his wife nor I had heard a
single note of the finale. Brusquely, he declared: 'Right,
the finale . . . uninterrupted, all right? For the very first
time!' Madame Mahler, sitting on the only spare chair
that could be found in a search of the neighbouring halls,
was back by the wall in the last row of the cellos. Janko
Càdra and I had been placed by the Master at the foot of
his podium. sitting directly at his feet, at the centre of the
orchestra that was ranged all around us. And there for
the first time we heard the immortal sunrise of that
glorious finale, opening with a frenetic clash of timpani
reminiscent of the first bars of *Die Meistersinger*. Fired
by the presence of the woman he idolized for her beauty
and Makart-like[8] Viennese gracefulness, the Master

---

7. Music critic.
8. Hans Makart (1840-84), lush Austrian painter with propensities for Rubens
figures.

threw himself about like a madman, seated, standing, dancing, leaping like a jack-in-the-box, in all directions at once, conducting to the right, to the left, in front, behind, completely oblivious of me and giving me several hefty kicks in the kidneys. But what enthusiasm! such delirium! And how we were carried away! And, indomitably Czech though they were in their response to a German conductor, the orchestra was conquered, swept off its feet . . .

'Souvenirs sur Gustav Mahler,'[9] *Revue Musicale Suisse*, vol. 101/1 (Jan.–Feb. 1961), pp. 29–39.

Ossip GABRILOWITSCH (1878–1936)

The Russian-born pianist and conductor came to Vienna in 1894 to study with Leschetizky. In 1905 he took up the baton and in the following year watched Mahler rehearse the Sixth Symphony in Essen. When they met in St Petersburg in November 1907 Mahler found Gabrilowitsch prepared 'to pull down the sky for me'.[1] Weeks later in Paris, Gabrilowitsch confessed to Alma that he was falling in love with her; he begged her to help him over it so as not to hurt Mahler.

He felt for my hand in the dark. The light was switched on and Mahler came in; he was affectionate and kindly and the spectre vanished.[1]

In 1909 Gabrilowitsch married the soprano Clara Clemens, Mark Twain's daughter. From 1910 to 1914 he conducted the Konzertverein Orchestra of Munich, and in 1918 he founded the Detroit Symphony Orchestra. At the time of his association with Mahler, he was said to look 'like a Kishinev Jew after a pogrom'.[2]

Mahler is to me the very incarnation of the highest ideals,

---

9. Ritter's reminiscences are quoted at length in HLG1, 2 and 3.

1. AMM, p. 300.
2. AML, p. 30, quoting Emil Zuckerkandl.

artistic and human. I did not believe such ideals could ever be realized until I met him. To have known him made life seem nobler – more worth living. He had the kind of limitless devotion to a high cause that only a saint has. He was the one artist I have ever known to whom personal success meant nothing. Not one atom of vanity was in his disposition. His was the childlike *naïveté* of the true genius.

Indifferent to his own success, he was incapable of understanding those to whom success meant everything. No man ever had a more loving or truly sympathetic heart than Mahler, but with those who placed their art beneath their ego, he had no patience.

It is not often given to a great genius to be understood and appreciated by his contemporaries . . .

Mahler might be described as the most impersonal artist that ever existed. He once told me how as a boy he succeeded (at the price of many privations) in attending one of the concerts Richard Wagner was conducting in Vienna. The effect of Wagner's music on the young chap

was overpowering. But when at the end of the programme Wagner was tendered an ovation, young Mahler
did not stay to see it, nor did he make an attempt to get
nearer the stage for a better look at the adored master.
The programme was finished – that meant the end of the
concert for Mahler. The personal element did not
interest him. He walked out of the hall.

Private papers quoted in Clara Clemens, *My Husband,*
Gabrilowitsch, New York (Harper and Brothers), 1938, pp. 128–30.

Clara CLEMENS
(1874–1962)

Mark Twain's daughter trained as a singer. After 1909 she gave
recitals in Europe and the US accompanied by her husband,
Gabrilowitsch.

Mahler filled one with the kind of awe one always feels
before an overpowering personality. I can imagine Beethoven, Savonarola, Caesar having much the same effect
on their fellow men. He seemed forbidding in his
strength and scornful of the human being. But he only
seemed so at first. The moment he smiled one felt that a
childlike sweetness and simplicity lay beneath the rugged
exterior.

He was not one who could use the ordinary means for
entering upon an acquaintanceship with anybody. He
was either burning with eagerness to talk about something which deeply interested him (and then he talked
with the eloquence and brilliancy of a genius), or he was
nobly silent like an Egyptian sphinx. One instinctively
hunted about in one's own nature for big qualities with
which to meet him. I have never known a greater
personality.

Gustav Mahler – The Composer, the Conductor, the Man;
Appreciations by Distinguished Contemporary Musicians, New York
(The Society of the Friends of Music), 9 April 1916, pp. 8–9.

Otto KLEMPERER
(1885–1973)

It says much for Mahler's magnetism that he attracted followers as
diverse as the worshipful Zemlinsky and adversarial Schoenberg, the
agreeable Walter, the submissive Fried and the contrarily strong-
willed Klemperer. Nor were they drawn by the allure of power and
high position. Young rebels like Schoenberg and Klemperer were
more inclined to resist powerful men than to adhere to them.

It was as a child in Hamburg that Klemperer caught his earliest
glimpse of Mahler.

> One day as I was walking home from school, I saw an
> odd-looking man beside me. He was holding his hat in
> his hand and seemed unable to walk properly. He had a
> jerky gait, halted abruptly from time to time, and
> appeared to have a club-foot. Regarding him with inordi-
> nate curiosity, I told myself: 'That's Kapellmeister Mah-
> ler from the Municipal Theatre.'

> *Klemperer on Music: Shavings from a Musician's Workbench*, ed.
> Martin Anderson. London (Toccata Press), 1986, pp. 132–3.

> At that time he had a habit of pulling strange faces,
> which made a tremendous impression on me. I ran along
> shyly after him for about ten minutes and stared at him as
> though he were a deep-sea monster.

> Letter to Alma Mahler, November 1911, cited in Peter Heyworth,
> *Otto Klemperer, his Life and Times*, Cambridge (Cambridge
> University Press), 1983, p. 1.

Although he saw Mahler no more than five or six times as an adult,
the encounters were decisive for Klemperer. Mahler's testimonial
launched his career and his example as a conductor was one that
Klemperer felt bound to follow. Fifty years after Mahler's death, in a
previously unpublished letter, he recalled that Mahler's conducting
could not be separated from his personality:

> I heard Mahler conduct on only a few occasions – in the
> opera house in *Walküre* and *Iphigenie in Aulis* and in
> concert in a mixed programme of *Tristan*, *Meistersinger*
> and *Bartered Bride* overtures and Beethoven's Seventh

Symphony. I also heard him rehearse his own Eighth Symphony.

. . . It is hard to say anything individual about [his conducting], his art and personality hung so closely together. The main things appear to me to be the simplicity of his music making. His tempos were absolutely natural[1] and accordingly convincing. The same holds true for his expressive gestures.

. . . He was, as man and musician, without vanity – therefore incorruptible. More, for the life of me, I cannot say.

> Unpublished letter to Jean Matter, dated 29 April 1972;
> German original in the possession of Lotte Klemperer.

Klemperer was twenty when he met Mahler professionally, directing the off-stage instruments in Oskar Fried's performance of Mahler's Second Symphony on 8 November 1905 in Berlin, where Mahler had conducted it first himself ten years before:

Mahler was present in person at the full rehearsal. When I went over to him and asked if the off-stage orchestra had been satisfactory, he said: 'No, it was frightful – much too loud.' I ventured to point out that the score said 'fortissimo'. 'Yes,' he replied, 'but in the far distance.' I took this to heart and prevailed on my musicians (who were much too close) to play very softly during the actual performance. It was, as I have said, an unqualified success. After taking innumerable bows, Mahler came down to the green-room. When he caught sight of me he promptly shook my hand and said, 'Very good.' I was overjoyed.

From that day forward my one dream was to work with Mahler, who was then directing the Vienna Hofoper. When I asked Fried's advice on how to arouse his interest, he told me: 'There's only one thing in the world that interests Mahler, and that's his own work.' I at once sat down and wrote a piano arrangement of the Second Symphony for two hands. (This has never been published.)

---

1. *Selbstverständlich.*

Some months after the above-mentioned performance
of the Second Symphony, Mahler himself conducted the
Third, in place of Artur Nikisch. Once again, I was
entrusted with a minor responsibility, in this instance the
off-stage side-drum. A much more important duty,
however, was to accompany Mahler from a rehearsal in
the Köpenicker Strasse to the Augsburger Strasse, where
he had been invited to eat with Richard Strauss. We had
to use the overhead railway, a novelty which did not seem
to interest Mahler unduly. Suddenly he said: 'You
compose, don't you?' Not regarding my academic exercises as compositions proper, I prevaricated. 'No, no,' he
laughed, 'you compose, I can see you do!' The Third met
with enormous success in Berlin, especially the first
movement . . .

My third visit to Vienna proved a watershed in my
career. Going to Mahler armed with my piano arrangement of the Second Symphony, I played the scherzo to
him by heart. When I had finished, he said: 'Why do you
want to become a conductor? You're an accomplished
pianist.' I confessed that it was my unshakeable ambition
to become a conductor, and asked him for a recommendation. He refused. 'A testimonial of that sort can
always be faked,' he said. 'But go and see Rainer Simons,
the Director of the Volksoper, tomorrow morning and
tell him I sent you.' Having done so without success, I
went back to Mahler and told him that a written recommendation was essential. He took a visiting card from his
pocket and wrote a testimonial which opened every door
to me. I have it still. It reads:

Gustav Mahler recommends Herr Klemperer as an
outstanding musician, who despite his youth is already
very experienced and is predestined for a conductor's
career. He vouches for the successful outcome of any
probationary appointment and will gladly provide further information personally.

Mahler was, in effect, my *creator spiritus*.
I sent photostats of this testimonial to all the major

opera-houses in Germany. Most of them did not reply at all, and the few that did so merely hinted at the possibility of an unsalaried post, which I could not entertain for obvious reasons. I would have made the effort only if it had been a question of working in Vienna under Mahler, but the Hofoper accepted no unsalaried staff. Eventually, with the aid of Mahler's testimonial, I secured my first appointment, which was a contract as chorus-master and resident junior conductor under Angelo Neumann in Prague . . .

In 1909, Mahler visited Prague again to conduct the first performance of his Seventh Symphony, for which he held about two dozen rehearsals. His technique was remarkable. Each day after rehearsal he used to take the entire orchestral score home with him for revision, polishing and retouching. We younger musicians, Bruno Walter, Bodanzky,[2] von Keussler[3] and I, would gladly have helped him, but he would not hear of it and did it all on his own.

We usually spent the evenings with him at his hotel. He was relaxed and extremely amusing, holding forth uninhibitedly and rather loudly about his successor at Vienna and declaring that he was even further from Wagner than he himself. Weingartner, who was the man in question, had made such enormous cuts in *Die Walküre* that patrons in the fourth gallery of the Hofoper had walked out, hissing and booing.

Mahler also spoke at great length about Hugo Wolf, whom he disliked exceedingly. Young puppy that I was, I had the effrontery to contradict him and assert that the *Mörike-Gebet* ('Herr, schicke was Du willst' [Lord, send what Thou wilt]), was very fine. He shot me an angry glance, at which I could only mumble: 'With all due respect, it's only my opinion.'

The Seventh Symphony was not a success. The Berlin critic Leopold Schmidt, in particular, came out strongly

---

2. Artur Bodanzky (1877–1939), assistant to Mahler in Vienna, later conduct at Berlin, Prague, Mannheim and the Metropolitan Opera, New York (1916–31).
3. Gerhard von Keussler (1874–1948), conductor and composer.

against the work. True, the first and last parts are still difficult, even today, but the three middle movements are deeply affecting in their simplicity.

In the winter of 1909 I had a difference of opinion with my director, Angelo Neumann, which resulted in my leaving Prague at the end of the season although I had actually been engaged for five years. In my hour of need I cabled Mahler, who was in New York, asking him to put in a word for me at Hamburg, where there was a vacancy. I heard later that he had sent a brief wire to the director, saying: 'Grab Klemperer'. He grabbed, and I found myself under contract.

Then came the glorious summer of 1910, during which Mahler rehearsed his Eighth in Munich with the Munich Philharmonic Orchestra. To be frank, it was not until then that I understood Mahler's music well enough to realize what a great composer he was. Unfortunately, I only heard the rehearsals with orchestra, soloists and children's choir. I was not present at the first performance in September because I was conducting at the Municipal Theatre in Hamburg . . .

During the rehearsals for his Eighth Symphony, Mahler quarrelled with the leader of the Munich Philharmonic (I think that was the name of the orchestra) because he wanted an absolutely first-class violinist who was familiar with his style. He sent for Arnold Rosé, who naturally took over the leader's place. At that, the rest of the orchestra rose and quitted the platform with one accord, leaving Mahler and Rosé alone. They did not return until Mahler had agreed that their leader should play in all future rehearsals and performances. This happened in 1910, when we still had monarchies and some respect for authority still remained. What would Mahler say today? . . .

When Oskar Fried performed Mahler's Second Symphony at Berlin in 1906, Mahler was present at the full rehearsal, seated in the stalls. Fried's programme comprised three works: a cantata by Max Reger, songs with orchestra by Franz Liszt, and the Second Symphony. Fried had only reached the second movement of the

Mahler Symphony by the close of the three-hour rehearsal. When told that he must stop, he flew into a towering rage, seized the nearest chair and flung it into the auditorium with all his might. (Luckily, no one was injured.) Mahler, who remained absolutely calm and unruffled, took Fried back to his hotel and discussed the whole work with him.

Next evening, before the concert began, Fried went to the members of his orchestra and told them: 'Gentlemen, everything I did at rehearsal was wrong. This evening I shall be using entirely different tempos. Please follow me.'

He often said that I reminded him of his brother, a namesake of mine. Mahler thought a great deal of Otto, who later committed suicide, and always said he was much more talented than himself.

Mahler's treatment of Schoenberg and Zemlinsky is typical of him. Schoenberg, whom he considered to have great talent, he enabled to compose by supporting him financially, and he took Zemlinsky on at the Hofoper and did all he could to include him in the repertoire. He also accepted his opera *Der Traumgörge*.[4] . . .

Mahler always said that a Jew came into the world 'with a short arm' – i.e., that he had to do much more than others to achieve a comparable result. Faced with the choice of becoming Director of the Vienna Hofoper or remaining a Jew, he chose the former course and embraced Roman Catholicism, to which he was anyway very close. This is demonstrated by the last movement of his Fourth Symphony, the *Wunderhorn* song in the Third ('Es sungen drei Engel einen süssen Gesang') and the ancient Latin hymn *Veni creator spiritus* from the first movement of the Eighth Symphony. When Alfred Roller asked him to compose a mass, however, he declined on the grounds that he could not write a credo.

Mahler was a thoroughgoing child of the nineteenth century, an adherent of Nietzsche and typically irreligious.

---

4. But did not remain long enough to perform it. The opera was finally staged in Nuremberg in 1980.

For all that, he was – as all his compositions testify – devout in the highest sense, though his sort of piety was not to be found in any church prayer-book. During his lifetime he was attacked both by anti-Semites and philo-Semites, neither group approving of him. He was simply an outsider . . .

Klemperer on Music: Shavings from a Musician's Workbench, ed. Martin Anderson, London (Toccata Press), 1986, pp. 133–47. Quotations reproduced by permission of Lotte Klemperer and the publisher.[5]

Interlude 2: Interview

Though unusually adept at manipulating a section of the Press, Mahler rarely gave formal interviews. His method was to cultivate a small core of critics sympathetic to his objectives and, when he wanted to release information, drop it to them casually in apparently off-the-cuff remarks.

The following conversation took place in August 1906 when Mahler, travelling to Salzburg, shared a compartment with Bernard Scharlitt, a Viennese musician, critic of the *Musikalisches Wochen-blatt*. Five years later, a week after Mahler's death, an abridged account of their conversation appeared in the *Neue Freie Presse*.

'I shall depart', said Mahler, 'in the next year from the Court Opera because in the course of time I have become convinced that the idea of a permanent opera company directly contradicts modern principles of art. It stems from an age whose artistic understanding differs greatly from ours. In an epoch of opera gluttony it was an easy

---

5. Klemperer's Mahler recollections were first recorded in 1960 as *Meine Erinnerungen an Gustav Mahler und andere autobiographische Skizzen* (Zurich: Atlantis), enlarged in English translation in 1964 (London: Dennis Dobson) and revised in *Klemperer on Music*, the most comprehensive version, from which these extracts are taken. Further Klemperer observations on Mahler may be found in Peter Heyworth, *Conversations with Klemperer*, London (Victor Gollancz), 1973; rev. (Faber Paperbacks), 1978.

matter to stage a hundred performances a year at the same artistic, or rather unartistic, level. A modern opera director, even if he is a genius like Wagner, could never cope with such numbers if he wants to do justice to today's concept of artistic perfection.

'Perfect performances merely validate criticism that all other performances leave much to be desired. To separate the artistic direction [of the Opera] from the administrative is also unthinkable. Such a division of labour would be possible anywhere except on the opera stage. Here, to take an example from everyday life, the cook must not only prepare the meal but buy the ingredients himself.

'A modern music stage in Vienna would be another matter – a theatre in which Wagner and Mozart could coexist – built perhaps on the Kahlenberg, with a short summer season that would not compete with the Court Opera. But that, for Vienna, is a long way off, the 'music of the future'.[1]

'Everything, by the way, outlives its own time. Me, too, and my achievements. I am no longer a novelty for Vienna. So I will depart at a time when I can still expect that the Viennese may appreciate in future times what I have achieved.

'From now on I want to devote myself quietly to composing. I am well aware that as a composer I will not find recognition in my lifetime. That can be expected only beyond my grave. That distance is necessary for an adequate assessment of a phenomenon like me, the *conditio sine qua non*[2]. As long as I am the Mahler who wanders among you, 'a man among men',[3] I as a creator must expect all-too-human treatment.

'I shall first have to shake off the dust of the earth before justice is done to me. I am, in Nietzsche's expression, a man not of his own time. This applies above all to my kind of works. The truly timely one is

1. Wagner's phrase: *Zukunftsmusik*.
2. Indispensable condition.
3. A description originally applied to Jesus Christ.

Richard Strauss. That is why he can enjoy immortality
while still alive. I rate his operas higher than his symphonic works and believe posterity will do the same.'

To my remark that he and Strauss shared a point of
contact in having set Nietzsche to music, Mahler
retorted: 'The explanation is simply that we both, as
musicians, sensed what might be called the "latent
music" in Nietzsche's mighty works. You once called
Nietzsche, not without justification, an "unachieved"
composer. That he was, in every deed. His *Zarathustra*
is born of the spirit of music, absolutely "symphonic" in
its construction. By the way, Nietzsche's talent as a
composer was far greater than is generally assumed . . .'

Neue Freie Presse, 25 May 1911

Dr Richard HORN[1]

Returning to work at the Opera in September 1906, Mahler stayed
for a while outside Vienna at the Dornbach villa of Ilse Conrat, a
friend of Alma's family. Here he would take afternoon walks with
Horn, a lawyer with whom he enjoyed discussing scientific
problems.

The alarming guest did not make such an upset as they
expected. When he found his apples for breakfast, lunch
and dinner and the first volume of Bielschowsky's biography of Goethe at Dornbach and the second in Walfischgasse,[2] he was in heaven; Goethe and apples are two
things he cannot live without.

We had many philosophic walks together; it was all I
could do to snatch my afternoon siesta. Mahler is a
notable thinker after the pattern of his fiery spirit, a deep
and often an inspired one, but usually a thinker by fits
and starts.

AMM, p. 103.

1. Dates unknown.
2. Frau Conrat's town apartment.

Berta SZEPS-ZUCKERKANDL
(1864–1945)

It was at the home of Berta and Emil Zuckerkandl that Mahler had fallen in love with Alma Schindler. Berta, arts patron and daughter of the newspaper proprietor Moritz Szeps, was Alma's intimate friend. Mahler had met her sister, Sophie, in Paris, where she was married to Paul Clemenceau, whose brother became French Prime Minister in October 1906. He also befriended Berta's husband Emil Zuckerkandl (1849–1910), a distinguished anatomist.

Berta's autobiography[1] contains pleasant recollections of Mahler's French fans. The following unpublished letters to her sister record Mahler's farewell to Vienna.

(*16 March 1907*)
An Old Vienna garden. Tall walnut-trees overhang a gravel path lined with rose-bushes. It is Emil Zuckerkandl's

Emil Zuckerkandl, anatomist.

---

1. Berta Szeps, *My Life and History*, London (Cassell), 1938.

garden. And Gustav Mahler is walking with him to and fro. Mahler glances now and then at the walnut-trees, because he knows that Beethoven once sat and worked beneath them.

'I'm aware', said Mahler melancholically, 'that I am leaving behind a task that's unfinished. I shall make that point in my farewell letter to the members of the Philharmonic. When all is said and done, they are a body of artists. They will understand what I mean.'

'I doubt it,' Emil replied. 'You are too inclined to assume, my dear friend, that other people share your artistic idealism. And you forget all the obstacles that this very orchestra placed in your path. None of them will ever understand that your severity is a matter of artistic principle. You have achieved what no one else has ever achieved. And only because you refused to make concessions.'

'All the same, I find like you that there is no sense in lying, and that is why I am so solidly with you. Though it saddens me to think that ten years ago I had a rock-solid belief that I could achieve perfection.'

'You've learned something that I recognized a long time ago: the things of this world are no more than tokens. This realization is the essence of tragedy.'

'How I love your garden,' said Mahler. 'The gentle sway of the walnut-trees and the sacred recollection of Beethoven. Perfection . . . well, if it can be achieved at all, the best that can be managed when recreating a work of art is a brief resurgence of the flame. Because perfection means fulfilment. And both imply a momentary respite in the restless progress of time. Each time I prepare to conduct an opera, I am aiming at perfection. But when I am blessed with success, it is like a flash of lightning passing through my soul. Extinguished no sooner than it illuminates.

'That's why I want you both to come to the first night of Gluck's *Iphigenie* the day after tomorrow. I have brought you tickets for a box. It's my final confession. I have put everything I am and everything I am capable of into *Iphigenie*. So perhaps for this farewell we shall really have the *Glück* – the good fortune – to experience that rare thing, perfection.'

Dearest, it is you I have to thank for the fact that I got to know Mahler all those years ago . . . yes, when he was conducting in Paris it was you who asked him to look us up in Vienna . . . so I want to tell you immediately about all the events that give Mahler's departure from Vienna such symbolic importance. He bared his heart and soul again in Gluck's *Iphigenie* and it was as if everything else conspired to fulfil his dream of perfection. He got the casting absolutely right. The orchestra gave of its best in a tough set of rehearsals. The setting was arranged behind a very thin curtain of gauze which produced a dreamlike impression of ancient Greece and a feeling of heightened reality. As the characters moved to and fro, this veil gave them that much more of a pictorial quality . . . And one thing is certain: despite all the art treasures the Greeks left behind, our view of antiquity is not how it was in real life. Mahler succeeded in making his vision of a Greek Iphigenia wonderfully homogeneous. He tailored it to Gluck's music, which has a controlled passion that under Mahler's baton gradually shrilled into bitter tragedy.

How deeply Mahler immersed himself in this work prior to his departure. The following story shows how he lived in a kind of trance.

Emil was crossing the road in the Ring on the day of the first performance [18 March] when he saw Mahler standing in front of an advertisement pillar with theatre bills on it. He was smiling with delight as he gazed at the bill for *Iphigenie*, so Emil asked him appropriately: 'What are you reading with such reverence?'

And Mahler replied with a childlike naïvety: 'I can't take my eyes off the poster for *Iphigenie*. I stop at every billboard and can't believe it's really happening now – that this very evening these singers and this orchestra will be taking their cue from me. It makes me feel so happy!'

Emil came home quite emotional. He said there had been something holy about Mahler.

'Mahlers Abschied' (manuscript), undated copy at the Bibliothèque Gustav Mahler, Paris. Quoted by permission of Emile Zuckerkandl, Palo Alto, California.

Lilli LEHMANN[1]

I was on the point of departing one evening[2] after my engagement when I was held back, as though by a higher power, for another day, so as to enjoy *Tristan* in all peacefulness at night with Mildenburg and Mahler and Roller's scenic decorations. I had talked with people all day long, and was so exhausted at night that I could neither see nor hear, and only by exerting all my powers did I drag myself to the Opera, where Mahler's box was at my service, in which I found his wife and sister. Both ladies hurried in quest of Mahler after the second act, and asked me to go with them. But being completely used up, and fearing, moreover, to bother Mahler after his tremendous labour and before what was yet to come, I urged the ladies to leave me to my fate alone in the box. All my entreaties seemed in vain; they would not rest until I had joined them, and we sat together in a large room with Mahler, who was taking some tea and talking animatedly, and with at least thirty other persons.

I listened quietly, only wondering how it was possible for him, in such confused chatter, to keep his head clear for his most difficult task, when suddenly the superintendent rushed into the gathering with the announcement that Herr Schmedes (Tristan) had become hoarse and would not sing any more. I admired Mahler's composure as he sent for the score so as to cut out all that it was

1. See. p. 58. Lehmann was now fifty-eight years old.
2. 19 May 1907.

possible to omit, and notified Schmedes that he must go on to the end of the opera. The dispute continued for a long time back and forth, and it was far from settled when the superintendent appeared a second time with the ominous tidings that Fräulein von Mildenburg, likewise, was hoarse and did not wish to sing any more. That produced the effect of throwing a burning torch into a keg of gunpowder, for Mahler exploded from his calm like a jumping devil out of a box, hopped about the room as though possessed, and could not stop from rage and excitement. Over an hour had elapsed meanwhile, and, after Schmedes had declared that he would go on singing, Mahler shouted: 'Mildenburg shall not sing at all, she shall shut up; I will cut out the lament, and the "*Liebestod*" the orchestra shall play alone!' – whereupon the whole crowd betook themselves to the stage so as to arrange for the orchestra the cuts that had been selected.

Frau Mahler and I were left behind alone in the tea-room; I silently shook my head, for anything like this I had never yet experienced. As we were on the point of going below, I said to Alma, whom I had known for some time as the youngest of Schindler's daughters and the stepdaughter of Carl Moll: 'If I had suspected that this would have caused such commotion I would have sung Isolde's few measures.' 'Oh, Lilli, would you really do it?' 'Yes, if you think that it would be a favour to Mahler.' Away she went and brought Mahler back beaming, who asked me if I would really sing? 'You may fetch me out of my grave if you ever need me, Lilli; and I will conduct anything where and what you like.'

My Path through Life, New York (Putnams), 1914.

Josef Bohuslav FOERSTER[1]

Mahler, in 1901, had summoned Berta Foerster-Lauterer to Vienna, 'the best Sieglinde I have ever heard'.[2] Two years passed before her husband could afford to join her; he finally found employment teaching and writing music reviews for *Die Zeit*. Foerster attended many of Mahler's rehearsals and performances, marvelling at his conducting and stage direction. But the daily intimacy they shared in Hamburg had vanished, there was time only for snatched conversations. Mahler had married and found new friends; Foerster's name does not appear in Alma's memoir.

> Right at the beginning of 1907, Mahler's last year at the Court Opera, it was clear even to the uninitiated that preparations were in hand to topple Gustav Mahler. On the first of January, if I am not mistaken, the government newspaper *Fremdenblatt*, which until then had acknowledged the marvellous activities at the Opera, published a magisterial *feuilleton* against his direction. No one could mistake the change of atmosphere.
>
> He also felt the storm-clouds gathering above his head. He knew his Vienna, one day glowing with love, the next icy cold. Day after day one had to struggle anew for recognition. In the opera-house, he prepared new productions of *Walküre* and Gluck's *Iphigenie in Aulis* with relentless devotion . . . On 15 October Gustav Mahler took the podium at the Court Opera for the last time . . .
>
> We talked once of publishers and printers. It was a day when Mahler was irritated and depressed by attacks on him in the Press. He said: 'If I had no children, it would never occur to me to bother with publishing my compositions. How long does a work survive? Fifty years? Then along come other composers, another time, another taste, other works. What's the use of it? I need such a great apparatus [for my music], and who can take the trouble to produce it well? And even if someone invests the enthusiasm and the time, how can I be certain that he

1. See p. 72.
2. *Der Pilger*, p. 515.

understands my intentions? Better no performance at all than a bad one.' . . .

When I went to see Gustav Mahler for the last time in the offices of the Court Opera, not long before his departure for America, I found him serious, unbroken but in amazingly tender mood. Understandably, I did not utter a word about his resignation, about the ingratitude, or the strange, insidious illusion of public opinion. But the shadows of the unsaid, the silent sorrow that filled his heart and mine lay heavily on our souls.

'So the decision is made – you're leaving Vienna. Perhaps for ever. That is what saddens me so.'

But Mahler smiled. 'I am going, but you should know that my contract provides long holidays, part of which I shall spend in Vienna. I am keeping my apartment, there are various members of my family here, a few friends. On the contrary, we two can once again have friendly relations with one another. Our Hamburg days – do you remember them? – will be revived. Until now I have been so busy we could hardly ever see each other. Now it will be different and I look forward to our relationship. By the way, have you read Giordano Bruno?'[3]

From that moment, he was as if transformed. Diederichs of Jena had just begun publishing Bruno's writings and Mahler, and coincidentally I, had both read the first volume.

'What a man, what a thinker!' enthused Mahler. 'Have we made any progress since then? Doesn't Bruno know everything that we know today?'

That was him absolutely. A single instant could make him forget everything that oppressed him, all the ingratitude, the bitter disappointments, the painful impressions of the last days and hours, the treachery of hangers-on and admirers who turned their backs and left him deserted, stripped of his power and authority. This hero, dethroned by impure hands, swung aloft on spiritual

---

3. (1548–1600), Italian pantheist philosopher, burnt at the stake in Rome for insisting that other worlds exist apart from ours. His works had just begun to appear in German.

wings into the realms of divine joy, where all earthly
concerns are forgotten.

Der Pilger, Prague (Artia), 1955, pp. 702–5.

Jean SIBELIUS
(1865–1957)

In Helsinki to conduct a Beethoven–Wagner concert in November
1907, Mahler heard some pieces by Sibelius. He described one of
them as 'kitsch served up with nordic harmonizations as a national
dish' but on meeting the composer found him 'extremely sympathetic, like all the Finns'.[1] Sibelius, who had just completed his Third
Symphony, touched in their conversations on a fundamental
divergence of symphonic philosophy.

> Mahler and I spent much time in each other's company.
> Mahler's grave heart-trouble forced him to lead an ascetic
> life and he was not fond of dinners and banquets.
> Contact was established between us in some walks,
> during which we discussed all the great questions of
> music thoroughly.
>
> When our conversation touched on the essence of
> symphony, I said that I admired its severity and style and
> the profound logic that created an inner connection
> between all the motifs. This was the experience I had
> come to in composing. Mahler's opinion was just the
> reverse.
>
> 'Nein, die Symphonie muss sein wie die Welt. Sie
> muss alles umfassen.' (No, the symphony must be like
> the world. It must embrace everything.)
>
> Personally Mahler was very modest. He had heard that
> the Gambrinus restaurant was a popular resort of orches-
> tral musicians and spoke of dining there. When I sug-
> gested that a Mahler ought, perhaps, to visit a

1. AMM, p. 196.

higher-class restaurant, he replied curtly: 'Ich geh' wohin ich will.' (I shall go where I please.)

A very interesting person. I respected him as a personality, his ethically exalted qualities as a man and an artist, in spite of his ideas on art being different from mine. I did not wish him to think that I had only looked him up in order to get him interested in my compositions. When he asked me in his abrupt way:

'Was wollen Sie dass ich von Ihnen dirigiere?' (What would you like me to conduct of yours?) I therefore only answered:

'Nichts.' (Nothing.)[2]

Karl Ekman, *Jean Sibelius; The Life and Personality of an Artist*, Trans. Edward Birse, Helsingfors (Holger Schildts Förlag), 1935, pp. 190–1.

Alban BERG
(1885–1935)

Long before he began studying with Schoenberg, Berg kept portraits of Mahler and Ibsen in his room as 'my living ideals'.[1] After the Viennese première of Mahler's Fourth, he sneaked into the conductor's room and stole his baton as a trophy.[2] He joined the retinue of acolytes but had only one private conversation with Mahler, reportedly during a lull in an evening's revelry in a Grinzing tavern:

MAHLER: And do you also want to be a conductor?
BERG: No.
MAHLER: You're quite right. If you want to compose, don't go into the theatre.[3]

---

2. Mahler programmed two works by Sibelius in his 1911 New York season but fell ill before he could conduct them. In 1909 Sibelius composed *In Memoriam* (op. 59), containing echoes of Mahler's Fifth Symphony. His next symphony, the austere Fourth (1911), starkly contradicts Mahler's sound-world.

1. Letter to Hermann Watzenauer, 1 August 1904.
2. Reich, p. 19.
3. Berg related this episode in a letter to Watzenauer (HLG 111, p. 509) and in conversations with H. F. Redlich (DMir/1980, p. 299) and Reich (p. 34).

The events surrounding this brief encounter were recalled by Berg:

One evening he left his Döbling apartment to go to the nearby restaurant zum Schutzengel and meet 'the young people'. Using Zemlinsky and Schoenberg as his mouthpieces he had let it be known that he liked to spend time together with young people. They came, found him in a private room and listened. For Mahler talked, talked almost alone; the others hardly dared to throw in a word. It was not long before he came to speak of his beloved Dostoevsky. But it was apparent that he was not really being understood, because hardly anybody knew Dostoevsky's books in any detail. Mahler: 'You must change that, Schoenberg! Have your pupils read Dostoevsky, that is more important than counterpoint!' Silence. Then Webern raised his hand like a little boy in elementary school and said very timidly: 'Please, we've had Strindberg.' General laughter . . . Gradually the noise became too much for such a small room. Everyone went out. A couple of hangers-on took their departure, but the rest of us walked over the Hohe Warte and entered the Casino Zögernitz. There too we quickly found a back room, and Mahler was again surrounded. He spoke enthusiastically of Schumann and told of his repeated efforts to get the symphonies to sound better by changing the instrumentation. But that could never have satisfied him . . . As we took our leave, he said, warding off admiring words about his work at the Opera: 'Those were only experiments. The real thing still lies ahead . . .'

Willi Reich, *The Life and Work of Alban Berg*, trans. Cornelius Cardew. London (Thames and Hudson), 1965. pp. 31–2.

The date of this meeting is uncertain. Berg placed it in the spring of 1908 or 1909, Specht in May 1909 and Paul Stefan in 1910. Alma Mahler, whose account amplifies theirs, was certain it took place late in 1907 shortly before Mahler's first departure for America:

Schoenberg and Zemlinsky and their friends wanted Mahler to spend an evening with them before he left Vienna, and so they all foregathered at the Schutzengel at

Grinzing. I stayed at home, as I always found such gatherings a weariness. Mahler came back at midnight in great spirits, but his clothes smelt so strongly of smoke that he had to change before giving me an account of the proceedings which kept us laughing until the early hours. He said that as soon as he joined them a religious hush descended on the company; and so to liven things up he called for the bill of fare. The waiter brought the soup with both thumbs in the plate. Mahler sent it back. The waiter next brought a roll in his hand and Mahler demanded another one. The waiter retired to the sideboard, put the same roll on a plate and brought it back again. It dawned on Schoenberg's assembled pupils, who had so far watched all this with wonder and awe, that Mahler was making fun of the man; the ice was broken, and the fun became so fast and furious that no one could hear himself speak.

Mahler found the noise worse than the solemn hush and was now eager to get home. He arranged with Schoenberg and Zemlinsky that he would jump off the tram at the Restaurant Zögernitz. They were to follow his example and by this means they would be quit of the mob of students; but the students too jumped with one accord from the swiftly speeding tram, and there they all were again, crowded together, enveloped in smoke, and reduced once more to an embarrassed silence, which gave way to merciless din.

Mahler shouted out above the racket: 'What do you fellows think about Dostoevsky nowadays?' A chorus of youthful voices replied: 'We don't bother with him any more. It's Strindberg now.' This evidence of the transience of reputations gave us a lot to think about. Mahler made a vigorous retort; but the young have to have their god of the moment – yesterday Strindberg, today Wedekind, tomorrow Shaw, the day after tomorrow a rediscovered Dostoevsky and so on *ad infinitum*. It does not matter that fashion changes their gods. The chief thing is that they have gods of some sort.

We talked it all over while he sat on the edge of my bed, smoking, and eating the supper I had hastily

Zemlinsky, the most loyal of Mahler's followers.

produced for him. He had been too nauseated to eat
anything all the evening.

ANN, pp. 125–6.

The depth of Berg's adoration of Mahler is revealed in a contemporary letter to his fiancée Helene Nachowski:

I was unfaithful to you tonight. It happened in the finale
of the Mahler Second Symphony, when I gradually felt a
sensation of complete solitude, as if in all the world there
were nothing left but this music – and me listening to it.
But when it came to its uplifting and overwhelming
climax, and then was over, I felt a sudden pang, and a
voice within me said: what of Helene? It was only then I
realized I had been unfaithful, so now I implore your
forgiveness. Tell me, darling, that you understand and
forgive!

Letters to his Wife, London (Faber and Faber), 1971, p. 32.

Egon WELLESZ
(1885–1974)

The day after he heard Mahler conduct Weber's *Freischütz* in 1899, the schoolboy Wellesz began to compose.[1] He studied with Adler and from 1905 with Schoenberg, connections that gained him privileged access to Mahler's rehearsals. His account of Mahler preparing his farewell to Vienna, the Second Symphony on 24 November 1907, is uniquely detailed.

I think I was the only one among Schoenberg's pupils who admired Mahler from the beginning. I remember that Anton Webern was rather shocked by this march in the Third Symphony when he first saw the score. We had a miniature score and there was a good arrangement of the symphony for two players. I persuaded Webern to play through the work with me before the first perform-ance in December 1904, when Mahler conducted the Vienna Philharmonic Orchestra. It was some time before Webern overcame his prejudice against the realistic features in Mahler's music. Finally, however, he became more and more enthusiastic and later conducted his symphonies.

I had heard all the great conductors of that time, but Mahler's rehearsing and conducting of his symphonies was an experience which I shall never forget. The reading of Mahler's scores by Bruno Walter comes near to it, but he lacks Mahler's intensity and breathtaking power in building up a climax.

Mahler left the Vienna Opera in the spring of 1907 and signed a contract for New York. Shortly before his departure he conducted his Second Symphony in a concert of the Gesellschaft der Musikfreunde, which did not admit any listeners to its rehearsals. I was very keen, however, to be present at the last rehearsals before Mahler left for New York and waited with my fiancée for

1. See Egon Wellesz, 'Erinnerungen an Gustav Mahler und Arnold Schönberg' *Orbis Musicae* (Department of Musicology, Tel Aviv University), vol. 1/1 (summer 1971), pp. 72–83.

his arrival. When Mahler came he asked us to wait until
he had talked to the orchestra. A few minutes later one of
the ushers came and said: 'Director Mahler asks you to
come in.' We went into the empty hall. Mahler was
already standing at the conductor's desk. He turned
round, waited a moment until we were seated, raised the
baton, and began.

At the end of the first theme he stopped and asked the
violas and cellos to delete the trill on B natural (p. 7, bar
3), which was now played only in the flutes, oboes and
clarinets; the sound became clearer and stronger when
played in that way.

Looking at the passionate melody which forms the
bridge to the second theme (p. 7, bar 6) one may ask why
all the woodwind start fortissimo, and instantly make a
decrescendo to piano. In fact this is the best way to get
the effect of a piano from the beginning, after the two
bars in which the brass hammers its rhythm fortissimo,
the four trumpets even forte-fortissimo.

Shortly afterwards there is a great crescendo of the
whole orchestra. At the climax (p. 12, bar 2) Mahler
stopped and said: 'Something was wrong in the woodwind.' At that moment the door of a box opened, and
Bruno Walter rushed in and shouted: 'The second oboe
played B flat, not B natural.' Even Mahler was astonished
at Walter's fine ear. And so the rehearsal went on.

The two last movements of the symphony, the song
'Urlicht' and the choral movement 'Auferstehn' with the
middle section for soprano solo and alto solo, are played
without interruption. Before the movement the choir
stood up, but Mahler gave them a sign to wait and told
the orchestra and the singers what he meant to express
when he composed the symphony.'It is the wrestling of
Jacob with the Angel', he said, 'and Jacob's cry to the
Angel: "I will not let thee go, except thou bless me."'

Never before had I seen Mahler in such an elated
mood. He never used to explain his ideas to the orchestra
and the singers, but would restrict his remarks to points
of orchestral technique, dynamics, and so on. When it
came to the famous duet between solo soprano and solo

alto: 'O Schmerz! Du Alldurchdringer!' it was obvious
that the chords in the trombones, though they were to be
played pianissimo, were covering the voices of the
singers. Mahler tried out everything to reduce the
dynamics of the passage, but to no avail. The voices did
not come through in the low middle register. Though
there are no other sustained chords in the score, Mahler
suddenly decided to strike out the trombones (p. 197, bar
12, p. 198, bars 2–7) and said in a solemn way, very
unusual for him: 'Hail to the conductor who in the future
will change my scores according to the accoustics of the
concert hall.'

'Reminiscences of Mahler', *The Score* (28 January 1961), pp. 54–6.

Paul STEFAN
(1879–1943)

Pseudonym of Dr P. S. Grünfeldt, music critic, supporter and biographer of Mahler. His books include a pro-Mahler polemic (1908), fiftieth-birthday tribute to Mahler (1910), a full-scale biography (1910, seven editions) and a Viennese chronicle (*Das Grab in Wien*, 1913) containing copious references to the Mahler era.

In the early days of December Mahler, accompanied by his wife, began his journey to America. Shortly beforehand word went out that the faithful could catch a last glimpse and see him off at the station. When we finally found out the date of his departure, some of his friends sent out a short note:

> The admirers of Gustav Mahler will gather to take leave of him on Monday, 9 December before 8.30 a.m. on the platform of the Westbahnhof, and invite you to attend and to inform any like-minded friends. Since this demonstration is intended to surprise Mahler, it is vital that no one connected with the Press should be informed. [The note was signed by Anton von Webern, Karl Horwitz, Heinrich Jalowetz and Stefan himself.]

Anyone who saw the greetings of those who turned out (there were about 200), who saw how whole-heartedly and unrestrainedly each one pressed Mahler's hand, how amicably and happily he responded – how he, normally so sparing with words, spoke in such friendly fashion to these loyal followers – no one who saw this could have found it in his heart to begrudge him – or rather them – this last pleasure.

It had all been arranged overnight, no 'official' personages had been informed. There was not a scrap of artificiality: just an urgent desire to see him once again, this man to whom we owed so much . . .

The train moved off. And Gustav Klimt gave voice to what we all felt and feared: 'It's over!'

Das Grab in Wien, Berlin (Erich Reiss), 1913, p. 92.

From Alma's memoirs:

When we drew slowly out it was without regret or backward glances. We had been too hard hit. All we wanted was to get away, the further the better. We even felt happy as Vienna was left behind. We did not miss our child, who had been left with my mother. We knew now that anxious love was of no avail against catastrophe, and that no spot on earth gives immunity. We had been through the fire. So we thought. But, in spite of all, one thing had us both in its grip – the future.

'Repertory opera is done with,' Mahler observed during the journey. 'I'm glad not to be staying on to witness its decline. Up to the last I contrived to hide from the public that I was making bricks without straw.'

AMM, p. 126.

V

I am lost to the world
(1907–11)

Chronology of Mahler's Life and Work

1908	1 Jan.	Opens at the New York Metropolitan Opera with *Tristan*.
	summer	Returns to Austria. Rents summer home at Toblach in the Tyrol, where he composes *Das Lied von der Erde*.
	19 Sept	Conducts Seventh Symphony at Prague.
	winter	Returns to New York.
	2 Dec.	Conducts his Second Symphony there.
1909	June	Sits for Rodin in Paris.
	summer	Starts Ninth Symphony at Toblach and Göding.
	2 Sept.	Toblach: Mahler completes his Ninth Symphony.
	winter	First season with the New York Philharmonic Orchestra.
1910		Orchestral tour of upstate New York.
	Apr.	Conducts Second Symphony in Paris.
	June–July	Alma, at a spa near Tobelbad, has an affair with the architect Walter Gropius, while Mahler at Toblach works on his Tenth Symphony.
	7 July	50th birthday: a volume of tributes is published. Discovers Alma's infidelity and fears losing her.
	25 Aug.	Travels to Leiden, Holland, to consult Freud on his marital difficulties.
	12 Sept.	Triumphant première of Eighth Symphony in Munich.
	Oct.	Returns to New York.
1911	20 Jan.	Conducts his own music for the last time, Fourth Symphony in New York.
	21 Feb.	Against doctors' orders, conducts his last concert, including the première of Busoni's *Berceuse élégiaque*; critically ill with a blood infection.
	Apr.	Receives serum treatment in Paris.
	11 May	Returns to Vienna.
	18 May	Gustav Mahler dies at Loew Sanatorium, aged 50.

Contemporary Events

1908   Theodore Roosevelt, US President, withdraws from politics at the
        age of 50.
        Bulgaria declares independence.
        Arthur Schnitzler's *Der Weg ins Freie* examines the dilemma of
        assimilated Jews in anti-Semitic Vienna.
        Arnold Schoenberg abandons formal tonality.
        William Howard Taft is elected 27th President of the USA.

1909   Blériot flies the English Channel.
        Henry Ford produces the first Model T automobile.
        Marinetti and the Futurists publish their manifesto in Milan.
        Diaghilev brings his Russian Ballet to Paris.
        Marcel Proust begins *A la recherche du temps perdu*.

1910   Stravinsky, *The Firebird*.
        10 Dec., New York Metropolitan Opera: Toscanini conducts the
        première of Puccini's *The Girl of the Golden West*.

1911   26 Jan., Dresden: Richard Strauss, *Der Rosenkavalier*.
        Amundsen reaches the South Pole.
        Theodore Roosevelt resumes his political career.
        Walter Gropius designs Fagus factory, Alfeld.
        First collection of poems by Franz Werfel, 21.
        Thomas Mann writes *Death in Venice*.

Samuel CHOTZINOFF
(1889–1964)

Russian-born pianist, critic and manager. In 1936 he persuaded
Toscanini to conduct the NBC Symphony Orchestra and was
himself appointed the network's director of music.

On the night of Mahler's American début, in *Tristan and
Isolde*, a large contingent of Katz's customers lined the
railing of the Metropolitan's top gallery. Mahler came out
hurriedly and climbed swiftly into the conductor's chair.
His profile was sharp and arresting. He looked and
behaved quite unlike Hertz.[1] His gestures were economi-
cal and precise. The prelude sounded different. It was
not as lush as with Hertz. There were fewer retards and
accelerations. There was a severity about this interpretation that, strangely enough, heightened both its sen-
suousness and its suspense. The curtain went up, the
invisible sailor sang his precarious measures, and suddenly the orchestra and Isolde plunged me into waves of
strong, beautiful, rugged sound. For the first time I
could remember, I heard distinctly the words Isolde was
singing. My eyes turned to Mahler to find a reason. He
was 'riding' the orchestra with the calculated sureness of
a master trainer, at one moment curbing it to a crafty
balance between it and the voice on the stage, at another
giving it its head as it raced alone. Perhaps at certain
climaxes he was too solicitous for the voice. Though I
heard the words and the voice, I was sensible of the reins
on the orchestra, and I did not feel the thrill and elation
of a great fusion of both, which I had expected. Nevertheless, it was an entirely new *Tristan* for me. Now at last
I knew how Wagner should sound. Hertz had misled us.
Wagner could be as clear, as understandable, as lucid as
Aida . . . At Mahler's début performance of *Tristan*

---

1. Alfred Hertz (1872–1942), principal conductor of German opera at the
Metropolitan Opera, 1902–15, thereafter conductor of The San Francisco Symphony
Orchestra.

Caricature by Caruso, posted by Mahler to his Iglau teacher, Fischer.

that season Olive Fremstad[2] sang Isolde for the first
time . . .

Indeed, Fremstad's Isolde was so vivid and, because of
Mahler's concern for the audibility and diction of singers,
so clear, that every detail of her characterization was
instantly apprehended and related to the drama as a
whole. Not a false move, gesture or nuance marred this
extraordinary impersonation . . .

Mahler became my idol. I attended all his performances. Hertz still conducted many of the Wagner operas,
but I stayed away. Under Mahler I heard for the first
time *Fidelio*, *Don Giovanni*, *The Marriage of Figaro*, *The
Bartered Bride* and *Pique Dame*. *Fidelio* overwhelmed
me. I had accepted the widely held opinion that Beethoven's genius was not suited to opera, and that *Fidelio*

2. Olive Fremstad (1871–1951), outstanding Wagnerian soprano of Swedish birth.

was a serious but unsuccessful attempt. Yet it moved me in a way that no other music drama had . . . Throughout the opera I was on the verge of tears, and often I felt helpless under the constant attacks of the music and the story on my emotions. I could hardly bear the moment when the tattered prisoners emerge from their cells like wraiths and greet the sun with hushed wonder and awe, as if for the first time; the digging of the grave in the hopeless dungeon; the colloquy there; Florestan's innocent 'Oh dank!' for a crust of bread; the shattering pianissimo trumpet call from afar; the spiritual summing up of the drama in the Third *Leonore* Overture played in the darkened opera house between the scenes of the last act; the final scene in the full blaze of the sun, so reminiscent of the finale of the Ninth Symphony and as liberating – these tore at my heart and made me weep for pity and joy.

The following year Mahler became the conductor of the Philharmonic Society. I attended all of his concerts religiously. In the concert hall Mahler generated the dramatic excitement of opera. As if to make up for the absence of singers and action, he drove his orchestra hard in building up dramatic tension. I remember his harsh but wildly dramatic interpretation of the first and last movements of Beethoven's Fifth. Though I hardly dared admit it to myself, the performance was technically ragged. But its tragic power more than compensated for its want of refinement. And I was much taken with the solitariness of the man; for Mahler appeared isolated and lonely. He was not a favourite with the public, and he conducted to ever-diminishing audiences. I bitterly resented his lack of popular appeal; yet it secretly pleased me, for it proved that I was one of the elect, one of that small number of connoisseurs who was not attracted by virtuosity, but sought out the nobler attributes of interpretative art. I heard stories of the dissatisfaction of the Philharmonic board with Mahler's programmes, which they held to be so austere as to repel the general public, and of their futile endeavours to make him play the popular repertoire, especially the symphonies of the always magnetic Tchaikovsky, and this made me hold the conductor in even greater esteem. Yet my heart ached for him when he came on to the stage of Carnegie Hall and faced half a house. One Sunday matinée I remember particularly. The audience was unusually small. Mahler played, among other things, two excerpts from Busoni's opera *Turandot*. The composer was present in a box. But when the pieces were over there was hardly any applause, not enough at any rate to give Mahler an excuse for pointing out Busoni. Mahler stood irresolute for a while in the disconcerting silence, and then walked sadly off the stage.

After concerts I would walk around the block to the stage door and slip into the green-room to gaze at Mahler adoringly, as he shook hands with admirers and conversed with friends. I was too timid to approach him. But it was enough for me to stand around and look at him. Very often his wife was in the room. I thought she was the most beautiful creature I had ever seen. It seemed somehow just that Mahler, whose face was plain, and who wore spectacles, should by his force and genius attract so lovely a woman. Sometimes she did not appear in the green-room, and Mahler's friends would presently depart, leaving him quite alone, except for me huddling against the wall near the door. He would put on his coat and hat, stare absent-mindedly at me and leave for the Plaza Hotel, where he lived. I would follow, walking right behind him. He seemed always intensely preoccupied as he walked, his body bent forward, his hands clasped behind his back. He looked like the picture of Beethoven walking in the suburbs of Vienna. At street crossings he would advance a few paces before he became aware of automobiles and carriages rushing past him, dangerously close. I longed to take his arm and lead him safely across, but I never could summon the courage. On these nightly shadowings I discovered, to my delight, that Mahler was superstitious, like me. He would suddenly pause without warning, swing his right foot behind him, and with the toe touch the heel of his left foot. It was not an easy thing to do. But he must have done it for a long time, for he managed the operation swiftly and skilfully. Once, when I was too close behind him, his sudden stop took me unawares, and I bumped against him, and in a scared voice I begged his pardon. He looked at me blankly and walked on. But half a block further he repeated the manoeuvre, unaware that I was still behind him, though at a safer distance. When he entered the hotel I ran across the street into Central Park and sat on a bench facing the Plaza, and watched for a light to go on in a window which would certainly indicate his room. I would wonder whether he would go to bed at once, or sit up and work on one of his long symphonies.

Day's at the Morn, New York (Harper & Row), 1964, pp. 122–7.

Fritz KREISLER
(1875–1962)

Austrian-born violinist and composer.

I crossed the ocean with Mahler and had occasion to spend hours and hours with him going over his remarkable scores and hearing them explained by the composer. I can truthfully say that in certain effects of orchestration Mahler has no superior, nor does any writer of music exist who outdoes him in sincerity and in the desire to express only what is in him without the slightest conscious use of sensational or extraneous means.

The whole world is bound to give him unreserved and enthusiastic recognition before long . . .

Interview in *Musical Courier* (New York), 9 November 1909.

Sergei RACHMANINOV
(1873–1943)

As the highlight of his first American tour, the Russian pianist and composer gave the première of a new piano concerto, his Third in D minor, in New York on 28 November 1909, Walter Damrosch conducting. He repeated it two days later, and again on 16 January 1910 at Carnegie Hall, with Mahler as the conductor.[1]

At that time Mahler was the only conductor whom I considered worthy to be classed with Nikisch. He touched my composer's heart straight away by devoting himself to my concerto until the accompaniment, which is rather complicated, had been practised to the point of perfection, although he had already gone through another long rehearsal. According to Mahler, every detail of the score was important – an attitude which is unfortunately rare amongst conductors.

The rehearsal began at ten o'clock. I was to join it at eleven, and arrived in good time. But we did not begin to work until twelve, when there was only half an hour left, during which I did my utmost to play through a composition which usually lasts thirty-six minutes. We played and played . . . Half an hour was long passed, but Mahler did not pay the slightest attention to this fact. I still remember an incident which is characteristic of him. Mahler was an unusually strict disciplinarian. This I consider an essential quality for a successful conductor. We had reached a difficult violin passage in the third movement which involves some rather awkward bowing. Suddenly Mahler, who had conducted this passage *a tempo*, tapped his desk:

'Stop! Don't pay any attention to the difficult bowing marked in your parts . . . Play the passage like this,' and

---

1. 'Judicious curtailment would help the concerto to a deservedly long term of life,' observed Henry Krehbiel in the *New York Daily Tribune*.

he indicated a different method of bowing. After he had made the first violins play the passage over alone three times, the man sitting next to the leader put down his violin:

'I can't play the passage with this kind of bowing.'

Mahler (quite unruffled): 'What kind of bowing would you like to use?'

'As it is marked in the score.'

Mahler turned towards the leader with an interrogative look, and when he found the latter was of the same opinion he tapped the desk again:

'Please play as is written!'

This incident was a definite rebuff for the conductor, especially as the excellent leader of the Moscow Philharmonic Orchestra had pointed out to me this disputed method of bowing as the only possible way of playing the passage. I was curious to see how Mahler would react to this little scene. He was most dignified. Soon afterwards he wanted the double-basses to tone down their playing of a passage. He interrupted the orchestra and turned to the players:

'I would beg the gentlemen to make more of a diminuendo in this passage,' then, addressing the argumentative neighbour of the leader with a hardly perceptible smile:

'I hope you don't object.'

Forty-five minutes later Mahler announced:

'Now we will repeat the first movement.'

My heart froze within me. I expected a dreadful row or at least a heated protest from the orchestra. That would certainly have happened in any other orchestra, but here I did not notice a single sign of displeasure. The musicians played the first movement with a keen or perhaps even closer application than the previous time. At last we had finished. I went up to the conductor's desk, and together we examined the score. The musicians in the back seats began quietly to pack up their instruments and to disappear. Mahler blew up:

'What is the meaning of this?'

The leader: 'It is after half-past one, Master.'

'That makes no difference! As long as I am sitting, no musician has a right to get up!'

Rachmaninov's Recollections, told to Oskar von Riesemann, trans. Dolly Rutherford, London (Allen & Unwin), 1934,[2] pp. 158–60.

Olga SAMAROFF-STOKOWSKI
(1882–1948)

Starting life in San Antonio, Texas, as Olga Hickenlooper, she launched her solo career as a pianist in 1905 and six years later married the young conductor Leopold Stokowski; their union lasted a dozen years. She appeared with Mahler in the Grieg Concerto in New Haven on 23 February 1910, and was due to perform the Beethoven G major Concerto with him two weeks later in New York but withdrew with appendicitis.

The years during which Mahler was conductor of the New York Philharmonic do not form a very creditable page in the musical history of the city. Doubtless he was irascible and difficult, but he was a great man, and New York never gave him his due.

He had not been long in America when the Charles Steinways invited me to meet him and his wife at dinner. I was so excited over the prospect that I arrived a full half-hour too soon. Mrs Steinway greeted me with the words:

'I am seating you beside Mahler at table tonight, but do not expect him to speak. He cannot be made to talk at dinner parties.'

. . . I responded to the challenge, but when Mahler arrived my courage sank. There was something so remote about him at first glance that I could scarcely imagine his taking part in any ordinary conversation. When we sat down to dinner he never even glanced at me. Oysters on

---

2. Rachmaninov dissociated himself from these memoirs after Riesemann's death, but this account is supported by members of the orchestra.

the half-shell received his undivided attention. He did not seem quite so much interested in the soup, however, so during that course I ventured a timid introductory remark. Without looking up he said '*Ja*,' and then relapsed into silence.

I racked my brains for a provocative subject of conversation, but nothing I could find in the animal, vegetable or mineral kingdom elicited any response . . .

Finally, I remembered that before dinner, when Mahler appeared to be utterly oblivious of everybody present, he had taken *The Brothers Karamazov* off the bookshelf and turned over the pages as though searching for a special passage. I decided that the Dostoevsky masterpiece was this drowning woman's last straw. But I also knew that if I did not succeed in establishing a controversial basis of conversation, I would merely get another '*Ja*.' So I boldly asked him if he did not consider *The Brothers Karamazov* a much overrated book.

'Not at all,' said Mahler fiercely, putting down his knife and fork. 'You ask that because you do not understand it.' He thereupon launched into a long discourse on the subject of Russian psychology and Dostoevsky's supreme understanding of it, while I settled down to the enjoyment of my dinner (and my triumph!), only throwing in an occasional provocative question when Mahler paused to eat a mouthful.

. . . Mahler followed me out into the drawing-room and spent the rest of the evening looking for passages in *The Brothers Karamazov* with which to illustrate his points and complete my conversion. I have often wondered what would have happened if he had known we were discussing one of my favourite books.

. . . Playing a concerto with the Philharmonic under Mahler's direction was a privilege I repeatedly[1] enjoyed. The first time I was soloist in one of his concerts on tour was in New Haven. By that time he and I had become good friends, and I had conceived a great liking for his lovely wife, who was one of the most beautiful women I have ever seen. She was not with him on this particular occasion and he felt the need of company at supper after the concert. I had lured my dear friend Miss Dehon[2] to accompany me to New Haven. It sometimes amused her to 'go on the road' when I played in cities near New York. When Mahler asked us both for supper she pleaded fatigue and went back to the hotel. Probably she had visions of shop talk in German, for Mahler spoke very little English, so she deserted me.

Being in a university town, Mahler expected to find gay cafés filled with students in multicoloured caps. When we had searched in vain for something more enticing than a corner drugstore, and our hotel had refused to serve what we wanted at such a late hour, his dismay was pathetic.

'*Was für eine Stadt!*', he murmured bitterly. 'What kind of students do they have here? No wine, no songs, and not yet midnight!'

1. Unless she means rehearsals, her memory has misled her.
2. Unidentified.

It did not seem to comfort him at all when I assured him that Yale students did sing at other times and had pretty much what they wanted to drink on occasions . . .

It later proved to be fortunate that Miss Dehon and Mahler made friends that night in New Haven over milk and crackers. When his health began to fail before his final departure from America he lay in bed for weeks at the Netherlands Hotel, weary from his struggles with people and conditions he could not understand, and hurt by the hostility of the New York Press. As his strength waned and he sensed that the end might not be far distant, he strove desperately to finish his last symphony, sitting up in bed with his manuscript before him and looking like the ghost of his former self.

He always disliked American hotel food and during these trying weeks it was almost impossible to induce him to take any nourishment. His wife, beside herself with anxiety, told me about this and I repeated it to Miss Dehon who had inquired about his condition. After that Miss Dehon constantly sent him soup and dainty dishes prepared by her own splendid Swedish cook.

An American Musician's Story, New York (Norton), 1939, pp. 158–62.

Henry Theophilus FINCK (1854–1926)

German-educated writer, music editor of the New York *Evening Post*, 1888–1924, Finck ranked with Krehbiel and Huneker as the senior music critics of Mahler's New York era. Finck considered Mahler 'a giant among conductors'. His sympathy and support, wrote Mahler in a parting letter,[1] were 'among the few experiences that made New York worth while for me.'

---

1. Finck, *My Adventures*, p. 424.

[An] unforgettable thrill Mahler gave me was in the funeral march of Beethoven's 'Eroica'. I had heard this given by a dozen of the world's leading conductors, yet none of them had made me realize as Mahler did to what sublime heights of overwhelming, tragic grief Beethoven's colossal genius could rise. Yes, Mahler was the greatest of Beethoven conductors, and acknowledged as such abroad. Yet in New York he was persistently abused, and, strange to say, most violently by Krehbiel,[2] the American high priest of Beethoven.

Krehbiel spent years of his life editing, completing and putting into shape for the printer Thayer's wonderful life of Beethoven[3] and he did it without hope of ever getting any pecuniary reward for all this toil. For this I take off my hat to him. Yet, simply because Mahler made changes here and there in Beethoven's antiquated orchestration – changes which Beethoven himself would have undoubtedly made had he lived a century later – Krehbiel jumped on him with both feet.

My Adventures in the Golden Age of Music. New York, 1926, p. 425.

Henry Edward KREHBIEL (1854–1923)

Mahler's bitterest American critic started out as a general reporter on the Cincinnati *Gazette*, joining the New York *Daily Tribune* in 1880 to cover music, yacht-races and, occasionally, politics. Devoted to Brahms, Dvořák, Wagner and above all Beethoven, he 'had a place in America . . . of commanding influence and authority. He had put the profession of musical criticism upon a higher plane of knowledge

---

2. See the following extract.
3. Alexander Wheelock Thayer, *The Life of Ludwig van Beethoven*, ed. Henry Edward Krehbiel, New York (The Beethoven Association), 1921; revised edition, Princeton University Press, 1967.

and competence . . .than it had ever occupied in America before his day.'[1]

Mahler, however, was anathema to Krehbiel. His *Tribune* obituary, an unabashed exercise in character assassination, is a classic example of Mahler's ability to arouse violent hostility in an otherwise honourable and well-informed follower of music.

> It was as a composer as well as a conductor that his friends, a well-defined party, or clique, sought to impress the world with a sense of his greatness . . . It was a singular paradox in Mahler's artistic nature that while his melodic ideas were of the folk-song order his treatment of them was of the most extravagant kind, harmonically and orchestrally. He attempted in argument to reconcile the extremes by insisting that folk-song was the vital spark of artistic music, but in his treatment of the simple melodies of his symphonies (some of them borrowed without acknowledgement) he was utterly inconsiderate of their essence, robbing them of their characteristics and elaborating them to death. He should have been an ingenuous musician – a musician, had he had that genius, like Dvořák. Instead, he tried to out-Strauss Strauss and out-Reger Reger, and not having the native force of either of them he failed. We cannot see how any of his music can long survive him. There is no place for it between the old and the new schools.
>
> There remains much to be said about his activity for two years in connection with the Philharmonic Society. A very large endeavour was made by the management, especially during the season which has just closed, to arouse popular interest in the concerts of the venerable society. It failed. Not only did the general public fail to respond to the loud appeal, but the subscription list grew steadily smaller. For this no one was to blame except Mr Mahler. It is a fatuous notion of foreigners that Americans know nothing about music in its highest forms. Only of late years have the European newspapers begun to inform their readers that the opera in New York has some significance. Had their writers on music been

---

1. Richard Aldrich, quoted in Max Graf, *Composer and Critic*, New York (W. W. Norton & Co.), 1946, pp. 315–16.

students they would have known that for nearly a century New Yorkers have listened to singers of the highest class – singers that the people of the musical centres of the European continent were never permitted to hear. Mr Mahler early learned a valuable lesson at the opera, but he never learned it in the concert room. He never discovered that there were Philharmonic subscribers who had inherited not only their seats from their parents and grandparents, but also their appreciation of good music. He never knew, or if he knew he was never willing to acknowledge, that the Philharmonic audience would be as quick to resent an outrage on the musical classics as a corruption of the Bible or Shakespeare. He did not know that he was doing it, or if he did he was willing wantonly to insult their intelligence and taste by such things as multiplying the voices in a Beethoven symphony (an additional kettledrum in the 'Pastoral', for instance), by cutting down the strings and doubling the flutes in Mozart's G minor, by fortifying the brass in Schubert's C major until the sweet Vienna singer of nearly a century ago seemed a modern Malay running amok, and – most monstrous of all his doings – starting the most poetical and introspective of all of Schumann's overtures – that to *Manfred* – with a cymbal clash like that which sets Mazeppa's horse on his wild gallop in Liszt's symphonic poem. And who can ever forget the treatment of the kettledrums which he demanded of his players? Wooden-headed sticks, not only in Beethoven's Ninth Symphony, but even in Weber's *Oberon* Overture! But the man is dead and the catalogue might as well be closed. Of the unhappy relations which existed between him and the Philharmonic Society's promoters it would seem to be a duty to speak: but the subject is unpleasant; those most interested know the facts; the injury that has been done cannot be undone, and when it becomes necessary the history may be unfolded in its entirety. It were best if it could be forgotten.

'Death of Mr Mahler; His Influence on Music in New York',
New York Daily Tribune, 21 May 1911. The complete text may
be found in DM2, pp. 407–13.

Krehbiel's tirade provoked Ossip Gabrilowitsch to risk his American career by launching a strident personal attack on the critic in a pamphlet distributed throughout the Press.

An Open Letter to the Music Critic of the 'New York Tribune'.
'Sir:
    'When, after a long agony of suffering, Gustav Mahler died in Vienna, you published an article in the *New York Tribune*, where, in language full of hatred, you insulted the memory of that great artist.

'The time has come when it seems necessary to disclose the true character of your attitude towards the Philharmonic Society's late conductor.

'When during Mahler's lifetime you took every occasion to attack and abuse him, you at least tried to make believe (and maybe some simple-hearted people did believe) that yours was bona fide criticism, not prompted by any personal animosity. But when Mahler died and on the very next day you piled up in the columns of your paper every possible calumny that could be invented against the man and the artist – then you showed your cards. No *critic* would be so eager to throw a pail of mud on a fresh grave. Only an enemy would do that . . . When Mahler died the newspapers and periodicals gave as much space and attention to him as is usually given only to kings. He was recognized as king in the realm of art. Of the glowing tributes paid to Mahler's memory after his death it would be easy to quote enough to fill volumes. The keynote of all these tributes is best formulated in one sentence, a sentence by which the leading European musical publication, *Die Musik*, opened its pages after Mahler's death:

'"The world has lost its greatest artist. Gustav Mahler is dead."

'It was this artist whom Mr Krehbiel denounced as "prejudicial to the good taste of the American people", and to whom he undertook to give lessons as to the interpretation of musical classics! . . .'

Clara Clemens, *My Husband, Gabrilowitsch*, New York
(Harper and Brothers), pp. 131–2.

Anon.

'America', he told us one day after his return, 'is altogether different from Europe. One feels there first and foremost a human being, with no one above you. If you want to, you can greet the President – "Good morning, Mister Roosevelt" – and if you don't want to, you don't.'

'All very well,' we replied, 'but is there a musical culture over there?'

'Culture, no, not that. But what do you want, one can't demand everything. One goes over there a couple of months each year to make money, then comes back to Europe, to music.'

Unsigned article in the Frankfurter Zeitung,
following Paul Bekker's obituary, 19 May 1911.

Marianna TRENKER[1]

In the summer of 1907, his family, health and future crumbling around him, Mahler fled to Toblach leaving Alma to dispose of the Maiernigg house, blighted by their daughter's death and his own illness. He had pursued inspiration in the south Tyrol intermittently since 1897; now he came in search of consolation. He found both while reading in Toblach Hans Bethge's *Die chinesische Flöte*, a cycle of Chinese poems given him by a friend, that supplied the text for *Das Lied von der Erde*.

The following year, Alma booked summer lodgings at an isolated inn between the villages of Toblach and Altschluderbach, on the railway network from Vienna and Munich. At some distance from the house, there was a simple hut in the woods where Mahler had peace to work. It was the last of his summer residences, source of *Das Lied*, the ninth and tenth symphonies, and scene of the great crisis in his marriage.

1. Dates unknown.

Carl Moll's sketch of Mahler's composing hut near Toblach.

Mahler and his household lived on the upper floor of the rambling fifteenth-century inn. The Trenker family, who still own the property, occupied the ground floor and observed his activities with frank amazement. Their adopted daughter, Marianna, wrote a brief reminiscence in 1938.

Three pianos would arrive each year in springtime and had to be installed in the little summer-house in the spruce woods five minutes from the house.[2] There he spent the greater part of the day and was to be disturbed by no one, not even his wife. At the crack of dawn his breakfast had to be laid out: tea, coffee, butter, honey, eggs, rolls, fruit and poultry.

Director Mahler would go to work at 6 a.m. A full-sized stove furnished the little house; he would light it himself and prepare his meal on it. The little house had

2. Probably a mislocution. The hut was just large enough for a divan, desk and chair and one upright piano. The others must have been installed in Mahler's living-room in the big house.

to be surrounded by a fence 1.5 metres high for one kilometre around. Once, two itinerant workers climbed over the fence and pestered the famous composer for alms. After that, the fence had to be provided with barbed wire.

Once, a vulture chased a raven that flew, seeking refuge, into Mahler's work-room. Highly agitated, the Director went to old Trenker, owner of Altschluderbach, and complained bitterly about the impudent intruder. Herr Trenker laughed in his face, and Gustav Mahler had to laugh with him.[3]

Another time, it was the house cockerel that disturbed him, waking him too early. 'What does one have to do to teach the cock not to crow in the morning?' demanded the Director. 'Ah well,' said Herr Trenker, 'you simply wring its neck.' But Gustav Mahler did not want to hear of that.

In his contacts with people, he was warm-hearted and unassumingly friendly. He often told us how as a child of a poor, large family he would have only a piece of bread to live on all day long in order to pay for his studies. Impoverished itinerant workers would gather round him on the street [at Toblach] and he would give them money to clothe and take care of themselves so it would be easier for them to find work.[4]

'Der Aufenthalt Gustav Mahlers in Altschluderbach' (16 August 1938), in Bruno Walter's legacy, Library of the Performing Arts, Lincoln Center, New York. Quoted in *Gustav Mahler in Toblach*, Vienna (Internationale Gustav Mahler Gesellschaft) and Dobbiaco (Gustav Mahler Komitee), 1980, pp. 7–8.

---

3. 'All at once "something terribly dark" came rushing in by the window and, when he jumped up in horror, he saw that he was in the presence of an eagle which filled the little room with its violence. The fearsome meeting was quickly over and the eagle disappeared as stormily as it had come. When Mahler sat down, exhausted by his fright, a crow came fluttering from under the sofa and flew out.' (Walter GM, p. 62.) Roller, who was also told the story by Mahler, has the more credible detail of a hawk chasing a jackdaw. See p. 164.
4. His local reputation for generosity explains the two intruders above.

Ernst DECSEY
(1871–1941)

The urge that drove Natalie Bauer-Lechner to preserve Mahler's every utterance for posterity was shared by Decsey,[1] music critic of the Graz *Tagespost* and from 1908 its editor. Unlike Natalie, he did not commit Mahler's comments immediately to paper but struggled to resurrect them in two long articles produced at the time of Mahler's death.

A skilled writer – he published biographies of Wolf, Bruckner, Lehár, Strauss and Debussy and created librettos for Salmhofer and Korngold – he made no attempt to edit his Mahler memoir professionally or present it in chronological sequence. It was, he said, raw material that could not be brought to life because the personality that infused it was dead. It remains, none the less, one of the most candid and least known portraits of Mahler, never apparently reprinted or translated since its appearance in the fortnightly *Die Musik* in June and August 1911.

---

1. Pronounced Déjai.

Born in Hamburg, Decsey graduated as a lawyer in Vienna in 1894 but took parallel music courses at the conservatory with Bruckner and Robert Fuchs. He had heard of Mahler before moving to Graz in 1899 as a music critic[2] and did not apparently meet him until June 1905, when Mahler conducted various of his Lieder in the Styrian town. He later visited Mahler at both his southern summer residences, and begins his memoir at Toblach in June 1909.

Decsey returned to Vienna as a critic in 1920 but was sacked in 1938 when the Nazis seized power.

'*Vita fugax*'[3] . . . I can still hear the deep, metallic voice pronouncing these words as the sun went down over the snow-fields of Toblach, casting on them its reddish glow. It was one of his favourite sayings and will remain in my memory for every, for when he uttered it . . . *vita fugax* . . . there was a hint of his desperation at not being able to check the headlong rush of this fleeting life, at not being able to fill every hour of his existence with the riches of his imperial mind, at not being able to turn every moment into one of action. He was a man who was consumed by himself. A fire glowed constantly within him; one never spent an hour with Gustav Mahler in which it did not burst forth, in which one did not gain something from him. This way he had of throwing himself into things, which gave his life fulfilment even if his work remained unfinished, was not a matter of impulse, it was his fundamental nature. That is why every moment spent with him was profitable. I have set down some of my experiences without attempting to draw conclusions or force them into a pattern. A degree of modesty prevents me from giving any more than raw material; but I am also forced to say that even properly edited it will remain raw material because the finest thing within it, the personal musicality, is gone for ever and no art can conjure it back into life.

June in Toblach was rainy. The clouds rolled down from the mountains into the Puster Valley. Even so, he

---

2. His opposite number on the other Graz daily was Wilhelm Kienzl, who had known Mahler from Budapest, see p. 60.
3. This fleeting life.

went out walking every afternoon. One evening he said: 'I get such pleasure from the world! How beautiful the world is! How can any fool say: I am indifferent to it all. Anyone who says that is a clod. Man is a marvellous machine, of course, but anyone who says that is a heap of dirt.'

That evening he stood at the veranda window gazing out over a footpath that shone palely in the twilight, winding its way up through the fields to Old Toblach. 'What a story that path has to tell!' he said and smiled as he looked at it, like someone listening to a folk-song. 'To be happy is a gift,' he resumed some time later. A musician from Berlin[4] whom he greatly admired was staying with him. This musician told us about a concert where they had booed Mendelssohn but he had just sat still: 'God,' he said, 'they can abuse Mendelssohn, it doesn't concern me.' 'But of course it concerns you,' Mahler burst out angrily. 'That's the trouble with Europe, that everyone says: it doesn't concern me. The whole world concerns me . . . ' And he really laid into the musician, despite the man having done him great service. The more complacently the visitor reacted to the attack, the more furious Mahler became. He wound up with violent words: 'And only an individual who shares our compassion is truly one of us!'

Another day he explained the basis for his belief in God. He urgently recommended us to read an essay by the Russian physicist Choolson[5] entitled 'Hegel, Haeckel and Kossuth' in which Haeckel's materialism is examined. 'When you see a complicated machine, a motor car, you assume, don't you, that there is no means of propulsion involved, because you can't see it? Well, don't you think there exists a concealed driving force within man?'

A great many books were piled high in his living-room. On one table were all the volumes of Brehm's encyclo-

---

4. Oskar Fried, according to de La Grange (HLG3, pp. 527–8). The present clash may have contributed to Mahler's growing disaffection with Fried.
5. Oreste Danilovich Choolson (1852–1934); see HLG3, p. 528.

paedia of animals, but most of what I saw were philosophical writings. Of an evening, he would often stretch
out and have someone read aloud to him. I chose a few
passages from the newly published diaries of Hermann
Bahr, and he was pleased to find that Bahr's thinking was
similar to his own, although he said he knew him only in
passing. When I told Mahler that Bahr intended to use
him, Mahler, as one of the characters in one of his
forthcoming novels he became worried. 'For heaven's
sake,' he said, 'people will think it's another conspiracy.'[6]

But mostly he asked me to read from Goethe: *Faust*,
Part II. It enabled him to savour passages he already
knew by heart. One evening when I had been reading to
him for over an hour, I had a curious experience
concerning his countenance. Mahler was stretched out on
the broad divan away from the direct light; his eyes were
closed and he seemed to be lost in thought. As I carried
on reading the verses and cradling him in Goethe, a
change seemed to come over his lowering, dark satanic
features. I could scarcely believe it but I have to say he
looked just like Goethe. His face was ennobled by
contemplation, his nose became more pronounced. I
gazed at him for a long time and the impression was
confirmed: like Goethe. When I recounted this later to
Hans Rudolf Bartsch, he said: 'Yes, of course, it's the
striking family resemblance between all highly gifted
people that Schopenhauer mentions.'

After one such evening of Goethe, Mahler also spoke
about a personal experience when he had just begun
composing the Eighth – he was working on the score in a
little pavilion near the house in Altschluderbach.[7] He
had got hold of the text of the old hymn *Veni creator
spiritus* from somewhere and was setting it to music
when half-way through the work he noticed that the
music was overflowing the text, like water spilling over a
full basin. In other words, the structural concept of the

6. Mahler took pains to avoid Bahr, who was summering nearby with his new wife,
Anna von Mildenburg.
7. The Eighth was composed at Maiernigg in 1906.

music was too big for the length of the verses. He
lamented his problem to a friend, a philologist,[8] who
pointed out to him that this was perfectly natural. The
version he was using was incomplete: about a verse and a
half were missing. So Mahler rapidly arranged for Luze,[9]
the conductor of the Court Orchestra in Vienna, to
obtain the complete text for him. And when the hymn
arrived he found to his absolute astonishment that the
words were exactly the right length to cover the music –
that his sense of form had made him compose too much
but now all the new words fitted effortlessly.[10]

Another time, he talked about the evolution of music.
Someone had remarked that Delius[11] was an artist who
showed little respect for anything. He considered Bach,
for example, outmoded. 'He's quite right,' Mahler
retorted, 'he is outmoded, but that doesn't mean he isn't
great. Every age has its own idiom and a later age cannot
naïvely appreciate the earlier one. It has to learn to
appreciate it intellectually – but then it often makes the
mistake of thinking that the Bach it appreciates is naïve! I
should like to perform the two hundred cantatas, but the
rest . . .? His arias are too long, and in general he lacks
contrast, the way Haydn introduces it. Haydn invents
two themes, so does Beethoven – no, with Beethoven it's
two different worlds! Music is still very young. With
Bach, polyphony reached its high point, then suddenly
the thread broke. Folk-music forced its way in, Haydn
and Beethoven opened the door; but looked at *cum grano
salis*,[12] they were not as great scientists as Bach. The
ideal for the future would be composers who are as

8. Fritz Löhr. For Mahler's 'very urgent' request, see GMB, pp. 291–2.
9. Karl Luze, former member, then conductor, of the opera chorus.
10. Alma relates: 'He composed and wrote down the whole opening chorus to
half-forgotten words. But words and music did not fit – the music had overlapped the
text. In a fever of excitement he telegraphed to Vienna and had the whole of the
ancient Latin hymn telegraphed back. The complete text fitted the music exactly'
(AMM, p. 102). Donald Mitchell (DM3 pp. 524, 597) suggests that the exactness of
the matching need not be taken too literally.
11. Frederick Delius (1862–1934), British composer resident in France. Mahler did
not conduct any of his music.
12. With a grain of salt.

excellent in the science of Bach's polyphony as they are singers of folk-music.'

His ideas were always fascinating, even if they were very one-sided. Time and again he would enthuse over Schumann's Symphony in E flat major,[13] saying it was Schumann's greatest work. It needed re-orchestration, sensitively, with respect for the original. In such matters, it was the conductor in him that came to the fore.

On another occasion he said that *Parsifal* was not a work by Wagner but one by a Wagnerite. He could not grasp Reger and similarly he declared – at least at the time – that he was incapable of 'reading' the score of a quartet by Schoenberg,[14] although he was indignant later on when he learned that they had catcalled Schoenberg in Vienna. – There was an up-and-coming writer on music[15] who was making some extremely useful efforts to reform the concert scene but Mahler would have nothing to do with him. He stamped his left foot and suddenly burst out: 'Let's have none of this nonsense about lowering the lights in concert halls! It's up to us to make music so well that people are blind and deaf to the world. Well, blind, anyway!' he added with just a touch of a smile. – One day he declared Peter Rosegger to be the most important contemporary poet. 'He's the greatest,' he said. 'With all the others it's more or less just a case of birth pangs . . . *cum grano salis*,' he said again, quickly pacifying his conscience, '*cum grano salis*.'

In Tobelbad (where he was staying a year later) he was preoccupied with Richard Strauss. He came down from the Strauss Festival in Munich and declared almost ecstatically: '*Don Quixote* is a masterpiece. Of course, the descriptive element is secondary. The whole thing is first and foremost a tone poem, but done with such art – everything is converted into sound, there's no longer any solid matter!'

---

13. The Third Symphony, op. 97, the 'Rhenish'.
14. Schoenberg's Second String Quartet, op. 10, completed July 1908, was performed amid audience uproar on 21 December 1908.
15. Paul Marsop of Munich.

At an orchestral rehearsal in Graz[16] he felt the strings
were not producing an even sound when they had to hold
a long, loud note in the Adagio of his Third Symphony.
He tapped for them to stop, then explained to the
players: 'The reason is that you're playing the violin
according to the book. Music should never be made
according to the book! With long-drawn-out forte notes,
you can happily move the bow up and down as often as
you like: the more times it passes over the strings the
better. I know the schools teach you: into the note, out of
the note. But the bow has no power in its tip. The right
thing is to do it according to life and experience, not to do
what the professors say!'

At the same rehearsal he was not very happy initially
with the ladies' choir, so he told them in his usual
forceful way to 'follow the example of children! Children
always pronounce things clearly because they really
emphasize the words, especially the consonants. Singers
naturally tend to concentrate on the sound: they are more
concerned with singing well than in conveying the
meaning; but a child wants to communicate and hasn't
yet learned to be coquettish with its voice.' After this
very practical explanation – and possibly the most effective thing about it was the way he said it: as usual he used
sound for effect, like a true musician – he got just what he
wanted from the ladies' choir: they sounded fine and,
quite unusually for a bevy of 'trilling songbirds', you
could really understand them.

He spoke curiously about *Das klagende Lied*. Originally it had been intended as a fairy-tale for the stage and
he wanted to publish it as a study piece. So he submitted
it to the official music society, the Allgemeiner Deutscher
Musikverein, but they turned it down. 'I don't hold it
against those gentlemen,' he said. 'After all, if somebody
nowadays was too advanced for me, heaven knows how I
would react!' But he said the piece, begun in 1878, has a
downright Straussian pòlyphony. In Hamburg he looked
at it again with a conductor's eye, and shortened and

16. December 1906. The symphony was performed on the 3rd and 23rd.

simplified it into its present form. If he had not gone into the theatre, it might have become a stage work, but as a theatre man he inclined more and more towards symphonic composition.

Once he also spoke fondly of his years with the Court Opera. He would have liked to put on a new complete *Ring*, followed by *Tannhäuser* and the *Meistersinger*; and then, something he had always wanted, to stage Cornelius's *Barbier von Bagdad* the way it should be done, as a fairy story. His ideas for the second act would have made the work completely accessible. (One of the main things was that he would have had Abul Hassan singing in full view of the roof of a house while Nureddin waited beside Margiana.) 'After these productions, to leave of my own accord – that's what I should have wished. And in general – I should have liked to found in Vienna a small court theatre for Mozart and the operettas to relieve the pressure on the big one. It would only have cost a million. Do you think I could have put together the million in Vienna?'

Perhaps I might explain how I came to enjoy this friendly relationship with Mahler, particularly because it says something about Mahler. In an essay about his Third Symphony I had mentioned that in order to understand the trumpet passage in the C minor section one had to think of Lenau's poem: 'Gentle was that night in May / Silver cloudlets sailing'. Exactly as the lonely notes reverberated through the woods in the poem, so they should sound here. This amazed Mahler. He asked me to come and see him. 'That's precisely what I had in mind,' he said. 'I was thinking of the same poem, the same mood – how did you know?' From that moment on, I was in his confidence, even though I was a *socius malorum*.[17] And when I happened to knock at the door of his house in Toblach late one night just to say good evening, he would not let me leave. He served the food himself at table – he was quite alone – tipped over the water glasses while he was offering the gravy, made the

---

17. An ally of the evil ones – presumably because Decsey was a professional critic.

bed – until suddenly he stopped and reminded himself:
'Oh, perhaps I had better ask the chambermaid . . .'
He said this very pianissimo and grinning like a little boy,
but, genuinely worried, he added: 'I had better be sure to
ask her. It's not good to get on the wrong side of her.'
The king, afraid of the butler.

At the kind invitation of the publisher,[18] I am continuing
my notes, which give a 'picture' of Gustav Mahler
equivalent only to what can be expected of an amateur
photograph. The hours I spent with Mahler were richer
than those I have spent with any other artist because he
was a generous giver. He never uttered empty fifths but
was always productive, even among friends. You never
came away from him without being stimulated in some
marvellous, dynamic way. And afterwards, you often had
Eckermann-type[19] impulses. This relationship, which
gave me such pleasure, began with a quarrel, quite a
serious quarrel, about Hugo Wolf: or more precisely,
Mahler quarrelled with himself about Wolf while I more
or less stood by as a spectator.

    Mahler had come to the Speech and Music Festival at
Graz.[20] The public were fascinated by him but a bit
unsure and a bit nervous of him as if he were the
hell-born Satan of music. The orchestra players joked
about him before rehearsal but when he stepped on to the
rostrum there was deathly silence; it was the teacher
standing before the class . . . He was rehearsing his
orchestral song 'I am Lost to the World,[21] in the
Stefaniensaal and I could not help noticing his totally
absorbed features. He had his eyes closed and looked as if
he was far away, lost, completely submerged in a musical
world of his own . . . *aquis submersus* . . . or like
Goethe's 'thus one is smelted on one's own coals . . .' I

18. The start of the second instalment of Decsey's memoir in *Die Musik*.
19. Johann Peter Eckermann (1792–1854) published a verbatim record of his
conversations with Goethe (English publication 1850 et. seq.).
20. June 1905.
21. 'Ich bin der Welt abhanden gekommen', from the Rückert Lieder, first sung in
Vienna, 29 January 1905.

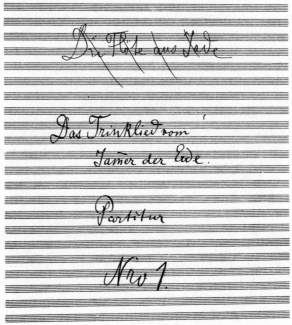

First page of *Das Lied von der Erde*, showing Mahler's original title.

had imagined him to be the toughest of nuts, in which case why did he seem now to be completely engrossed in and overcome by the sadness of his own song? With my friend Julius von Weis-Ostborn,[22] whom he completely won over on this occasion, I went to see him at Maierling[23] with my heart full of doubts and determined to find out his true nature before I was prepared to cry 'Galilean, thou hast conquered!'

The conversation turned at once to Hugo Wolf and Mahler grew distinctly strident, to such an extent that I thought to myself 'Watch out, the sparks are about to fly! he's obsessed with Wolf!' He spoke dismissively of 'Weyla's Song',[24] saying it was 'not a song in the artistic

22. (1862–1927) conductor at Graz.
23. A Freudian slip. Mayerling was where Crown Prince Rudolph shot himself and his young mistress on 30 January 1889. Mahler's summer residence besides the Wörthersee was at Maiernigg.
24. 'Gesang Weylas', 1888.

sense. Those strummed fourths with the melody super-
imposed on them, where's the song in that?' It was
apparent that he could sense greatness but did not want
to admit it: the natural egotism of genius was in conflict
with his own intelligence. Before getting up and leaving,
I felt I had to draw his attention to the impressionist
qualities, the Böcklin-style conceit in the simple
rhythmical construction of the piece. Then the sparks
really hit the roof. He simply would not let me speak.
'Oh, come on,' he said, 'anyone can produce a tone
poem! But what I expect of a song is not just a bit of a
trill when there is a bird in it and a bit of rumbling about
in the bass when a wind comes along – I expect a theme,
the development of the theme, some working out of it,
the real use of the voice, not de-cla-ma-tion!' And he
underlined every syllable by striking his open palm with
his fist. I had the feeling it wouldn't be long before he
exploded. His nature, I thought, is like nitro-glycerine;
you only have to wave a peacock's tail feather at it and it
blows sky high. The atmosphere grew oppressive. He sat
there in pained silence while the room sparkled with
blinding sunlight reflected off the Wörthersee. But I was
pleased that he had uninhibitedly said what he felt and
not shown any deference to his visitor, when even the
greatest people are inclined to wag their tail to the
smallest of critics. So I stayed put. I liked this man, so
naïvely at war with himself and so wrong-headed with it.
For it was the same with Wolf as with his own music:
some songs had a thematic treatment and some did not –
but Mahler seemed not to know this, or not to want to
know. In a word, Wolf was a sore point with
him . . . but after this outburst we never talked about
him, it was like a tacit understanding and he had the tact
to maintain this *modus vivendi*.

The conversation gradually relaxed and turned to the
subject of artistic technique. In due course Mahler said:
'A man who seeks to develop will never come to the end
of the road . . . and this saying of Goethe's applies to no
one better than to Goethe himself. Goethe never ceased
his apprenticeship, he went on developing right to the

end. That's an open secret.' He smiled wryly and one or two shadows crossed his face: 'If you take *Faust*,' he said, 'Goethe put a lifetime's work into it but the average person, at least German opera-goers, only know it from Gounod's *Margarethe*[25] . . . this is the form they are familiar with. And the most dangerous thing about *Margarethe* is – that it's so well done!' In those days he did not like to speak about his own work. 'I am Lost to the World', that lonesome creation of his, was, so he said, literally composed in deepest isolation 'six years ago' up there in the pine forests of Meierling.[26] When I made particular reference to one or two finer points of harmony and commented that at the end of 'The Song of the Night Watch'[27] there was a remarkable evolution of the dominant chords that produced an ever-rising tension, he refused to accept the point. 'Dominant chords!' he said. 'Oh, go on! Just accept things with the simplicity with which they're intended.' Another time, much later, Julius von Weis-Ostborn referred to the leap of a seventh *(Septensprung)* at 'Tu *sept*iformis munere' in the Eighth Symphony, and the return to the major key, D major, where it says: 'He returns . . .'. But Mahler was truly not aware of these things and laughed at the well-meaning enthusiasm of friendship. He confessed incidentally that he had no sense for what music experts refer to as 'banal'. 'What is "banal"?' he demanded, not really looking for an answer. 'You should just go ahead and write what comes to you!' There was a lot of talk about all his success in Graz and the big impression made by the *Kindertoten-lieder*. 'I've reached the ripe old age of forty-five,' he said, 'before enjoying my first success. And now certain Vienna papers find that it is too early, that all this public acclaim makes one think there is something funny about anyone who has that kind of success. But that's hogwash . . . And woe betide if a single individual should hiss during a concert! Then they immediately say the

25. As the Faust opera was known to German-speaking audiences.
26. Maiernigg.
27. From the *Wunderhorn* Lieder.

work was hissed off the stage. But I know what goes on. I have a good many friends who are too genteel to clap: but my enemies, they're not quite so genteel, they're quite prepared to hiss!'

Mahler suffered from an incurable disease. It was called idealism. He related an 'episode' in the long history of his illness that took place in the first year of his appointment in Vienna and shows incidentally how much energy it cost him to put the house in order. He was doing the first run-through of *Walküre* with the orchestra of the Court Opera and found that a brass soloist (I forget which) was rushing his notes in the third act and not putting any expression into them. He rehearsed the passage with this man, taking him through it individually and persevering until he was satisfied. The night of the performance, Mahler was looking forward particularly to the third act. – Along came the passage they had been rehearsing, he gave the entry sign but no sound was heard – 'their stillness answering his cry . . .' The brass player's chair was empty. Mahler was in such a state of trembling exasperation that he could scarcely wait for the end to come. No sooner was the act over then he rushed up to the stage and demanded: 'Where is that b—?' 'Well, Herr Direktor,' they just shrugged helplessly, 'there's really nothing to be done. The man lives in Baden [outside Vienna] and the last train departs at 9.45, so he has the right to leave at 9.30. He has had that for a long time.' Mahler was almost speechless. He dispatched an express telegram to Baden saying: 'YOU WILL SEE ME TOMORROW MORNING SEVEN O'CLOCK AT THE OPERA'. So at 7 a.m. along came the brass player as required, though at first he tried to brazen it out. That is to say, he stuck out his chest and insisted on his due. But he didn't know the new Director. 'Either you leave your home in Baden,' thundered Mahler, 'or you leave the Court Opera' – and that settled the matter. The brass player, who had allowed himself to be rehearsed all to no purpose, was reduced to a whisper and promised to give up his place in Baden, I believe with some sort of financial compensation. 'But the worst part about this interview,' said

Mahler, still looking drawn at the recollection and smiling ruefully, 'was that I had to get up at 6 a.m. too!'[28]

He also told many stories about Johannes Brahms, whom he particularly admired, including the following anecdote. Mahler was in Hallstadt once and went by bike to Ischl to visit Brahms. (I cannot guarantee these place-names.)[29] Brahms was having one of his bad days and railed against modern composers. 'What do they think they're doing?' he said. 'There's no such thing as a new invention, music has come to a dead end. It can't be developed any further!' Mahler listened in silence. They went out for a walk and when they were crossing a bridge Mahler stopped suddenly, pointed excitedly at the water and called out: 'Look, Herr Doktor! Look at that . . .' 'What is it?' asked Brahms. 'Down there, down there!' shouted Mahler, leaning over the parapet. 'Can't you see, there goes the last wave . . .!' And Brahms was forced to concede a smile as he gazed after the last new wave.[30]

There is another anecdote that is appropriate here. A young musician who wanted a job at the Court Opera was once recommended to Mahler. Someone remarked that he was only a beginner but that he was terribly modest. 'Ah, but does he have anything to be modest about?' responded Mahler, who thought that modesty was only for people with real talent.

I went away from Mahler that first time with a humbling thought: one should never make public pronouncements about an artist before coming to terms with his personality. The world generally knows a famous person not in portrait form but as a rough cartoon; if it is properly acquainted with only two aspects of his make-up, it tends to draw conclusions from those that are prejudicial about his character rather than flattering.

28. Natalie relates the same incident (NBL, pp. 99–100), differing in certain details. In her account, the offending player was a timpanist living at Brünn. When summoned to Mahler early next morning, he explained that he could not live in Vienna with his family on 63 guilders a month. Mahler's reaction was to seek a pay rise for the orchestra. See p. 141.
29. Mahler was staying at Steinbach am Attersee, some 30 km. from Ischl.
30. Alma relates the same incident (AMM, p. 111).

There is an old Jesuit saying: *Quilibet habetur malus,
donec probatur bonus*![31] Does this not inadvertently
reveal something about the general character of ourselves, the world at large? What I mean to say is that
having seen how naïve Mahler was in his everyday life, I
accepted the genuineness of his youthful songs, his
excursions with the French horn in the C minor section
of his Third Symphony and his folk-song 'Galiläer, du
hast gesiegt!' (Galilean, thou hast conquered!)

A few years before I was at the Café Parsifal, haunt of
Viennese musicians, opera-goers and lovers of art and
music; Mahler was the subject of conversation. The talk
was of dreadful sackings and terrible scenes with singers.
The whole world was up in arms about the Court Opera.
One critic had coined the phrase 'Mahler the Meyerbeer
of modern music' and the others copied it: 'Mahler the
Meyerbeer of modern music . . . overrefinement of
expression . . .', doom and gloom. The 'disintegrating'
opera programme disintegrated even more. The 'empty'
opera house grew more and more empty: in short, they
lambasted Mahler and the more his faults were spoken
of, the more they grew. In fact, the strangest thing was
that you could discuss them for hours and they still
remained fascinating. People were no longer referring to
'Mahler' but simply to 'that fellow' . . . when all of a
sudden someone shouted: 'There he is!' Everyone got up
and rushed to the window. They stood there pressed up
against each other, peering out. On the other side of the
Walfischgasse, Mahler was walking along with his wife.
He was swinging his hat back and forth in his right hand
and stamping down with his left foot from time to time as
if he was trying to pacify the ground. He laughed, partly
devil-may-care and partly with the ease and innocence of
a child, and then fenced again with his hat. Everyone
stared at this bare-headed little man and then, of an
instant, all awoke from their staring and looked at each
other. They smiled at one another, perhaps trying to
diminish the fact that this 'bungler', this 'so-and-so'

31. Anyone may be considered evil until proven good.

whom they had just been tearing to pieces over their coffee, was able to make such an impression and was possibly greater even than themselves. All took back a piece of his personality to their café tables and were silent or talked about other people while they visibly chewed it over. Mahler . . . that is the way it always was. Behind his back, raised fists. But when his eye was on them, only a tingling of the flesh. Like the loudmouths in Auerbach's cellar,[32] holding their heads in bewilderment at the thought that they had been holding the devil. This time, though, Mephisto had merely walked past the café window.

It was also about this time that Mahler astonished a critic by telling him: '*Rienzi* is Wagner's greatest opera, truly the greatest . . .' But it was not difficult to work out why he said this: Mahler had begun to study the score because he was planning to revive it at the Court Opera, so he immersed himself in *Rienzi* and being so involved with it, thought it the greatest of all.

At a performance of *Tristan and Isolde* at the Vienna Court Opera in December 1906, I observed the way Mahler conducted. I was sitting in the second row of the stalls, behind and a little to the side of him, and could follow his every move. Roller had recently created new sets and costumes for the work and I must say that I have never seen such a 'dramatic' setting; the way it looked said literally what the work was about. The curtain rose to reveal a ship placed diagonally across the stage and rising two storeys high. Below, the quarters of Isolde, a noblewoman's quarters with the green sea sparkling through the casements. Above, the deck space, separated from the living-quarters by yellow curtains, the colour of which suffused the whole set. At the back of the set, high up at the wheel – Tristan. Isolde could see him but not hear him (at least, that was the impression given); on the other hand, she could hear Kurwenal plainly because when he was preparing to sing his ridiculing song, he

32. In *Faust*.

moved forward and sang it over the head of Isolde, who was down in the body of the vessel. The delicate lighting changes in Act II were more than just attractive, they actually made sense. Bathed in white light, the tower of the castle stood out against the deep violet of a moonlit night, while in the background the light shaded away into a fathomless darkness relieved only by the glimmer of an occasional star. The suggestion was of a vast tract of heath and moorland where even the sounds of Mark's horn were lost. The light was used as a living entity that contributed to the plot because it altered according to the action, unobtrusive in the way it moved hither and thither or subtly faded away. And when Mark returned to find Isolde in Tristan's arms, it was not the usual idiotic stage dawn that filled the sky but an excruciating greyness that made you shiver at the very sight of it. Act III was perhaps a little over-ambitious: the tree under which Tristan suffers in torment was set on an artificial knoll, built about a metre high, and dominated the scene, whereas the sea, which ought to establish the mood of this act, was very little in evidence. In fact, the newly designed production was sharply attacked on this very point, but the thing was an experiment and even the misses of a creative artist who is searching for something new are more to be prized than the safe shots of a mediocrity who sticks to the same old ways.

Mahler explained to me later that this new Tristan had been conceived over cups of black coffee. He had made the acquaintance of Roller at a dinner and, though he was a man of few words, had got into a conversation with him about the works of Wagner. Roller had let it be known that he had been working on designs for some time and at the end of the meal he immediately did a rough drawing of a new set of décor for Tristan. Shortly afterwards, he said, Roller had produced a model and Mahler was captivated by the beauty of it all and the ideas behind it. Although expensive and a huge risk, the decision was taken to order the sets and costumes. I told Siegfried Wagner about the arrangements when he visited Graz, but I was on slippery ground. He shook his head, indicating disapproval. 'My father mounted the production of *Tristan* himself in Munich,' he said, 'so I'm afraid that's it and that's how it will have to stay.' He may have been right from a sentimental point of view, but in 1865 Richard Wagner would not have had the technical facilities to hand that were available forty years later. He managed with what he had, and he did not have a man like Roller whom I would characterize as the living expression of a new age in the theatre, an age that is attuned to musical drama.

But I must speak about Mahler. I had never heard such a thoughtful and sensitive rendering, such freedom combined with textual fidelity. It realized Wagner's intentions by taking the bare notes of the score and suffusing them with the spirit of the work. Just as the light altered to suit the scene, so did the coloration of the music. If I may dare to use the word 'alteration' – for I had the distinct impression that he did it – Mahler altered the orchestration of the work during the course of conducting. He trimmed the balance of the orchestra and he improvised, i.e. sometimes he would motion two desks in the first violins to be still so as to let the second violins be heard better, then he would bring the first violins back up. He would halve the violas and then use their richness of tone to greater effect: in a word, this was musical direction by the nerve-ends. The sensitivity of his modern tastes would not allow him to miss nuances, while an overseeing intelligence always kept an eye on the main directional line. With Hans Richter and his broad brushstrokes, you had the feeling that the main line was composed of almost unbroken swathes whereas with Mahler it was a series of dots. His body was racked with movement and in the semi-darkness he looked like some kind of fairy-tale goblin engaged in a flurry of hocus-pocus. In the harsh spotlight that lit up the rostrum his face was fascinatingly ugly and had a ghostly pallor, ringed as it was by his waving hair. Every little shift of the orchestra was reflected in the sensitive features: one moment he would be damping something down, which would knot the skin around his eyes into grim folds

accompanied by a lifting of his nose; the next moment he
would be smiling in confluence with the sweet strains of
the orchestra, radiating his approval and enjoyment, so
that it was a case of both devils and angels crossing his
visage by turn. Lightning flashed from his spectacle
lenses with each sharp movement of his head, and from
behind the lenses his eyes shone forth, watchful, asser-
tive and demanding attention – every inch of his frame
was simultaneously both an instrument of command and
a means of expression. Girardi[33] included a caricature of
a similar conductor in his satire *Er und seine Schwester*,
showing him extracting long streamers of sound from the
players with outstretched arms and indicating the
kettledrum by pointing a dagger at it. As in all caricatures, there was something true about this one. As time
went by, in fact Mahler became gradually more sedate:
but no one could ever escape the spell of his presence.

The Court Opera orchestra took on tremendous stature in 'Brangäne's Song'; it became one huge riot of
sound and colour and it made me think: this is the very
breath of harmony, because the music swelled from the
orchestra in mighty sobbing chords like the heaving of a
breast moved by passion. The players and Mahler himself were so transported by their own playing that they
looked almost like priests engaged in a religious service.
And what a contrast this was with the same orchestra
when I had seen it once under a different conductor in a
performance of *Lakmé*! I shall never forget one viola
player who never looked at the conductor at all but sawed
away at his instrument with his head turned to one side,
chatting with his neighbour who was showing him
something.

Mahler in this *Tristan* showed what he meant by 'the
supremacy of the conductor'. He fastened them all with
his eye and seemed to be the conductor of the whole
scene rather than just of the orchestra. He continually
lifted his head and gave leads to the singers, directing
them with his look, keeping them in time with his look –

---

33. See p. 313, note 1.

it is amazing how many places his eyes could be in at the same time! Just before the second curtain I heard him say aloud to the artist singing Tristan: '*O König, das kann ich dir nicht sagen!*' He enunciated every syllable, spreading the sides of his jaw and literally forcing the words into the soloist's mouth so that, urged along in this way, the singer had no alternative but to copy him and articulate '*O König, das kann ich dir nicht sagen!*' loudly and clearly. This prompting by Mahler – which he did again at various important points – could truly be called conducting, Wagner-conducting, in the highest sense. You could appreciate what the word really means. The effect was plain to see: he was, you might say, the overall director of the entire artistic production.

Reading this now on paper, people might tend to look critically at the advantages and disadvantages of this style of direction. But those who were in the audience came out in a state of trance; it was total ecstasy even though frankly the singers were not in perfect voice and often came over too low. In the interval it was all I could do to stutter 'Wonderful . . .' to Hermann Bahr, who was rushing about excitedly. I was beginning to love Mahler, Vienna was becoming my Bayreuth.

Mahler spoke afterwards about the difficult job he had had with the singers. 'These people always want to "act",' he said. 'They all overdo it. Right from Act I they start waving their arms about and screwing up every limb – so what are they going to do in Act III when the climax comes? "Stand still!" I'm always saying to Tristan, don't fiddle about, don't wave your arms – sing in three-four time, Herr Tristan, sing in three-four time – one, two, three!' And to give this the necessary emphasis, he stamped the beat on the floor: one, two, three! In other words, he believed in a certain economy of expression, achieving an effect with only the smallest use of gesture, since even the tiniest movement on the stage will register on the audience: and in saving more pronounced expressions for the few moments of climax since a large gesture is effective only if it comes in the middle of small ones or none at all.

Finally Mahler, like the old music master he was, demanded that the singing should be strictly in tempo, since only by adhering to the composer's exact notation could the intended musical effect be achieved. That was something close to his heart. He put everything he had into conveying it to the orchestra and singers, which was why his manner often became unpleasant. Nevertheless, it was the way he captured the true spirit of Wagner in Vienna, and how in the production of *Figaro* in Salzburg he captured the essence of Mozart.

Last summer [1910] I saw him one last time in Tobelbad. There had been a rumour going around then that they wanted him back at the Vienna Court Opera but he merely smiled at the idea. He had returned home from America and spoke a lot about the way things were with American orchestras. In general he thought that a nation of English stock did not have enough temperament,

Jacket of Decsey's novel, *Beloved Vienna*,
published in the year of Mahler's death.

enough feeling for Art; though the ninety-six players he
had under his baton had paid more attention to him than
any previous orchestra because he had been in sole
charge. About Paris, where he had conducted his Second
Symphony on the way back, he was full of enthusiasm.
'Such *joie de vivre!*' he said. 'Such civilization!' The
symphony had been very warmly received. A choir of a
hundred professional singers, really first-rate people
much better than in Vienna, had been put at his disposal.
Altogether everybody had been very accommodating;
only the artists – and he named a name – had been
envious and had tried to make difficulties for him. The
performance, as mentioned, went very well and the
people were enthusiastic, though somebody in the audience suddenly called out *'A bas la musique allemande!'*[34]
'But', he added, 'my Second Symphony has become
different from my other compositions. If it takes root
somewhere, that doesn't really do anything for the rest of
my works.' Then he spoke about Munich and the early
rehearsals for the Eighth Symphony. 'The singers from
Leipzig', he said, 'are far more disciplined and hard-
working than the Viennese. They are the most depend-
able of people: it's a pleasure to work with them. I wasn't
used to that from Vienna. But the Viennese can sing
better!' Of Strauss's *Don Quixote* he spoke with the
warm appreciation of a musician. He also recalled the
production of *Salome* that he had not managed to stage in
Vienna. Never had he met such resistance: it had been
virtually set to appear when suddenly it was all off. 'I
know who was behind getting it stopped,' said Mahler:
'Kutten!'[35]

One rainy night he came over to Graz. He loved the
ancient architecture of the town and enjoyed spending
time there. We had spent hours one winter evening
stamping about in the deep snow all over the Schloss-
berg, looking at the old houses. When he saw the
delightful Italian Renaissance of the Krebsenkeller, he

34. Down with German music!
35. Unidentified.

was quite carried away. 'What a pity I've already done
The Taming of the Shrew!' he said. 'What a pity! It would
be just right to have Petrucchio standing here, Kate there
and Bianca over . . .' and he began setting it all up right
there in the middle of the courtyard, filling the place with
characters from Goetz's opera. I could not tear him
away. But the time he came over from Tobelbad, he
carried on to Munich later in the night. He was utterly
mild and transfigured, wholly affectionate with myself
and Weis-Ostborn. He talked about America and his
terrible vexations with Customs and hinted that he was
hoping that problems with the contract would keep him
from having to return there again. He seemed worn out
to us, worn out from America; he was also more
concerned than usual about his health. He showed us
cigarettes that were without nicotine and 'did not harm
the heart', and he ordered caffeine-free coffee. I told him
about the young composer Josef Marx[36] and his great
admiration for Mahler. 'It's really the song of the pris-
oner in the tower[37] that made him such a devotee,' I
explained. 'That's extraordinary,' Mahler replied,
pleased and rather touched. 'That song did not go down
well in Berlin originally. But an artist is like an archer in
the night. He shoots his arrows into the darkness not
knowing if they will hit anything, but they do hit the
mark . . .'

He went back to America after all and I never saw him
again. And how I regret now that I did not set down
every conversation I was lucky enough to have with
Mahler. How it pains me that I didn't imitate Eckermann, because Mahler expended a large part of his
personality in conversation. I relied far too much on
memory and even learned a few things he said by heart.
But memory alone is like a beam that is rotted from the
centre: it will carry the weight for a time, then the whole
thing collapses. Only one thing consoles me: that many,
indeed most, of the things that Mahler said had to be

36. (1882–1964), born in Graz.
37. 'Lied des Verfolgten in Turm', from the *Wunderhorn* Lieder.

heard direct from the man himself, with his unique inflection and with his own deep voice that boomed solidly from his chest like the very voice of creation. You were aware that in this voice was the essence of the man. How often we are let down when a heroic figure with an eagle's nose and a beard like Wotan's opens his mouth – and out comes the thin voice of a second tenor. But when you heard Mahler's voice, you looked up and were entranced. You immediately gained a different perspective, and all the tales of the arrogance of singers or the indolence of musicians took on a different aspect. There was something special at work, something roared from the hidden depths of the cave. You understood the integrity of this character. If people were discussing a new man, he himself often asked: 'Is he to be taken seriously?' If you heard Mahler's voice, you had no need to put such a question. So when quoting his words it ought really to be possible to put in all the inflections to reproduce the words exactly. Only the gramophone could have done the job adequately, and if now I read through everything I have set to paper it seems wooden and lifeless . . . With the loss of Mahler, a window on the universe was shattered and we can do no more than gather up a few splinters of glass.

And should I allow his death to convince me that he is completely dead: this hot seething, restless spirit, as hot, seething and restless as life itself . . .? It is childish but I often tell myself: he isn't dead, he is only 'gone away', as it says in his *Kindertotenlieder*. There are men and women who live on beyond their death: Ahasuerus or Barbarossa or Capet . . . all those who become the stuff of legend – whence they return to walk among us for ever.

'Stunden mit Mahler', *Die Musik* (Berlin), vol. 18 (Gustav Mahler-Heft), pp. 352–6; vol. 21, pp. 143–53, June and Aug. issues, 1911.

Anna Mahler with her father, Toblach 1909.

Anna (Justine) MAHLER
(1904–1988)

Mahler's second child was just under seven years old when he died. Raised in Vienna, she left home at sixteen, married, divorced and became a sculptress. She was married to the composer Ernst Krenek, the publisher Paul Zsolnay and the conductor Anatole Fistoulari; she had two daughters. Active in political and artistic Vienna in the 1930s, she escaped after the *Anschluss* and rebuilt her career in Britain and the United States. This interview took place at her house in London in December 1985.

You were born into a fin-de-siècle *life.*

I didn't notice much. I was an only child. I hated other children and always loved being alone.

Do you remember your elder sister at all?

No. I am quite sure that was for me very lucky. She was

very wild and apparently treated me very badly. I have one glimpse of recollection. I was three when she died. I don't remember it.

What is your earliest memory?

I suppose Putzi, my sister. And the house at Maiernigg. I was sitting on a high table having my nappies changed and this sister whom I feared was lower than me. I looked down upon her. That surprised me.

Was your mother in that memory?

No, a nanny. I saw my parents only at mealtimes, which was very bad because the mealtimes were no pleasure. I wasn't allowed to talk. I can understand as a grown-up that the chatter of children can be quite awful. I should have been left to eat in the kitchen, it would have been much nicer.

Was it your father who commanded silence?

Absolutely.

Was it that he wanted to talk to your mother?

No, silence. He was always overworked. But to subject a child to that kind of atmosphere was awful.

Do you have any close memories of him?

Yes. Oh yes. When he did take notice of me he was very, very kind. And understanding.

You have said that you remember his smile, his eyes.

You can see it in some of the pictures. There is a very typical one from Toblach and he is with the two children, wearing a cap.[1] He smiles. That smile I absolutely remember.

---

1. Only with one child.

Do you remember Toblach at all?

I remember going for a walk with him, seeing him going up a hill and me behind. Just pictures, there are no stories.

There are many descriptions of his strange way of walking.

Oh, I saw that. It was a nervous tic. He just changed pace, right and left, then back again. But he could control it. From my mother I know that they had a word that she could tell him and then he would control it. It wasn't absolutely necessary for him. When I was allowed to walk with him, I noticed it very strongly.

Did you give him presents, or do any childish drawings for him?

Heavens, no.

Was there a time of day when you could go to him?

In the morning when he worked, before he went out. Children wake up very early. I was very silent by nature and I was allowed to watch him working on his scores. Not composing, of course, but preparing the parts during the winter. I remember that in New York. I remember his room and his writing-table. I would stand to the left, watching him. I remember his hands, their shape and the flatness of the fingers from playing so much. I can see the page he was working on, the shape of the knife he used to cut the notes out.

Alma tells the story that you exclaimed one day, 'Papi, I wouldn't like to be a note.' 'Why not?' he asked. 'Because then you might scratch me out and blow me away.'

I was told that. I can't remember it.

Did he make any sound while he worked?

No. Silence.

Was he a physical man? Did he occasionally embrace you? Did you receive any warmth from him?

If so, I don't remember. He took me for walks once or twice in New York, in Central Park. I remember snow and – something else. Roller-skates. I had some roller-skates, and I was terrible at any kind of sport. I was always on the floor and I remember him picking me up again and not ever being angry or cross when I fell down again immediately. He had quite a lot to do putting me on my feet again.

Did you talk to him as you walked?

I don't think so.

Were these long walks?

No, he wouldn't have had much time. Most of my memories are from the last year.

Did you ever go to his concerts?

I was once taken to the opera. It was *The Bartered Bride*. I was sickly. They knew when I was taken somewhere that the next day I had a high fever. A septic throat. I was too fat, you know, I was overfed and never exercised. A Viennese upbringing.

Did you have Viennese food in New York?

No, very bad food because Mahler was hypochondriac. He ordered these awful steaks, overcooked. He didn't want to be reminded that he was eating meat. It was not quite honest. If you feel so strongly about it, better not eat meat. He was convinced that he had to eat meat to be able to work. But he didn't want it to look like meat. He did eat it. But it tasted bad and that relieved him a bit. If it's no pleasure, it's not quite so bad.

Were there any favourite dishes?

No, it was only health, health, health. No pleasure. It was eating to stay as strong as he could.

You must have had an awesome consciousness of death from very early on?

Children take things as they come and think them natural.

When were you aware that Mahler was seriously ill?

I can't tell you. I had many dreams about it but I can't say if it was after his death or during.

Were you removed from kindergarten suddenly in New York to go back to Europe?

I must have been.

Were you conscious of a sudden decline in Mahler's health?

No, he had these illnesses very often. I had them too, these septic throats.

Do you remember the journey home?

I remember in Paris, the room he lay in at the clinic. Where the bed was, where he was. Just glimpses.

Were you frightened?

I don't know.

Were you on the train with him going back to Vienna?

He was in a special carriage. I don't remember anything. The memory is a strange thing. One remembers glimpses, the important things are wiped out, too strong. I was taken to say goodbye to him – in Vienna. I remember waiting outside the room, not the thing itself. I am sure that was rejected as being too strong. Children have an armour against these things. Apparently when my mother wanted to tell me of his death I said: 'Don't. I know.'

Alfred ROSÉ
(1902–75)

Mahler's nephew, son of his sister Justi and the violinist Arnold Rosé.

Can you, as a boy, remember Mahler at all?

I can only remember him personally, not as an artist. I was too young to be taken to the opera or to a concert at that time. But I remember that he liked me very much and usually when he came he gave a soldier's salute, then slapped me on my cheek. That was one of the usual greetings of Mahler.

Your mother was very attached to her brother, wasn't she?

Very close.

Did your mother talk at great length to you about Mahler?

Oh yes, she told me events from her early life – she had been his housekeeper for the twelve years up to 1902.

Your father was first violin of the Vienna Philharmonic. He was also a great friend of Mahler's.

They became very close too because Mahler appreciated the musical attitude of my father and brought him into his house, and that's the way he got to know my mother.

Your father and Mahler also played violin and piano sonatas together, didn't they?

Yes they did. It must have been very lovely. I am sorry I couldn't attend.

Do you happen to know the sort of music they played?

The Brahms. Over and over again the Brahms sonatas, that I know.

Taped interview (source unknown) at the Bibliothèque Gustav
Mahler, Paris.

(Sir) Rudolf BING
(born 1902)

Austrian-born impresario; manager of the New York Metropolitan
Opera, 1951–72.

Our family took summer vacations in the Dolomite Alps,
not far from where I spend my summers now, and I
would walk a great deal in the woods, alone. Once as a
very young boy, I remember, I met Gustav Mahler
thrashing through the woods, singing, looking almost
demented; and I fled.

5,000 Nights at the Opera, London (Hamish Hamilton), 1972, p. 8.

Sigmund FREUD
(1856–1939)

On the afternoon of 26 August 1910 Mahler met Freud at an hotel in
Leiden, Holland, and for the next four hours underwent an
impromptu psychoanalysis while strolling through the town. Freud
had broken his holiday on the North Sea because 'he could not refuse
a man of Mahler's worth'.[1] Mahler had overcome deep-seated
reservations about Freud[2] on discovering that Alma was having a

1. Ernest Jones, *The Life and Work of Sigmund Freud*, vol. 2, p. 88.
2. See p. 195. Mahler was almost certainly aware that Walter had sought help from
Freud in 1902 for psychosomatic pains in his conducting arm. See Walter TV,
pp.164–8.

passionate affair and might leave him for her young lover, Walter Gropius.[3]

Contact with Freud was made through Richard Nepallek, a Viennese neurologist related to Alma. Mahler cabled Freud for an appointment, then cancelled. He vacillated three times more until the analyst warned that he was leaving shortly for Sicily. Freud viewed Mahler's hesitation as a '*folie de doute* of his obsessional neurosis'.[4] In emotional turmoil, convinced that this was the only means to save his marriage, Mahler travelled from Toblach by train to Leiden, sending anguished missives to Alma along the way.

He and Freud were of similar age, origin and liberal outlook[5] but of opposing interests. Freud was indifferent to music; his preoccupation was with man and history. Mahler was concerned with pure philosophy and science, almost to the exclusion of their physical application. Yet an instant empathy seems to have formed between them. 'Although Mahler had no previous contact with psychoanalysis, Freud said he had never met anyone who seemed to understand it so swiftly,' wrote Ernest Jones, Freud's authorized biographer.[6]

The encounter was first revealed in Alma's memoir of 1940. Her report cannot, for obvious reasons, be altogether trusted but conforms in most respects with Jones's:

> He realized that he had lived the life of a neurotic and suddenly decided to consult Sigmund Freud (who was then on holiday at Leiden in Holland). He gave him an account of his strange states of mind and his anxieties, and Freud apparently calmed him down. He reproached him with vehemence after hearing his confession. 'How dared a man in your state ask a young woman to be tied to him?' he asked. In conclusion, he said: 'I know your wife. She loved her father and she can only choose and

---

3. Gropius (1883–1969) met and made love to Alma at a spa in Tobelbad in June–July 1910 while Mahler was composing at Toblach, then pursued her to the Dolomites to satisfy himself that her husband was aware of the episode. See HLG3, pp. 752–3 and Reginald R. Isaacs, *Walter Gropius, der Mensch und sein Werk*, vol. 1, Berlin (Gebr. Mann), 1983. Gropius married Alma briefly during the war and in 1919 founded the Bauhaus workshop, one of the primary influences in twentieth-century design.

4. Jones, op. cit., vol. 2, p. 88. Freud uses the identical term in his letter to Reik (see below). Mahler was equally indecisive when it came to having his bust made by Rodin. See Danièle Gutmann, 'La conjonction Mahler-Rodin' in the catalogue of the Mahler exhibition at the Musée d'art moderne de la ville de Paris, 1985.

5. They were born within four years of one another in small towns in Moravia to Jewish families deeply rooted in their communities and traditions.

6. Jones, op. cit., vol. 2, p. 88.

love a man of his sort. Your age, of which you are so much afraid, is precisely what attracts her. You need not be anxious. You loved your mother, and you look for her in every woman. She was careworn and ailing, and unconsciously you wish your wife to be the same.'

He was right in both cases. Gustav Mahler's mother was called Marie. His first impulse was to change my name to Marie[7] in spite of the difficulty he had in pronouncing 'r'. And when he got to know me better he wanted my face to be more 'stricken' – his very word. When he told my mother that it was a pity there had been so little sadness in my life, she replied: 'Don't worry – that will come.'

I too always looked for a small, slight man, who had wisdom and spiritual superiority, since this was what I had known and loved in my father.

Freud's diagnosis composed Mahler's mind, although he refused to acknowledge his fixation on his mother. He turned away from notions of that kind.

AMM, p. 175

Jones was not aware that Mahler had consulted Freud until, alerted by Donald Mitchell, he unearthed a 1925 letter from Freud to Marie Bonaparte[8] describing the analysis. The letter itself has never been released for publication; its contents were paraphrased by Jones:

Mahler was greatly impressed by a remark of Freud's: 'I take it that your mother was called Marie. I should surmise it from various hints in your conversation. How comes it that you married someone with another name, Alma, since your mother evidently played a dominating part in your life?' Mahler then told him that his wife's name was Alma Maria, but that he called her Marie! She was the daughter of the famous painter [Ger. *Maler*] Schindler, whose statue stands in the Stadt Park in Vienna; so presumably a name played a part in her life also. This analytic talk evidently produced an effect,

7. Nowhere in their written communications does Mahler call his wife anything but 'Alma' or a diminutive of that name.
8. (1882–1962) Princess George of Greece and Denmark, French psychoanalyst, confidante of Freud's and his liberator from Nazi Austria in 1938.

since Mahler recovered his potency and the marriage was a happy one until his death, which unfortunately took place only a year later.

In the course of the talk Mahler suddenly said that now he understood why his music had always been prevented from achieving the highest rank through the noblest passages, those inspired by the most profound emotions, being spoilt by the intrusion of some commonplace melody. His father, apparently a brutal person, treated his wife very badly, and when Mahler was a young boy there was a specially painful scene between them. It became quite unbearable to the boy, who rushed away from the house. At that moment, however, a hurdy-gurdy in the street was grinding out the popular Viennese air 'Ach, du lieber Augustin'. In Mahler's opinion the conjunction of high tragedy and light amusement was from then on inextricably fixed in his mind, and the one mood inevitably brought the other with it.

Ernest Jones, *The Life and Work of Sigmund Freud*, London (Hogarth Press) 1953–7, vol. 2, pp. 88–9.

Mahler emerged from the session ecstatic, believing his intimate problems to have been resolved. 'Be joyful!' he telegraphed Alma,[9] before returning to Toblach. Two weeks later, however, while Mahler rehearsed the Eighth Symphony he had dedicated to 'my beloved wife', Alma was consorting again with Gropius in a Munich hotel room.[10]

Independently of these sources, Theodore Reik, another Freud disciple, learned of his analysis of Mahler[11] while living in Holland in 1934. He had been toying with writing a psycho-history of Mahler and applied to Freud for information. Freud's letter, dated 4 January 1935, is hazy on detail but potent in his abiding impression of Mahler.

I analysed Mahler for an afternoon in the year 1912 (or 1913?) in Leiden. If I may believe reports, I achieved much with him at that time. The visit appeared necessary

---

9. Unpublished telegram (HLG3, p. 772).
10. See HLG3, pp. 773–780.
11. Reik does not say how. Could Mengelberg or another of Mahler's Dutch friends have been let into the secret?

284   HUGO VON HOFMANNSTHAL

to him, because his wife at the time rebelled against the fact that he withdrew his libido from her. In highly interesting expeditions through his life history, we discovered his personal conditions for love, especially his Holy Mary complex (mother fixation). I had plenty of opportunity to admire the capability for psychological understanding of this man of genius. No light fell at the time on the symptomatic façade of his obsessional neurosis. It was as if you would dig a single shaft through a mysterious building.

> Theodore Reik, *The Haunting Melody; Psychoanalytic Experiences in Life and Music*, New York (Farrar, Straus and Young), 1953, pp. 342–3.

This letter is Freud's only account to be made public. There was no further contact between the two men. On 23 May the following year, five days after Mahler's death, Freud wrote to his executor, Emil Freund, seeking payment of 300 crowns for a 'consultation of several hours in August 1910 in Leiden, where I had gone at his request from Noordwijk a. Z.' The fee was paid in full; the receipt is dated 24 October 1911.[12]

Hugo von HOFMANNSTHAL
(1874–1929)

Hofmannsthal had started out as a poet – a 'wonderful and unique phenomenon in whom our youth saw not only its highest ambitions but also absolute poetic perfection come into being in the person of one of its own age'[1] – but in 1902 began writing for the stage. He was adored by most of Mahler's friends, though not by Mahler, whose literary tastes were conservative. At the Opera, he rejected Hofmannsthal's earliest musical venture, Zemlinsky's ballet *The Golden Heart*, 'because I don't understand it'.[2] And of Strauss's collaboration with

---

12. Letter and receipt sold at Sotheby's London, 9 May 1985. The tone of Freud's letter suggests that he had not invoiced Mahler in his lifetime.

1. Stefan Zweig, *The World of Yesterday*, London (Cassell) 1943, pp. 45–6.
2. AMM, p. 4.

Hofmannsthal in *Elektra*, he mocked: 'Oh blessed, oh blessed a modern to be!'[3]

He first met the writer on holiday by the Attersee in the summer of 1896[4] and thereafter on sundry social occasions in Vienna, though Hofmannsthal counted only one real conversation.[5] He admired Mahler enough to overlook any personal slight and, in 1910, wrote the following fiftieth-birthday tribute:

Where a creative mind is at work, there is drama. Wherever such a mind operates, it clashes with matter; it is confronted with inertia, miscomprehension and incomprehension. As it wrestles with them, the atmosphere around the conflict becomes the point of interest: there is no need to fabricate it. A rhythmic process begins, perhaps the odd convulsion. A chaotic and truly

3. Letter to Alma, 16 August 1906, (AMM, p. 276).
4. Walter TV, pp. 90–91.
5. HLG3, p. 991. Among other connections, Hofmannsthal introduced Mahler in May 1909 to Edgard Varèse, visionary of electronic music.

heterogeneous entity takes shape, while hostile or indifferent elements band improbably together in opposition.
And to the delight of lovers of Art, and the reluctant
astonishment of philistines, it becomes apparent that out
of many dead elements a living whole can emerge, thanks
solely to the miracle of a creative mind. Such a drama
was Gustav Mahler's leadership of the Vienna Opera.

Paul Stefan (ed.), *Gustav Mahler: Ein Bild seiner
Persönlichkeit in Widmungen*, Munich (Piper), 1910, p. 16.

Lilli LEHMANN[1]

In Mahler's symphonic compositions, I was struck at
once by the fact that the effect was caused by the
simplicity of the melodies, which he knew how to
present, of course, with an immense apparatus. The idea
flashed into my mind, at the same time, that perhaps he
might be the very one who would be willing, especially
with regard to the machinery, to strike again into simple
paths, and I put the question to him. He replied with
scornful laughter, 'What are you thinking of? In a
century my symphonies will be performed in immense
halls that will hold from twenty to thirty thousand
people, and will be great popular festivals.' I was silent
but I thought, involuntarily, that the more music is
deprived of intimacy, the more it will be lacking in true
genius.[2] . . . I saw Mahler again and for the last time at
Munich, in 1910, when he led his Eighth Symphony;

---

1. See p. 51.
2. He told Max Graf: 'In forty or fifty years they will play my symphonies at
orchestral concerts as they now play Beethoven's . . . I have time to compose only in
the summer. During the short holiday, I have to write large works if I want to go
down into posterity.' (Max Graf, *Legends of a Musical City*, New York (The
Philosophical Library), 1945, p. 212.)

Riezl[3] and I had gone there especially for it. Mahler had aged greatly, and I was positively alarmed. His work, that was given with the aid of a thousand performers, sounded as though it came from one instrument and one throat. I was painfully moved by the second part of the symphony, that is based on the second part of *Faust*. I cannot say whether it was his music, his appearance, a presentiment of death, Goethe's words, the recollections of Schumann, or my youth – I only know that I was dissolved in emotion during the entire second part and could not control myself. When I went to him, the next morning, to greet him, and met him surrounded by a crowd of people, he was amiability itself, went after Riezl, who had waited for me below, and brought her up himself, and would not let us leave. Then came his fearful fate, his terrible illness and death!

My Path through Life, New York (Putnams), 1914, pp. 389–91.

Berta SZEPS-ZUCKERKANDL[1]

In October before sailing for New York, Mahler paid me a visit. The first time since Emil departed this life. With the exquisite sympathy he has shown for my grief, he refrained from offering any word of condolence. He knows there is nothing anyone else can say. I must work things out for myself. On the contrary, he tried to divert me. He talked cheerfully about his American impressions. It was a pleasure, he said, to take part in the emerging life of a young country. America was still a place of hectic beginnings, of untamed enthusiasm; of eagerness to learn, to indulge in wonderment, to make

---

3. Lehmann's younger sister, Marie (1851–1931), a retired soprano.
1. See p. 211.

something of one's self. This openness, the willing involvement, will make America the Eldorado of art and learning. Mahler is determined to carry his work forward in America.

Naturally we came round to talking about Vienna and what a confusing place it was, so attractive on the one hand and yet so depressing.

'Isn't there such a thing', I asked Mahler, 'as a psychology of cities?' Vienna especially had a complex character that was difficult to unravel: the genial Vienna that produced people of genius and the satanic city that killed the geniuses off?

'Yes, you are right,' said Mahler in reply. 'Freud should add a psychology of cities to his list of publications. What terrible inner struggles there must have been during Vienna's formative years. Conflicting influences that give the character its duality. Unfortunately, you can't uncover the subconscious of a city.'

'Mahlers Abschied' (manuscript), undated copy at the Bibliothèque Gustav Mahler, Paris. Quoted by permission of Emile Zuckerkandl, Palo Alto, California.

Interlude: Interview

At the start of his final season in New York, Mahler gave a lengthy, verbatim interview to *The Etude* in which he discussed the folk roots of music, speculated on the prospects for American music, and discoursed on his personal development in terms that reflect his recent encounter with Sigmund Freud. Nothing is known of the circumstances of the interview, which is unsigned. It was presumably conducted in German and translated into an English monologue, which amply conveys Mahler's forthright delivery.

The influence of the folk-song upon the music of the nations has been exhibited in many striking forms. At the very root of the whole matter lies a great educational

THE ETUDE

THE INFLUENCE OF THE FOLK-SONG ON GERMAN MUSICAL ART

From an Interview with the Eminent Composer and Director

GUSTAV MAHLER

Secured expressly for THE ETUDE

Mr. Mahler gave his opinions to our interviewer partly in German and partly in English. Consequently it has been impossible to employ his exact phraseology

[EDITOR'S NOTE—Gustav Mahler, who is now recognized as one of the very foremost composers and directors of our time, was born at Kalischt, Bohemia, July 7th, 1860. Neither his father nor his mother were musical. Notwithstanding this lack of hereditary influence, he manifested musical talent at a very early age, and started to compose when he was but a mere boy. Mahler now looks lightly upon these juvenile efforts, but they are said to have indicated his very pronounced talent. His first teachers were little known musicians located in small towns in Bohemia. Later he entered the Gymnasium at Iglau and later at Prague, Bohemia. The German Gymnasium corresponds to the high school and college in America. Mahler's academic education was completed at the University of Vienna, and his musical education was continued at the Conservatorium in Vienna, where he came under the influence of Bruckner. In 1880 he started his career as a conductor, which has made him one of the most renowned

PLAGIARISM?

In some cases we find that the great composers have actually taken folk-melodies as themes for some of their works. In most cases of this kind they have given the source of the theme all possible publicity. In some cases where they may not have done this a few critics with limited musical knowledge and no practical ability in composition have happened to find these instances, and being at a loss to write anything more intelligent, they have magnified these deliberate settings of folk-themes into disgraceful thefts. The cry of plagiarism is in most cases both cruel and unjustified.

truth which is so powerful in its effects, and so obvious to all, that one can almost make an axiom: 'As the child is, so will the man be.' We cannot expect an oak to grow into a rose bush and we cannot expect the water-lily to become a palm. No amount of development, care or horticultural and agricultural skill could work miracles of this kind. So it is with children. What occurs in childhood makes an indelible impression. The depth of this psychological impression must ever be the rock upon which all educational systems are founded. So it is in music, that the songs which a child assimilates in his youth will determine his musical manhood.

Assimilating Good Music in Childhood

The music which the masters have assimilated in their childhood forms the texture of their mature musical development. It cannot be otherwise and I am unable to understand why the great educators of our age do not lay even greater stress upon this all-important point. I have said assimilated – you will notice that I did not say appropriated. That is quite a different matter. The music is absorbed and goes through a process of mental digestion until it becomes a part of the person, just as much as the hair on their heads, or the skin on their bodies. It is stored away in their brain-cells and will come forth again in the minds of creative musicians, not in the same or even similar form, but often in entirely new and wonderful conceptions.

I have often heard composers who claim to seek individuality above all things state that they purposely avoid hearing too much music of other composers, fearing that their own originality will be affected. They also avoid hearing the songs of the street or folk-songs for a similar reason. What arrant nonsense! If a man eats a beefsteak it is no sign that he will become a cow. He takes the nourishment from the food and that transforms itself by means of wonderful physiological processes into flesh, strength and bodily force, but he may eat beefsteaks for a lifetime and never be anything but a man.

Plagiarism?

In some cases we find that the great composers have actually taken folk-melodies as themes for some of their works. In most cases of this kind they have given the source of the theme all possible publicity. In some cases where they may not have done this a few critics with limited musical knowledge and no practical ability in composition have happened to find these instances, and being at a loss to write anything more intelligent they have magnified these deliberate settings of folk-themes into disgraceful thefts. The cry of plagiarism is in most cases both cruel and unjustified. The master who has the skill to develop a great musical work certainly possesses the ability to evolve melodies. When he takes a folk-theme as the subject of one of his master-works, it is for the purpose of elaborating and beautifying it as a lapidary might take an unpolished diamond, and by his skill bring out the scintillating and kaleidoscopic beauties of the stone. After all, the handling of the theme is even more significant than the evolution of the theme. Consider for one moment the incalculable benefits to the literature of the world brought about by the Shakespeare treatment of plots which otherwise would have been absolutely forgotten. *Hamlet, King Lear, Romeo and Juliet, Julius Caesar,* all of them plagiarized but gloriously plagiarized . . .

A Grave Musical Question for America

Since my residence in America I have been so busily engaged in the mission for which I came to this country that I have not had, perhaps, the right opportunities to investigate musical conditions as thoroughly as possible. Nevertheless, what I have observed, and what has been related to me by experts who have lived in the country for a lifetime, leads me to believe that a musical condition exists in this country which makes it extremely difficult for the American composer to work with the same innate feeling which characterizes the work of some of his European contemporaries. I respect the efforts of American composers most highly, and shall gladly do everything in my power to assist them when possible, but the subject of the folk-song bears such a direct relation to this matter that I cannot fail to avail myself of this opportunity to discuss the matter.

I have previously expressed the somewhat axiomatic truths through which we learned that the musical influences which surround the child are those which have the greatest influence upon his afterlife and also that the melodies which composers evolve in their maturity are but the flowers which bloom from the fields which were sown with the seeds of the folk-song in their childhood. Therefore when I am asked whence the future American composer will come I am forced to enquire: 'Where is the American folk-song?' I cannot be quoted as an authority on American music, but depending upon the information received from friends whom I consider keen observers, and upon what I have heard myself, it seems to me that the popular music of America is not American at all, but rather that kind of music which the African Negro transplanted to American soil has chosen to adopt. It must be remembered that the music of the African savage, be he Zulu, Hottentot, Kafir or Abyssinian, rises but a trifle above the rhythmic basis. When these people, the ancestors of the present American Negroes, made their compulsory voyages from the jungles of the Dark Continent to the New World it should be remembered that they were in most cases savages pure and simple.

While I have the very greatest respect for the accomplishments of a few of the American Negroes who have risen above their surroundings to high places and to distinguished attainments, I cannot subscribe myself to the doctrine that all men are born equal, as it is inconceivable to me. It is not reasonable to expect that a race could arise from a savage condition to a high ethnological state in a century or two. It took Northern Europe nearly one thousand years to fight its way from barbarism to civilization. That the Negroes in America have accomplished so much is truly amazing. In their music they doubtless copied and varied the models of the white people to whose households they were attached. Their love for song and their sense of rhythm assisted them in this. But to expect that they would evolve a new, distinct and original folk-song is preposterous in itself. They are great imitators, I am told, but that is no reason why the American composer should imitate their distorted copies of European folk-songs. The syncopations introduced in Negro songs under the name of 'ragtime' are not original, but may be found in the folk-songs of Hungary and other European nations. Syncopation as a part of national folk-songs existed in Europe before the first Negroes were transported from Africa.

Just why the American composer should feel that he is doing something peculiarly American when he employs Negro folk-songs is difficult to tell. Hungarian composers are prone to employ gypsy themes, and the music of

Hungary has become marked in this way so that it has become gypsy music and not Hungarian music. Surely American music based upon the crude themes of the red-skinned aborigines, or upon the appropriated European type of folk-song which the African Americans have produced, is not any more representative of the great American people of today than are these swarthy citizens of the New World representative of all Americans.

So long as young Americans have to content themselves with the kind of trashy popular songs which are ground out by the thousand every year and howled mercilessly in the music halls of the country, just so long will America be forced to wait for its great master in music. But I am told by educators, America is awakening to this condition, and American children are being furnished with ever-increasing opportunities to hear good music. The music of the public schools is based upon the best folk-song melodies of all Europe. The music in the best churches, instead of being modelled upon the kind of tunes not very remote from crude Negro melodies in themselves, is now following the best models of the world and I know in my own sphere as a conductor that America is now being afforded splendid opportunities to hear the great masterpieces played by famous instrumentalists and sung by world-famous singers. America thus hears the music of all nations played by performers from all nations. One does not have to be a prophet to see that some day when this marvellous amalgamation of Teuton, Celt, Latin, Anglo-Saxon, Czech, Slav and Greek is more advanced, America may look for results in music far beyond the fairest dreams of the most optimistic.

Copy at the Bibliothèque Gustav Mahler, Paris.

Herman MARTONNE[1]

As a music student in Vienna, Martonne was so excited by Mahler that he followed him to New York, joining the first violins of the Philharmonic soon after Mahler's appointment.

Something Mahler never could stand was indifferent tone. He said, for instance: 'Where music is, the demon must be!' That's what he said: 'demon!'

There was a clarinet player that Mahler thought the world of, yet one day he tells him: 'Piano, piano.' 'But yesterday you said it was too piano,' says the player. So Mahler explains: 'Well, it all depends on our mood. Yesterday I thought it was too much, today too little.' He didn't say, 'What I say goes.' He just explained that it was all mood.

Mahlerthon

Benjamin KOHON[1]

Bassoonist, New York Philharmonic Orchestra.

He wouldn't take a cab into town or have a limousine sent for him: he used to take the subway. I was in the same car as him once. I tipped my hat to him, he looked around but I don't think he recognized me. He had very poor eyesight. But he'd see things you'd never think he saw, way in the back of the orchestra.

He never could get enough volume out of us to play the first movement of Beethoven's Fifth. He always wanted more and more, like a cataclysm, a volcanic eruption. He wanted something we really couldn't give him. Well, one day he finally got what he wanted. And he was really delighted. Genuinely delighted. He invited the entire orchestra to have a little after-concert snack with him.

He took ill and stayed away for a week or so . . . Came in a day or two before the concert and said, 'Well, we're

1. Dates unknown.

not really ready yet with this composition but I don't want to keep you gentlemen late on account of my sickness. I don't want you to suffer for it.' He didn't call for any overtime, though he was entitled to it. A week or so later he took really ill, and that was the end of it.

Mahlerthon

Ugo GIARDINI
(1888–1944)

Italian journalist and musicologist who lived for some years in the US.

It was generally known that Mahler had frequent conflicts with the women managers of the Philharmonic Orchestra who raised the large funds necessary to cover the deficits of the organization. One of these busybodies attended the rehearsal of one of Mahler's own symphonies and then went to the composer's room to congratulate him. She could not refrain from remarking that she thought he had played the first movement much too slowly. I could hardly believe my own ears. It was plain to see that Mahler had to struggle with himself not to give her the answer she deserved; but he won. The little man, ghastly pale, utterly exhausted from the long, gruelling rehearsal, simply turned away from her in silence.

New York made him frightfully nervous. A sea of meaningless stone, he called the city; he found it intolerable. Every hour he spent here he longed for the wide green parks of his Vienna, for his country house in the Alps. He considered that in making the short journey from his hotel to Carnegie Hall he was performing an act of self-sacrifice for which he was being paid. 'I can't breathe between these eternal walls,' he complained to me. 'They're crushing me, slowly but surely.'

Article in *Corriere della Sera* (Milan), date unverified. Trans. in Otto Zeff (ed.), *Great Composers through the Eyes of their Contemporaries*, New York (E. P. Dutton & Co. Inc.), 1951, pp. 446–7.

Maurice BAUMFELD
(1868–1913)

Director of New York's German-speaking Irving Place Theater, a
Viennese who emigrated to the US in 1900 after brief careers in
commerce, railways and journalism. On their first lonely New York
Christmas of 1907, he knocked on the Mahlers' door to insist on
sharing with them some seasonal jollity. Alma refers to him as 'that
good *Schlemiel*',[1] a Yiddish expression for a clumsy, well-meaning
fool; Mahler disparaged his stage production of *William Tell*.[2] His
perceptive insights into the marital relationship suggest that he
enjoyed Alma's confidence.

First performance of the Eighth in Munich. When
Mahler finally appeared on the podium the entire audience, as if responding to a secret signal, rose to its feet,
initially in silence. The way a king is greeted. Only when
Mahler, visibly surprised, gestured his gratitude did a
cheering erupt of a kind that is seldom heard at such an
event. All this, before the performance began.

It was a triumph for a man whose remarkable importance as a composer, a conductor and a human being was
increasingly being recognized throughout Europe. A
purely personal homage by adherents of differing schools
and types, rendered to an artist whose greatest strength
was his ability to command . . .

He was exceptionally stimulating in conversation, but
not the kind of thinker who never lets anyone else express
an opinion. If a counter-argument was genuine and
stated with conviction, he would be impressed, far more
so than by the vague enthusiasms that were the bane of
his existence. Sensitive to the highest degree, he had an
almost pathological aversion to falsity. The very thought
of it gave him physical pain. When he encountered it, he
would cast around for help from friends, wringing his
hands in a way that anyone who had seen it before could
not fail to recognize.

---

1. AMM, p. 130. Mistranslated in the English edition.
2. Letter to Alfred Roller, February 1909 (GML, p. 332).

That is why many thought Mahler short-tempered and moody. In fact, he was kindness personified, showing a touching friendship for all who managed to come close to him. It cannot have been easy. One has to appreciate that the immense wealth of his mind was bound to make his nature volatile. Quite apart from music, he was one of the best-read, most cultured and most original of minds. He just had to find the right partner in conversation and you would hear shaft after shaft of immortal utterances. But with the deep-rooted humility that critics often denied him, he took all this for granted. These sparring sessions with friends, he loved above all else.

His best hours were when, after conducting a successful concert, he gathered round him in his living-room at the corner of the Hotel Savoy[3] a few people who understood him and appreciated his true nature. People with whom he could be as he really was. He liked to lie on the divan until tiredness overcame him. Then he got up and said: 'Right, ladies and gentlemen, now you can enjoy yourselves and make merry: I'm past that. If it gets too hectic, I'll throw my boots at the wall. Then you'll know you are making too much noise.' A few hearty handshakes, and Mahler was off to bed.

That remark about being past merriment was, of course, untrue. He had a strong sense of humour which ascended a scale from savage mockery to childish glee. We could not stop laughing when, in high spirits, he mimicked well-known conductors and composers. He restrained neither the harshest words nor the most grotesque mimicry.

On the other hand, anyone who saw him playing with his little daughter[4] fully appreciated the gentleness, the lovableness, of this essentially private nature. Whether Mahler was the magician or the fairy, the wild beast or the faithful dog, whether he improvised his hilarious tales or worked them into a parable, he always showed

---

3. Hotel popular with Metropolitan artists, where the Mahlers lived in their last two seasons in New York.
4. Anna Mahler spent only the last New York winter with her parents.

that beautiful understanding of the child's awakening
soul that he expressed in so many compositions.   .

Equally deep and tender were his relations with his
wife, Alma. Though these had endured struggle and
crisis. The beautiful Frau Alma, herself a dazzling
musician and more than averagely gifted composer, did
not always have an easy time, for all the love he bore her.
It was many years before he accepted her as an equal.
Then, when he recognized that she was more than a
companion, that she could find her way through the
labyrinth of his unspoken thoughts, he shared everything
with her completely.

In this last winter, their harmony was of almost
unbelievable intensity. For this woman above all, he
composed, conducted, created, lived. If she once missed
a concert because of illness and he could not send up a
glance at her box before he began, it was as if his right
hand was gone. In his long illness, he would not let her
leave his side for an instant. I seriously believe that he
held on to her powerfully enough to fend off death itself.

Around Christmas, he once called me most secretively
into his room. 'You must help me buy presents for my
wife. You know her tastes. But she, for Heaven's sake,
must not get wind of it.' So we made a top-secret
rendezvous. I walked for hours with him around New
York stores and art shops. Nothing seemed to him good
enough or beautiful enough. He impressed on every
dealer that it was imperative not to deliver the items he
selected before a certain time and not to hand them to
anyone but himself. And when all the presents were
assembled he, with the eagerness of a small boy who has
just been allowed to spend his first dollar, asked me time
and again: 'Do you think we have found the right thing?
Will it take her breath away? Or should we perhaps buy
something more?'

Then he filled great sheets of paper with orders for
unimaginable treasures to be bought in Europe, above all
in Paris, under the personal supervision of Frau Alma
herself. He put the whole thing together piece by piece

on Christmas Eve, still doubting whether his treasure trove was beautiful or rich enough.[5]

His instructions for the future remained unfulfilled, as did his plan to build a house of his own high on the Semmering near Vienna, where he planned to live a contemplative life after finishing work in New York. This house must have been built and demolished a thousand times with his friends in New York last winter. Plans had been produced by members of Frau Alma's artist circle in Vienna, as well as by American architects. For it was to be uniquely special, utterly personal . . . We argued furiously about every single chair, about wallpaper and carpet designs. This house that will now never be built was his castle in the air. 'So long as you leave my working-room alone,' he would say, 'you can carry on building whatever you like. But the room where I shall write my next symphony is something for me to decide.'

This symphony, too, will never be heard by mortal ears. Early this year when he was preparing to depart, he called me into his room to say farewell. 'You have asked me often enough this winter,' he said, 'what I have been doing in my spare time. Now you shall see.' And he set before me the manuscript of his Ninth Symphony, complete but for the final orchestral retouches. What he told me then was that it would be something entirely new, containing the essence of his attitude to life, to which his stay in America had contributed in no small measure.[6]

Mahler often had sharp words for the philistines and snobs of New York, but he was not blind either to the city's greatness or its special character. He felt quite passionately about the New York sun. From the corner window of his living-room at the Hotel Savoy, he had a broad view over the greenery of Central Park and could

5. Alma confirms his boyish excitement (AMM. pp. 186–7).
6. Baumfeld contradicts himself: if the symphony was finished there was no reason it should not be heard by mortal ears. Might he also have been shown the unfinished Tenth, with its anguished private inscriptions to Alma?

sit for hours entranced staring out over its vibrant life. 'Wherever I am, the longing for this blue sky, this sun, this pulsating activity goes with me.'

Slowly, he also came to believe in New York's serious-ness about art. In the first half of the winter, when they had not yet begun to embitter his work with their petty meddling, we often spoke of his mission to create in New York a higher musical understanding.

For quite a while he doubted whether this was feasible. But he was as dedicated as a saint and when he began to perceive that the public was starting to appreciate him, he resolved to return and complete his task here. But then what happened? This is not the place to go into details, but they took this truly unstinting man and martyred him with every kind of tiny irritation. Hard-bitten, uncomprehending, they ignored his long-term aim and began to look for success only in terms of dollars. Moreover, something they can deny but not eradicate, they flayed and tore at his sensitive nerves until finally one day his sudden collapse resulted, the outbreak of his fatal illness. When he had been feeling better for a few days, Mahler had no thought other than to return straight to the concert hall, not suspecting yet that he was done for. As little as fourteen days before his departure, the first time he was out of bed, he arranged a rehearsal for the following day and discussed the schedule for the concert that was to be his farewell to New York for the present season. It was the final resurgent glimmer of energies that had been sapped to the roots. The very next day saw the severe attack that left no doubt that he had only weeks to live. Even his most intimate friends could no longer see him. Everything possible was done to smooth the way to the dread hour, be it the selfless ministrations of his friend and doctor[7] who stood firmly at his side, or the loving care of his wife and mother-in-law.[8] While the newspapers were still full of notices

7. Dr Joseph Fraenkel (1867–1920), Viennese-born New York physician.
8. Anna Moll arrived from Vienna on receiving Alma's telegram: 'Gustav's condition variable. Can Mother come.'

saying that Mahler would definitely be conducting on such-and-such a day, and while there were people in New York who insisted there was nothing to his illness but a contretemps with the ruling powers at the Philharmonic, he sank inexorably towards death, wasted away by a mysterious intractable fever.

The afternoon before his departure,[9] I took my leave of him. Wrapped in warm blankets, he lay as in former times on his divan before the open window, gazing out on the New York that was always in his memory. The short time I had not seen him had been enough to cause a noticeable ageing of his features. He had always been full of life and blessed with a richly expressive face but now he lay tired and haggard, almost as if he were already laid out on the bier. Whether Mahler knew it was goodbye for ever, I do not know. His little daughter was still playing around him happily. As in days gone by, he wanted me to tell him the latest news, in fact just like the good old days he risked a little stab at an argument. But it all seemed like a dim and distant echo. Earlier on, you had often enough had the feeling that Mahler was elsewhere in spirit, that he was in another world, but in this moment of parting I had the distinct impression that the person speaking with me was receding further into the distance with every passing hour. His hand, which used to return such a confident answering pressure, had grown hot from the fevers within. The eye of command that had so often cast its glare over us was already flickering out. There were only isolated moments when you were aware that here lay a great fighter who would not give in easily, even to death. For Mahler was bound to life by every fibre.

In the first half of the final winter he had been in a particularly happy frame of mind. Full of the most ambitious plans which, contrary to his usual custom, he actually talked about. He was filled with the sublime joy of life that is typical of advancing age. Since he knew that he and his family were financially secure for the rest of

9. They sailed for Europe on 8 April 1911.

his life, he wanted to spend a few years – 'it won't be all that long in any case' – enjoying the unfettered existence of an independent artist. Dedicated solely to his compositions, for which he expected full recognition only from a succeeding age, and to a time of blissful contemplation within the circle of those friends with whom he gladly spent hour after hour. Art has suffered an infinite loss in Gustav Mahler. But humanity has lost even more. For he was one of the few great men who knew how to give of his infinite riches with both hands. And now, when Gustav Mahler's lips are stilled, thousands will come to realize what they are deprived of and what they failed to appreciate while it existed so long in the abundant outpouring of his riches. His music will continue to communicate with us, but the most unique part of him, the titanic humanness, the inner wisdom born of kindness and understanding that allowed him to see beyond our own limited understanding – that is gone. Few people really knew him. But for those who did, it is not only a fine musician that has died, it is a truly great human being.

'Erinnerungen an Gustav Mahler von Dr Maurice Baumfeld',
New Yorker Staatszeitung, 21 May 1911. Transcript in the
Bibliothèque Gustav Mahler, Paris.

Ferruccio BUSONI (1866–1924)

Composer, pianist, philosopher, bibliophile, artist; his rich personality was bound to appeal to Mahler, ever attracted to musicians whose interests transcended music. Mahler conducted Busoni in Beethoven concertos five times between 1899 and 1910; he also performed Busoni's *Turandot* Suite twice in New York and, in the last concert of his life on 21 February 1911, his *Berceuse élégiaque*. 'I honour and love you equally as a man and as a musician . . . to be in your company has a purifying influence,'[1] wrote Busoni to Mahler. On the final sea voyage to Europe, he sought to divert the dying man with crazy specimens of counterpoint.[2]

New York, 22 February 1911 [to his wife, Gerda]:
At dinner Mahler said something very good. 'I have found', he said, 'that people in general are better (more kindly) than one supposes.' 'You are an optimist,' here interposed a fat American woman. 'And more stupid,' Mahler concluded, quickly, addressing the lady.

The first performance of the *Berceuse* took place yesterday evening. Toscanini came.

After two recalls for Mahler, I was obliged to bow twice to the audience (from my box). 'The audience doesn't like the piece, but it likes me' I remarked. The *Berceuse* belongs to a type of music which does *not* suit Mahler so well as the rhythm and drums of *Turandot*.

> *Ferruccio Busoni: Letters to his Wife*, trans. Rosamond Ley, London (Edward Arnold & Co.), 1938, p. 182.

Berlin, 25 May 1911 [to Irma Bekh]:
Since 1 May I have been working hard on my own account. It is the finest time of my life; the spring has come. I am free and healthy and deeply, profoundly grateful to Fate.

This seemed almost *unjust* to me whilst Mahler was lying on his deathbed; I had an uneasy conscience. I sailed back from America on the same ship as he and already then had no doubt as to the outcome. It had a dampening effect on our little party of travellers (Stefan Zweig[3] was among them) and in the midst of conversation we were often silent. Now that he is no more, he

1. AMM, p. 339.
2. AMM, p. 194.
3. See p. 304.

seems to me to grow ever more beautiful. A true artist
and a character of gold. What purity in that soul!
Enough, I weep.

> Anthony Beaumont (ed. and trans), *Ferruccio Busoni: Selected
> Letters*, London (Faber and Faber), 1986. Manuscript owned by
> Dietrich Fischer-Dieskau and reproduced by permission.

*Stefan ZWEIG
(1881–1942)*

On the final voyage home from America, Busoni told Alma that
'there was a young Austrian on board who wished to offer his
services to Mahler and me.'[1] He volunteered no help with the
luggage, however, and disturbed Mahler on the train to Paris by
telling his daughter a fairy story in a loud voice.

The unhelpful young man was Stefan Zweig, a rising poet and
dramatist who became a best-selling biographer of historical figures.
Zweig was drawn to famous men as a butterfly to flowers. He had
already made contact with Freud, Herzl, Rodin, Rilke and Rabin-
dranath Tagore and would add Strauss, Bartók, Ravel and
Toscanini to his portfolio of musical friends. He also assembled an
important collection of musical scores and artefacts including, at one
time, a desk used by Beethoven.[2] His brush with Mahler is described
in a newspaper article in 1915.

> To young people who felt the creative urge fermenting
> within us, the fiery and visibly exposed drama of such a
> man was indescribable. We yearned to submit ourselves
> to him, to be near him, but were inhibited by a puzzling,
> secretive shyness, in the way one would not dare
> approach the rim of a crater and gaze into the boiling
> lava.

1. AMM, pp. 195–6.
2. Zweig's scoops as a collector are detailed in his autobiography, *The World of
Yesterday*, London (Cassell). 1943, Much of what remains – including Mahler's
'Urlicht' song from the Second Symphony – was presented by his estate to the British
Library in May 1986.

We never tried to force ourselves upon him. His mere presence, the awareness of his existence near by in the same world, was happiness enough in itself. To have seen him on the street, in the café, in the theatre, always from a distance, amounted to an occasion, so greatly did we love and worship him. I still see him vividly today. I remember every single time that I encountered him at a distance. He was always different and always the same, for he continually radiated the vehemence of his spiritual expression.

I can see him at rehearsal: angry, twitching, screaming, irritated, suffering at all the inadequacies as if in physical pain. I see him again brightly chatting in the street with a natural childlike cheerfulness, as Grillparzer portrayed Beethoven (and with which his symphonies are amply spiced). He was always somehow swept along by an inner force, always totally animated.

Unforgettable, however, was the last time I saw him, for I have never sensed so deeply the heroic in a man. I was travelling over from America and he was aboard the same ship, mortally ill, a man dying. The first signs of spring were in the air, the crossing was smooth on a blue, lightly rolling sea. A few friends had gathered around Busoni, who played us his music. We were constantly tempted to be happy, but down below in the bowels of the ship, he lay half-awake watched over by his wife, a shadow over our bright day. Sometimes when we laughed, someone would say, 'Mahler! Poor Mahler!' and we fell silent.

Far below us he lay, lost, consumed by fever, only a small flame of his life flickering above deck: his child, playing happily and unknowing. But we knew: we felt him below, beneath our feet, as if in a grave.

Then on the quay in Cherbourg, as we disembarked, I finally saw him: he lay there, deathly pale, motionless, his eyelids shut. The wind had blown his greying hair to one side, his rounded brow stood out clear and bold and beneath it the hard chin, showing the vigour of his will. The skeletal hands lay folded wearily on the blanket. For the first time I saw him, the pillar of fire, in his frailty.

This silhouette – unforgettable, unforgettable – was set against the grey infinity of sky and sea. There was boundless sorrow in this sight, but also something transfigured by greatness, something resounding into the sublime, like music. I knew I was seeing him for the last time. Emotion drove me near, shyness held me back. Only from a distance did I see him and see him, as if in seeing him I could still absorb him, and be grateful.

'Gustav Mahlers Wiederkehr', *Neue Freie Presse*, 25 April 1915. Reprinted in Zweig, *Europäische Erbe*, Frankfurt (Fischer), 1960, pp. 177–9.

Epilogue

VI

My time will come

Posthumous chronology

1911	22 May	Mahler is buried at Grinzing, beside his elder daughter.
	20 Nov.	Bruno Walter conducts the first performance of *Das Lied' von der Erde* in Munich.
1912	26 June	Walter premières the Ninth Symphony in Munich. Alma has affair with the artist Oskar Kokoschka.
1915	18 Aug.	Alma marries Gropius in Berlin and bears his daughter the following year.
1918	2 Aug.	Alma bears short-lived child of the novelist Franz Werfel. Alma is divorced from Gropius.
1920	6–21 May	Amsterdam: international festival of Mahler's works.
	Sept.–Oct.	Vienna: Oskar Fried conducts a complete symphonic cycle.
1924	14 Oct.	Two movements of the Tenth Symphony are conducted in Vienna by Franz Schalk. Part of the score is published in facsimile, showing Mahler's anguished cries for Alma. First recording of a Mahler work, Oskar Fried conducting the Second Symphony in Berlin. Volume of Mahler letters (GMB) is published.
1929	6 July	Alma marries Franz Werfel.
1936		Walter publishes a memoir of Mahler and records *Das Lied von der Erde*.
1938		Walter records the Ninth in Vienna. In March, Mahler's family and many of his surviving friends become refugees after Austria's *Anschluss* with Nazi Germany.
1960	19 Dec.	Bertholt Goldschmidt conducts in London a partial completion of the Tenth Symphony by the British musicologist Deryck Cooke. Alma refuses them permission to continue, but later relents.
1964	13 Aug.	Cooke's completed Tenth is conducted by Goldschmidt.
	11 Dec.	Death of Alma Mahler in New York, aged 85.

Arthur SCHNITZLER
(1862–1931)

Vienna's foremost writer, Schnitzler was fascinated by Mahler and even dreamed about him.[1] Viennese by birth and temperament, he exposed sexual and racial tensions in a succession of witty plays, winning great fame with *Reigen (La Ronde)* (1900), *Der einsame Weg*[2] and *Der Weg ins Freie*.[3] In Mahler's last days of life, his diary reads:

15 May 1911
My birthday. Lovely summer's day. Flowers from Olga and the children . . . Dr Abels. Conversation with him afterwards about the Mahler case and questions of immunization . . .

16 May
[Dictated] At Loew Sanatorium. In the garden (after fleeting meeting with Bahr), J. Bauer and Chiavacci, lying one opposite the other in a circular flower bed. Chatted to both of them. Then along came Frau Rosé, Mahler's sister, looking lost.

19 May
Last night Gustav Mahler died. I spoke to him only once, late autumn 1905 at Rosé's. Saw him for the last time last summer on the Kärntnerstrasse and followed, if my memory does not deceive, a couple of paces behind him because his way of walking interested me.[4]

---

1. Schnitzler's diary: '*17 July 1910* First night dreams: . . . With Mahler at the Opera, large (rehearsal?) room – 'I bring you (me speaking) my birthday wishes . . . many happy returns . . . I wish you and us . . .' talking on some more. Mahler (cheerfully) waves me away; Me: Last night I was at your Eighth . . . (Ninth?) – was delighted by it. He finds fault with the first performance. I remark that it hadn't come off completely. He continues talking. It pleases me that we are inside the Opera. So will Mahler be Director again? Suddenly sitting in front of me are little Kraus and some others; also in conversation with Mahler – what about? – Kraus turns around towards me, I push ahead of him: Kraus cross.'
2. *The Lonely Way* (1903, Eng. trans. 1915).
3. *The Road to the Open* (1908, Eng. trans. 1923).
4. This contradicts Alma's account (AML, p. 165) of Schnitzler seeing Mahler soon after the death of his daughter in 1907 'sitting alone on a bench in Schönbrunn, his head bowed in mourning' and asking himself 'how can the man survive that?'

21 May
Mother for dinner. Played Mahler's Fifth with her. What
an autobiography!

Tagebücher 1909–1912,
Vienna (Österreichische Akademie der Wissenschaften), 1981.

Thomas MANN
(1875–1955)

Mahler's dying journey across Europe was reported daily in the
newspapers and followed in Italy by the novelist Thomas Mann.
Strained, unwell and irritable with his wife and brother Heinrich,
anxious about a cholera scare, blocked in the middle of *Felix Krull*
and troubled by his sister's recent suicide, Mann's thoughts turned
to Mahler. His greatest story began to take shape as Mahler's first
name, age and physical features were bestowed on the tragic figure of
Gustav Aschenbach in *Death in Venice*.

Nine months earlier, after hearing the Eighth Symphony in
Munich, Mann had sent his latest book to Mahler, 'the man who, as
I believe, expresses the art of our time in its profoundest and most
sacred form'.[1] In a letter to the illustrator of *Death in Venice*, Mann
explained how Mahler became Aschenbach.

The conception of my story, which occurred in the early
summer of 1911, was influenced by news of the death of
Gustav Mahler, whose acquaintance I had been privileged to make in Munich and whose intense personality
left the strongest impression upon me. I was on the
island of Brioni at the time of his passing and followed
the story of his last hours in the Viennese Press bulletins,
which were cast in royal style. Later, these shocks fused
with the impressions and ideas from which the novella
sprang. So that when I conceived my hero who succumbs
to lascivious dissolution, I not only gave him the great
musician's Christian name, but also in describing his

1. AMM. p. 342.

appearance conferred Mahler's mask upon him. I felt quite sure that given so loose and hidden a connection there could be no question of recognition by readers. Nor was it likely in your case as illustrator. For you had not known Mahler, nor had I confided anything to you about that secret, personal connection. Nevertheless – and this is what startled me at first glance – Aschenbach's head in your picture unmistakably reveals the Mahler type. That is certainly curious.[2]

> Letter to Wolfgang Born (1894–1949), 18 March 1921, in *The Letters of Thomas Mann 1889–1955*, ed. and trans. Richard and Clara Winston, New York (Alfred A. Knopf Inc.) 1970, p. 110.

On learning of Mahler's death, Thomas and Katia Mann cabled their condolences to his widow:

> For us, too, the announcement of the death of your dear husband signifies the terrible and definitive end of a prolonged and daily uncertainty between fear and hope. Our heart bleeds as well for that great and dear man . . . Stronger than all our pain must be the thought that the decease of such a man represents, for the civilized world, a case of immortality.[3]

> HLG3, p. 1053.

Berta SZEPS-ZUCKERKANDL:

To her sister, Sophie Clemenceau:

[May 1911]

> Dearest . . . You saw Mahler only a few weeks ago in

---

2. When Luciano Visconti filmed *Death in Venice* in 1971, he adopted as his theme music the Adagietto from Mahler's Fifth Symphony.
3. Although Schoenberg was his primary model, Mann drew from Mahler some aspects of Adrian Leverkühn in *Doctor Faustus* (1948), his ultimate musical creation.

Paris, the dying husband whom poor brave Alma had to bring home from America.

He died a few days ago in Vienna.

Did he suffer a great deal? Probably he never noticed a spectacle that, from so clear-sighted a thinker – a man who sought God in his work – would have drawn only a resigned shake of the head. Because the moment the Press announced that Mahler was seriously ill and the implication of his home-coming was grasped, this city of Vienna donned all the panoply of mourning – the very people who, when he was healthy and hard at work and sacrificing himself to produce things for their sake, had driven the man away.

Under sensational headlines the Press issued daily bulletins from his bedside. Sentimental anecdotes were peddled everywhere. In the salons and coffee houses, memories were sparked off like cheap fireworks – of the great age of opera that had existed under Mahler. His sparkling *Don Giovanni* . . . His magnificent *Fidelio* . . . His *Figaro* . . . His like would never be seen again. The same sneering somebodies who had done down every Mahler production were now keen to belong to the exclusive circle of Mahlerites.

And the Loew Sanitorium where the dying man lay, tended by Alma, was surrounded each day by hundreds of people.

Vienna was surrounded by an atmosphere of sadness and anticipatory dread. Then flowers rained down on the death-bed. But the most immense wreath of all, so heavy that it took two men to carry it – a wreath decked with broad, flouncy ribbons proclaiming in gold printed letters their overwhelming love for the immortal Master whom they had served under with heart and soul in profoundest gratitude – was the one placed on Mahler's grave by the Orchestra of the Vienna Opera: a parting gesture from the members of the Philharmonic.

I did not want to attend the funeral. I have always hated this business of saying goodbye surrounded by a horde of indifferent spectators. I could grieve in much greater peace at home. But dear old Girardi,[1] sympathetic as ever, came to join me. He could not bear to think of me alone. There in silence I followed the funeral train in my imagination. My maid entered, bringing the evening paper. Girardi began to read the sensationalized article which reported in every detail on the touching expression of general grief that the people of Vienna had paid to one of their greatest sons. It ended with a special mention of the wreath laid on the grave by the Philharmonic and the heart-breaking text of the dedication from his faithful friends.

I could not bear to listen to any more of this. 'Don't go on,' I told Girardi. 'It makes me sick. The crass stupidity of it, more than the lack of integrity. If it were some kind of comedy performed for the benefit of one's self and others . . . a Jesuitical trick for granting oneself absolution. But it isn't. They actually believe in their grief. They think they are genuine mourners! They have no awareness that once again they have been intellectual vandals.'

Girardi, with his sardonic smile, such a lovely mixture of the wise and the foolish, added simply: 'Indeed, the Viennese were always great ones for lying . . . in state.'

'Mahlers Abschied' (manuscript).

Paul STEFAN:

Mahler had wished for a simple burial unaccompanied by word or music, and people were thus deprived of their 'spectacle'. In order to deter those who 'wanted to have been there', and also because the small church and cemetery of Grinzing did not allow it, both were closed, and admission was allowed only to the holders of entrance-cards. And even then many who had them were obliged to wait outside the church. Thence the coffin was carried through streaming rain to the burial-place, and immediately on arrival interred without further cere-

---

1. Alexander Girardi (1850–1918), popular Burgtheater comedian who caricatured Viennese types.

mony. The crowd, still many hundreds, was scarce able
to speak. The rain had ceased, a wonderful rainbow
became visible, and a nightingale's voice was heard
through the silence. Then fell the last clods, and all was
over.

Stefan, *Studie* (US edition, 1912), p. 119.

Julius KORNGOLD:[1]

Mahler is the Bülow of the post-Wagner period, a Bülow
with a creative gift. He represents perhaps, at its most
particular, the type of the modern musician in whom
nervosity becomes a driving artistic force.[2]

Obituary, *Neue Freie Presse*, Vienna, 19 May 1911.

Paul BEKKER:[3]

One of the mightiest energies, one of the most
inconsiderate despotic natures, one of the most powerful
spiritual potencies in our public life has departed with
him. A will of unbending strength, of immovable
resistance, a temperament of demonic power has
destroyed the unprepossessingly weak shell.

Obituary, *Frankfurter Zeitung*, 19 May 1911.

---

1. (1860–1945), Eduard Hanslick's successor as chief music critic of the influential
Neue Freie Presse, 1902–34.
2. A perverse and peculiar eulogy by one of Mahler's chief sympathizers. In
comparing him to Bülow, Korngold acknowledges Mahler as a great conductor and,
apparently, as an advocate of music by his contemporaries but reduces his
compositions to 'a creative gift'. Korngold's concluding epithets, 'a great stimulator, a
great educator and a master of his art', fail to redeem Vienna's final verdict on Mahler.
3. (1882–1937), a former violinist in the Berlin Philharmonic Orchestra, Bekker
became a conductor then a music critic and biographer of progressive tendencies.
As a boy of fifteen, he heard Mahler conduct a movement of his Third Symphony in
Berlin. In 1921 Bekker published a full-length study of Mahler's symphonies.

Arnold SCHOENBERG:

Gustav Mahler was a saint.

Anyone who knew him even slightly must have had that feeling. Perhaps only a few understood it. And among even those few the only ones who honoured him were the men of good will. The others reacted to the saint as the wholly evil have always reacted to complete goodness and greatness: they martyred him. They carried things so far that this great man doubted his own work. Not once was the cup allowed to pass away from him. He had to swallow even this most bitter one: the loss, if only temporarily, of his faith in his work.

How will they seek to answer for this, that Mahler had to say, 'It seems that I have been in error.' How will they seek to justify themselves when they are accused of having brought one of the greatest composers of all time to the point where he was deprived of the sole, the highest recompense for a creative mind, the recompense found when the artist's faith in himself allows him to say, 'I have not been in error.' Let it be remembered that the creative urge continues, the greatest works are conceived, carried through and born, but the creator, who brings them forth, does not feel the bliss of generation; he feels himself merely the slave of a higher ordinance, under whose compulsion he ceaselessly does his work. 'As if it had been dictated to me,' Mahler once said, to describe how rapidly and half-unconsciously he created, in two months, his Eighth Symphony.

What the whole world would some day believe in, he no longer believed in. He had become resigned.

Rarely has anyone been so badly treated by the world; nobody, perhaps, worse. He stood so high that even the best men often let him down, because even the best did not reach his height. Because in even the best there is yet so much impurity that they could not breathe in that uttermost region of purity that was already Mahler's abode on earth. What, then, can one expect of the less good and the wholly impure? Obituaries! They pollute the air with their obituaries, hoping to enjoy at least one more moment of self-importance; for those are the moments when dirt is in its element . . .

'Gustav Mahler', *Der Merker*, vol. 3/5 (Mahler-Heft, March 1912. Trans. in Arnold Schoenberg: *Style and Idea*, ed. Leonard Stein, London (Faber and Faber), 1975. © Belmont Music Publishers.

Josef Bohuslav FOERSTER:

The life of Gustav Mahler is convincing proof of the truth of Flaubert's saying: 'The history of art is nothing but an unending martyrdom.'

Der Pilger, Prague (Artia), 1955, p. 350.

Hermann BAHR:

In his lifetime, his personality stood between his works and the public. His personal impact was so strong that most people could not reach over it to his work, some because of their admiration and love for him, others because of envy, fury and hatred. He had first to die for his work to become free.

Now, however, it is high time we remembered him. Not for his sake, but for ours. It is a crime against ourselves to leave the immensely vital force of his works lying dead any longer. It is a scandal that Vienna does still not know Mahler's works . . . There exists in Vienna a society for the promotion of tourism. I trust that it will take up Mahler's works, perhaps.

Feuilleton in the *Neue Freie Presse*, 1 May 1914. Collected in Hermann Bahr, *Essays*, Vienna (Bauer-Verlag), 1962, p. 281.

Alma MAHLER:

Mahler, it seems to me, discovered a new term in music: an ethical-mystical humanity. He enriched the symbolism of music – which already included love, war, religion, nature and mankind – with Man as a lonely creature, unredeemed on earth and circling through the universe, a lost child waiting in silent meditation in the greenwood twilight for its father to come. He set to music Dostoevsky's question to life: 'How can I be happy when somewhere another creature suffers?'

Introduction to Mahler's letters. GMB, pp. xiii–xiv.

Richard SPECHT:

Was he a happy man? To outward appearances, it seemed so. He must have been uplifted by the intoxication of power, this son of a simple Bohemian village trader before whom the greatest men of his time bowed deeply in gratitude . . . And anyone who saw him at home and witnessed the harmony of souls and comradeship with his wife must have had the impression of a happy man. But men of his kind are locked in solitude, and live mostly beyond happiness and unhappiness. He walked in a dream and a storm, barely noticing how he felt.

Only when his creations collided with everyday life was he aware of the blows and wounds. Time and again, he was shocked deeply by the lovelessness of a world that greeted with scorn someone who offered a new beauty or a new truth. His pained astonishment at those who could not accept what he offered with overflowing soul alternated with his conviction that his time would come. A time for which – in Wagner's expression – he would first have to prepare with his own suffering.

. . . Was he a good man? I once dared put this question to him, and he answered with quiet pride: 'There are no great men without some goodness.'

Specht, pp. 59–62.

Index

Page numbers in **bold** indicate main entries

320 INDEX

Fried, Oskar, xv, xixn, xxi, **173–6**, 178, 191, 202–5, 203–4, 206, 252n, 308: *Das Trunkene Lied*, 173
Fuchs, Robert, 25n, 251

Gabrilowitsch, Ossip, xixn, 192, **199–201**, 246
Giardini, Ugo, **295**
Girardi, Alexander, 268, 313
Gluck, Alma, xin
Gluck, Christoph Willibald von: *Iphigenie in Aulide*, 203, 212–13, 216
Goethe, Johann Wolfgang von, xiii, 43n, 130, 196, 210, 253, 258, 260–1, 287
Goetz, Hermann: *The Taming of the Shrew*, 193, 271–2
Goldmark, Karl, 59, 104: *The Queen of Sheba*, 114
Gounod, Charles: *Faust*, 261
Graf, Herbert, 102
Graf, Max, **101–3**, 286n
Greugg, Karl, 121
Grieg, Edvard: Piano Concerto, 239
Gropius, Walter, 230–1, 281, 283, 308
Grünfeld, Alfred, 17n
Grünfeld, Heinrich, 17n
Grünfeld, Moritz, 8, 17n
Grünfeldt, Dr P. S., *see* Stefan, Paul
Gutheil-Schoder, Marie, xvi, 86, 103, **115–17**

Haeckel, Ernst, 252
Haitink, Bernard, ix
Halévy, Jacques Fromenthal: *La Juive*, 57, 120
Hanslick, Eduard, 314n
Harris, Sir Augustus, 65, 66
Hartmann, Emil, 75n
Hassinger, Assistant Director, 118–19
Hauptmann, Gerhart, 178
Haydn, Joseph, 173, 254
Hellmesberger, Joseph, 8
Hellmesberger, Joseph Jr. (Pepi), 96, 142
Hermann, Abraham, xviin
Hermann, Isaac, xviin
Hertz, Alfred, 232, 233
Hertzka, Emil, xvi, xixn
Herzl, Theodore, xviii, xxi–xxii, 2, 55
Hesch, Wilhelm, 120
Hickenlooper, Olga, *see*, Samaroff-Stokowski
Hitler, Adolf, 55, 174
Hoffmann, E. T. A., xiv, 41, 61, 64, 73, 81
Hofmannsthal, Hugo von, xxii, xxiii, 50, 133, **284–6**
Holbrook, David, xin
Horn, Richard, **210**
Horwitz, Karl, 226
Hummer (Vienna cellist), 108–9
Humperdinck, Engelbert, 106
Huneke, James Gibbons, 242
Hynais, Cyrill, 27

Inbal, Eliahu, ixn

Jäger, Professor, 30
Jahn, Otto, 140

Jalowetz, Heinrich, 226
Jeral (Vienna cellist), 109, 110
Joachim, Amalie, 40
Jones, Ernest, 281, 282

Kafka, Franz, 5
Kähler, Willibald, **165–6**
Karpath, Ludwig, xiii, xixn, 32, 90, **104–8**, 134
Keussler, Gerhard von, 205
Kienzl, Wilhelm, **60–2**, 251: *Der Evangelimann*, 60
Klafsky, Katharina, 89
Klein, Herman, **65–6**
Klemperer, Otto, xixn, xxvi, 36n, 50, **202–7**
Klimt, Gustav, xv, xxii, xxiii, 97, 133, 134, 138, 165, 226
Klopstock, Friedrich Gottlieb, xx, 78–9
Knüpfer, Paul, 40
Kohon, Benjamin, **294**
Kokoschka, Oskar, 133, 308
Korngold, Julius, 250, **314**
Kralik, Richard von, 29
Kraus, Karl, xxvn, 55, 309n
Krehbiel, Henry Edward, 237, **243–6**, 246
Kreisler, Fritz, **236**
Kreisler, Kapellmeister, xiv, 41, 61, 73, 81–2, 99
Krenek, Ernst, 22n, 274
Krenn, Franz, 25
Kubelik, Rafael, ixn
Kurz, Selma, xvii, 103, **113–14**

La Grange, Henry-Louis de, xiii, 7
Lauterer, Berta, *see* Foerster-Lauterer
Lechner, Natalie, *see* Bauer-Lechner
Lehár, Franz, 250
Lehmann, Lilli, **57–8**, **214–15**, **286–7**
Lehmann, Marie, 287
Lenau, Nikolaus, 257
Lipiner, Siegfried, xv, xviiin, 26, 90, 134
Liszt, Franz, 206, 245; *Legend of Saint Elizabeth*, 174
Löhr, Friedrich (Fritz), xv, xviiin, 254n
Loos, Adolf, xxiii
Lortzing, Albert: *Der Waffenschmied*, 36; *Zar und Zimmermann*, 36, 103
Lösch, Franz, **71–2**
Louis, Rudolph, 61n, 195
Lueger, Karl, 55, 97
Luze, Karl, 254

Maazel, Lorin, ixn
Mahler, Abraham, xvii
Mahler, Alma Maria, (*née* Schindler), xi–xii, xvi, 6, 47, 67, 85, 90, 134–9, **143–8**, 154–5, 156–7, 178–9, 182, 198, 199, 211, 214–15, **220–2**, **227**, 235, 247, 280–1, 296, 298, **316**
Mahler, Anna Justine (daughter), xiii, xxvi, 101, 132, **274–9**, 297, 301, 304
Mahler, Bernhard (father), xvii–xviii, 8, 12, 15, 17, 24, 283
Mahler, Emma (sister), 67
Mahler, Ernst (brother), xviiin, 17